LETTERS FROM THE EDGE

LETTERS FROM THE EDGE

Outrider Conversations

MARGARET RANDALL

New Village Press • New York

Published in the United States by New Village Press
bookorders@newvillagepress.net
www.newvillagepress.org
New Village Press is a public-benefit, nonprofit publisher
Distributed by NYU Press

Paperback ISBN 978-1-61332-263-5
Hardcover ISBN 978-1-61332-264-2
eBook Trade ISBN 978-1-61332-265-9
eBook Institutional ISBN 978-1-61332-266-6

Library of Congress Control Number: 2024951470
Cover Photo: Barbara Byers

This book is dedicated to the art of risk,
a rare commodity in a society that shapes us
to be submissive to its interests, which are rarely ours.

"Against the ruin of the world, there is only one defense—the creative act."

—Kenneth Rexroth

CONTENTS

ABOUT THIS BOOK

Outriders[1]: those who live and work outside the norm. Who represent a rupture from tired values and a ferocious resistance to their imposition. Who have the integrity to reject society's seductive efforts to mold them into its cowering image of predictable acquiescence, thus making it more difficult for political and corporate powers to co-opt them to their advantage. Who reject the idea that there are only two choices, a "good" and a "bad," and demonstrate with their lives and in their work that we can all create other choices that enhance our journey.

---

1. The word *outrider* did not originate with me. I first heard it spoken by the U.S. poet Anne Waldman, who, in her book *Outrider* (Albuquerque: La Alameda Press, 2006), writes, "Outrider is a line of demarcation. It's words—obsession for the honor, dignity of a mind ill at ease, restless, jumping from desk to orally standing-at-attention, examining itself. A maker of poetry. Parallel to a maker of many things." Thank you, Anne, for this brilliant word, for curating Naropa University's Jack Kerouac School of Disembodied Poetics for five decades, and for so much else. *Outrider,* the 2024 documentary about Waldman, directed by Alystyre Julian, explores the term further. I use it here to define someone who has faced social stigma and pushed through that to create.

Outriders are often artists and others who are bridges—between cultures, between languages, between ideas. They can bring people together and strengthen communities. Sometimes they are forced into exile by political excess or violence and construct such bridges by their own examples. They must resist the very real possibility that cruel displacement may destroy their will. Those who do resist emerge at pivotal moments in history with a collective force, sometimes following periods of social oppression, censorship, and defeat. When they do, the communal explosion may be termed countercultural.

Although outriders are sometimes unifying forces, they can also be loners, determined to go their own way with neither thought nor concern for how they are seen by those in the mainstream. They project their own power and aren't tempted to go with the flow, even when doing so could make their lives easier. They are makers and doers who prioritize their need to stand for and express a singular curiosity, honesty, and commitment.

I have gathered five of them in this book: original thinkers all, two poets, an anthropologist, a public intellectual and publisher, and a painter. My life has been enriched by knowing such people, engaging with them, being sustained by their unfettered imaginations. They have enlarged my thinking and pushed my own art in unexpected directions. But there is an additional quality, something beyond the individual contributions these people make. They belong to a substratum of energy, risk, and courage that, from generation to generation, represents humanity's defiant and always struggling movement toward ever more visionary ways of seeing and creating. In times such as these, when destruction of the Earth, genocide, and everyday violence are the norm, these people continue to make us human.

These relationships were also deep friendships. These people and I loved and trusted one another. The two who are still alive accompany me with a beautiful consistency, and I accompany them.

A painter friend with whom I love discussing these issues said he thought that "[b]eing true to ourselves is the essential trait of all artists; if we aren't, we are derivative gibberish." I agree, but with one important caveat. I have known many artists who are true to themselves, but their own truth is narrow, elitist, or self-serving. Their creativity soars and their work may be successful by all commercial measures, but my definition of outriders goes beyond these qualities. Outriders are people—artists or not—who are not only true to themselves but possess an integrity sorely lacking in a world that increasingly rewards competition, overblown ambition, and deception. The South Korean painter Park Seo-Bo articulated an aspect of this when he said: "Art appears when one reaches great dignity.[2]

Outriders, intentionally or not, challenge predatory capitalism's efforts to mold us to its submissive cookie-cutter image. They express previously unimagined ideas, thus laying the groundwork for positive social change: not only the change that means improved lives with more inclusion, equality, compassion, and justice but also that which is capable of embracing the curiosity and imagination we need to envision an expanded aesthetic.

I have been fortunate throughout my long life to have been able to count on many such people: artists, writers, scientists, gardeners, health workers, social activists from different latitudes and cultures. The painters Elaine de Kooning, Pat Passlof, and Milton Resnick. Leonora Carrington, whose Surrealist

2. Park Sao-Bo (1931–2023) was a seminal figure in Korean contemporary art. His work was a synthesis between the traditional Korean spirit and Western abstraction.

vision led her to challenge such familiar references as time and space. The Franco-Mexican anthropologist Laurette Séjourné. The Communist poet Walter Lowenfels, whose poetic imagination freed him from Party dogma. Feminist biologist Ruth Hubbard and feminist historian Gerda Lerner. Revolutionaries Roque Dalton, Haydée Santamaría, Carlos Fonseca, José Benítez Escobar, Dora María Téllez, Sofía Montenegro, Milú Vargas, Kathy Boudin, and others, who fought imperial domination, local oligarchies, and colonizing ideas with creativity and sacrifice. Although I am an atheist, I have also been inspired by religious thinkers and writers Thomas Merton, Giulio Girardi, Frei Betto, and Ernesto Cardenal.

Extraordinary poets such as Juan Gelman, Raúl Zurita, June Jordan, Audre Lorde, Adrienne Rich, Sonia Sanchez, Joy Harjo, V. B. Price, and Anne Waldman, each of whom invented new language to say what they needed to say. Cuban photographer Ramón Martínez Grandal, who taught me that art form in challenging circumstances. Robert Schweitzer, who organized my first retrospective photo exhibition in 1988 and has supported my photography ever since. Radical U.S. lawyers Michael Ratner, David Cole, Michael Maggio, and Jules Lobel, without whose brilliance and hard work I wouldn't be here. South African novelist Mark Behr, who attended university thanks to the patronage of an uncle who demanded that he spy on fellow students belonging to the African National Congress (ANC), but they turned him instead and he became a double agent, reporting to that organization during the last several years of his country's fight against apartheid. Adventurous and generous editors Arnaldo Orfila Reynal, Karin Aguilar-San Juan, Bryce Milligan, Gisela Fosado, Alfredo Zaldívar, Bob Arnold, Lynne Elizabeth, and Zach Hively, who are artists in their own right and have curated my books with originality and the respect every writer needs. Poet and art historian Roberto Tejada, whose groundbreaking work always elicits my grateful response.

My children, grandchildren, and great-grandchildren, who have inherited the value I place on creativity, integrity, and independent thought, and have the confidence that they can move in their own directions. My life partner and wife, the painter Barbara Byers, with whom I can converse in person; our talks enrich me every day. Susan Sherman, philosopher, poet, and brilliant editor, whose personal/political story placed her outside the communities that should have embraced and supported her. Greg Smith, contemplative painter, whose work remains unappreciated by the mainstream and whose ability to see and know runs deeper than most. Rich Gabriel, artist whose wisdom punctuates his usually quiet demeanor.

These names comprise a partial list. I don't mention them to titillate or impress. Whether our relationships have been fleeting or enduring, every one of these people gave me what I needed precisely when I needed it. Even those long gone continue to speak to me; I hear their voices and am always grateful. Their outrider creativity has changed my life. They opened me to exploration and choice. Although many of them were older than I and experienced in areas of which I may only have had a passing knowledge, they never tried to impress me with a language calculated to intimidate or belittle. We were open with one another and asked lots of questions. Our relationships were rooted in mutual respect.

Conversations with these people have inspired and pushed me beyond any temptation to give in to society's suffocating norms. And it is these conversations that I have wanted to recreate in this book, through the correspondence we sustained at different periods in my life. These dialogues have taken place over endless coffees, in the old epistolary manner when letters traveled by train or ship and took weeks or months to arrive at their destinations, and that long once more to receive answers, and in today's emails, which are almost instantaneous in their ability to transmit connection, comradery, news, plans, ideas.

Back in the 1980s, the feminist biologist Ruth Hubbard and I collaborated on a book in which we used the letter format as a device through which we discussed issues important to us and to the larger community. The book was called *The Shape of Red: Insider/Outsider Reflections.*[3] Both Ruth and I had left our countries of origin as young adults, she forced by political circumstances, I enticed by a desire to know the world, and we were interested in exploring the ways in which that made us feel as if we belonged and the ways in which we felt at the margins of society. But the epistolary conversations with the people in this book took place in actual letters, bridging thousands of miles or sent through cyberspace, and written out of our need to exchange ideas in real time. Revisiting those letters and quoting from them here seems the best way to share the impact they've had on me.

At this late stage in my life, many of these relationships are reappearing. The chance discoveries seem magical. They shine a light on shared moments, energies, and accomplishments, sometimes moments I'd forgotten entirely. A sentence may reignite memory or lead to locating other letters that reveal important historical events, many of them pivotal in our lives.

The idea for this book emerged from a fortuitous encounter between my youngest daughter, Ana, and an old friend, Mai Jacobs, with whom she recently reconnected. Mai's grandfather was Walter Lowenfels (1897–1976), a poet and writer who first contacted me in the mid-1960s, when the bilingual poetry

3. Cleis Press, Pittsburgh and San Francisco, 1988.

journal I'd cofounded and was editing in Mexico City, *El Corno Emplumado/The Plumed Horn*, was already in its fourth year.

I had gone to live in Mexico City as an incipient but serious poet in the fall of 1961, taking with me my young son, Gregory. The Surrealist poet Philip Lamantia and his wife, Lucille, lived in a central part of that sprawling metropolis and hosted a nightly salon to which poets—both local and those passing through—went to share their work. I was fortunate to be one of them because those gatherings gave me an entrance to my new home and introduced me to Mexico's rich cultural life. Poets writing in Spanish and English read to one another, but our knowledge of one another's languages was rudimentary and good translation was hard to come by. Mexican poet Sergio Mondragón and I were moved to try to remedy the situation. Thus, *El Corno Emplumado/The Plumed Horn* came to be. It was a bilingual literary quarterly that over the next eight years would showcase more than seven hundred writers and artists from thirty-eight countries. In thirty-one book-length issues, we published work by Beat and Black Mountain poets, Surrealists and Dadaists, Language poets, the Concrete poets of Brazil, Indigenous writers, mystics, Catholic monks and priests, academics, Communists, and poets who were also guerrilla fighters in Latin America's armed- struggle movements of the time. We were delighted when established writers sent us their poetry and proud to publish newcomers whose work had merit. Quality alone was our criteria for inclusion.

We envisioned an independent book-length quarterly not beholden to any institution or clique, one that would feature good translations of young as well as established poets from both hemispheres. Sergio, who knew the Latin American poetry scene, and I, with my years in New York, were ideally suited to the task. Eventually we also published work from many other countries. But it was never easy. Throughout the magazine's almost eight-year run, we read submissions, wrote acceptance or rejection letters to everyone who sent us work, raised the funds, proofread each issue, oversaw the printing, distributed the finished product throughout much of the world, and handled billing. We might send a package with only five copies to a bookstore in Buenos Aires, San Francisco, Paris, or Mumbai, but those copies were passed from hand to hand and read by dozens. Decades before the internet, email, or digital printing methods, we networked in a way that seems astonishing to me today.

Walter and his wife, Lillian, were members of the U.S. Communist Party and, despite Walter's having been indicted under the Smith Act and Lillian's having lost her public school teaching job and having suffered a stroke that left her partially paralyzed for the rest of her life, they casually but proudly proclaimed their Party membership at a time when few others had the courage to do so.

These weren't your typical Communists; this was the first thing that caught my attention. They were nothing like my admittedly distorted idea of what a Party member would be like. They were committed to social justice and had walked the walk as well as talked the talk but defied narrow party-line rules and regulations. They were much too open and imaginative, freethinkers who believed in the possibility of a different world but one as protective of individual freedoms as it was dedicated to the common good. Artists, they inhabited the realm of imagination.

The Lowenfels visited us in Mexico, and we became immediate friends. In 1964, my coeditor and then husband, Sergio Mondragón, and I translated a book-length poem of Walter's, *Land of Roseberries,* and published it in a bilingual edition made even more meaningful by a series of original drawings contributed by the great Mexican muralist David Alfaro Siqueiros.[4]

Managing the translation across miles—the Lowenfels lived in Mays Landing, New Jersey—necessarily depended on the slow mail system of that time, requiring ample doses of patience and persistence. Securing Siqueiros's drawings was a drama in and of itself. Considered dangerous to the public good by the Mexican government, the artist had just been released after four years in prison. He was aging and in poor health. But the project eventually came together successfully, and the book remains a gem.

Mai Jacobs told Ana that she'd been spending time with her grandfather's archives at Yale University's Beinecke Library and had found hundreds of pages of letters between him and me. They covered the period of our early friendship, the process of translating his book and our attendant efforts to acquire Siqueiros's drawings, my giving birth to my third child, Ximena, our families, artistic lives, and constant struggle to raise enough money to keep the magazine going. She was kind enough to send me copies.

Reading those letters transported me back to moments I barely remembered, certainly not in any detail: the constant difficulties of keeping the journal going, the nature of printing with linotype and on old flatbed presses, the costs of paper and binding, the ever precarious finances of an independent project, and the solidarity of readers around the world who refused to allow us to go under, until a political repression caused us to

4. Walter Lowenfels, *Land of Roseberries/Tierra de moras*, translated by Sergio Mondragón and Margaret Randall de Mondragón (as per Spanish language custom at the time, I used my own and my husband's surnames, the "de" signifying "belonging to"), and with original drawings by David Alfaro Siqueiros (Mexico City: Ediciones El Corno Emplumado, Acuario Collection, vol. IV, 1965).

flee Mexico and we had to stop publishing. Our correspondence is filled with anecdotes that characterize the times and the people I knew who helped us push our dreams forward.

Walter and Lillian exposed me to the work of progressive U.S. poets—Sonia Sanchez, Clarence Major, Olga Cabral, and others—ignored by a system determined to silence them. They opened me to a whole world of which I was unaware. I also remember Lillian correcting my spelling, which was quite deficient at the time; she would firmly but lovingly admonish me: "Remember now, *mouths* doesn't have an *e*!" She did it in a way that didn't let me forget. Reconnecting with this correspondence so many decades later, I immediately thought, There's an interesting book here.

So, my initial idea was to create a book based on this material. I was eager to know if there were other letters in addition to what Mai had found. I contacted the Beinecke and discovered that it is one of a very few special-collection libraries that facilitate digital copies; I wouldn't have to travel there to examine them in a reading room and make the copies myself—difficult to impossible at my age. I viewed some of Walter's correspondence with others, providing background material that enhanced my understanding of the historical context. But as I reread our correspondence and pondered what it reflects, I began to think of other friends whose lives have a similar outrider quality of irreverence and resistance to the dulling status quo, poets and creators in other fields who have consistently gone their own way despite the hardships that entails.

Walter was definitely an outrider, one of those creative people who struggle at the margins of society, who persist in doing work that may never be awarded grants or honors, won't be accepted by the big commercial publishing houses, or shown in the major galleries or museums. They believe in what they are doing and stay true to their vision despite a lack of acceptance or financial support. Recognition rarely comes during their lives and often not even after they are gone. But their ideas and how they express them vibrate and inspire. They are part of an invisible and often ignored but always powerful current we sometimes call genius. They are threads in a brilliant and imaginative fabric that gives us something on which to build. I've had meaningful friendships with many such people and soon realized that a more exciting book would be one that included my epistolary conversations with a selection of people from among this larger group.

I settled on five: Walter Lowenfels, Laurette Séjourné, Arnaldo Orfila Reynal, Susan Sherman, and Greg Smith. Several criteria went into making these choices. Most important, each is profoundly original in her or his thinking and creative expression. Their art isn't influenced by fads. It is beholden to no one other than themselves. It may have been ignored, ridiculed, or even maligned at the time of its creation, sometimes only recognized later when the broader public caught up to its import. Then, too, correspondence with them took place at different periods in my life, enabling us to clarify and dig deep into ideas and issues relevant to each of those eras. I also wanted as much diversity as possible in terms of background, culture, expressive form, age, gender, and other variables; the selection is not as racially diverse as I would have liked. A determining consideration in each case was having enough correspondence from which to draw.

I've already described Walter Lowenfels and why our relationship begins this book.

Laurette Séjourné (1911–2003) was a Franco-Mexican archaeologist and anthropologist whose work on the Mesoamerican cultures of Teotihuacán and the Mayan world (particularly

Palenque) was considered too radical by Mexico's anthropological establishment when she began publishing her findings in the 1950s. They accused her of being speculative (rather than imaginative and brilliantly intuitive) and of lacking the methodology then considered a requirement in the field. They dismissed her as a woman and foreigner. They belittled her work and even managed to make some of it disappear altogether. Because her third husband, the publisher Arnaldo Orfila Reynal (1897–1998), believed in her and produced exquisite editions of her findings, she was never completely ignored. Late in life, the political establishments that had marginalized her admitted her great worth and rewarded it with important honors. And time has brought it the widespread acceptance it deserves.

Laurette, whose birth name was Laura Valentini Corsa, was born in Perugia, Italy in 1911. She and her family immigrated to France and settled in Paris after World War I. There she married Bernard Séjourné, took his surname, and changed her first name to Laurette. The name change may have been in response to the fact that her father was an outspoken admirer of Mussolini and she wanted to distance herself from him. Bernard introduced her to the world of cinema and facilitated her early work as a film editor. In that capacity she edited *Victoire de la vie* (*Return to Life*), Henri Cartier-Bresson's first documentary on the Spanish Civil War, made in 1937, and Ladislas Starevitch's *Le Roman de Renard* (*The Tale of the Fox*), one of the earliest animated films.

In the late 1930s Laurette was close to André Breton, Jean Cocteau, and Victor Serge. She eventually divorced Bernard and married Serge, with whom she immigrated to Mexico when he, a Belgian Jewish novelist and revolutionary, had to flee European fascism. They were antifascists in lived experience as well as ideology. In Mexico, Laurette continued to work in film for a while but also studied archaeology at the Instituto Nacional de

Antropología e Historia. After Serge's death, in 1947, she married Orfila Reynal, who had participated in the important University Reform Movement of 1918 in Córdoba, Argentina, and with whom she lived for the rest of their long lives. He was an important publisher, director of the prestigious Fondo de Cultura Económica, and later founder and director of Siglo XXI.[5]

Laurette Séjourné wasn't only an outrider in her interpretations of Mesoamerican culture, particularly Nahua and Maya and the cult of Quetzalcoatl. Her understanding of Marxism and religion were also unorthodox. In a number of circles, she was disparaged as a strong and brilliant woman, a foreigner, and someone who didn't take the traditional investigative routes to her conclusions. Mexico's anthropological establishment and political powers put every possible obstacle in her way, discrediting her with every tool in their arsenals. One definitive history of Mexican archaeology mentions her once but does not cite her at all.

Séjourné's experience reflects the patriarchal challenges that women faced at the time, and even do today, in being recognized as legitimate professionals, and provides insights into the circulation of ideas or lack thereof between different national contexts. She was also an anomaly among the Marxist thinkers of her day. She was interested in politics in a practical sense but wasn't taken in by narrow ideologies. She distrusted isms,

5. El Fondo de Cultura Económica received financial support from the Mexican government. When it published two books that government disapproved of—Oscar Lewis's *Children of Sánchez* and *Listen, Yankee,* by C. Wright Mills—Orfila was fired. A large group of Mexican and Latin American intellectuals and artists came together to help him create his own publishing house, Siglo XXI, free of government censorship. Siglo XXI's impressive publishing list over many years continues to contribute significantly to the decolonization of thought so necessary to understanding our history.

cliques, and party lines. One of her great contributions was that of consistently decolonizing current interpretations of history, whether the history of Mesoamerica's ancient cultures or the neo-Marxist dogma that presented a skewed view of the political struggles of the early twentieth century. In the words of Ian William Merkel, who has written at length about Séjourné, "Despite her Marxist and materialist predispositions for contemporary history, she attempted to treat Mesoamerican spirituality on its own terms." According to art historian Esther Pasztory: "Séjourné explored the heart and soul of the sites upon which she worked."[6]

Arnaldo Orfila Reynal had his own extraordinary history of struggle and accomplishment. At twenty-one years of age, he participated in the University Reform Movement in Córdoba, Argentina, an event that would change the face of Latin American higher education for decades to come. He became an internationally known publisher, producing a brilliant list of books that have influenced thinking throughout the world.

In 1965, he was ousted from his position as director of the Fondo de Cultura Económica. This didn't stop him. A large group of artists and intellectuals came together to help him create his own independent publishing house, Siglo XXI, where he continued to produce important titles.

I met Laurette Séjourné and Arnaldo Orfila Reynal soon after my 1961 arrival in Mexico City. Nancy Macdonald, with whom I had worked at Spanish Refugee Aid in New York City, gave me their names as people she thought I would like. I looked them up soon after I arrived, and we became instant friends.

6. Both these quotes are from "Art, Archaeology and Socialism: The Life and Work of Laurette Séjourné, Interpreter of Mesoamerica," by Ian William Merkel, Freie Universität Berlin, Belrose International Encyclopaedia of the Histories of Anthropology, 2022.

Arnaldo published several of my early books, and our correspondence includes details of a unique editor/author relationship. I often accompanied Laurette to her excavation at Teotihuacán when she made weekly visits to assess the work of those laborers doing the actual digging. We ate her exquisite picnics surrounded by ancient pyramids and artifacts, and she schooled me in the wonders of that complex, mysterious, and misunderstood culture.

Laurette was also supportive of my work. Merkel writes that she was an active participant in and benefactor of the review *El Corno Emplumado* and that her contributions there appeared alongside those of established poets such as Pablo Neruda and the literary avant-garde from across the Americas. "In terms of both her age and her politics," he also points out, "Séjourné straddled the Mexican nationalism of an earlier generation and the more radical aesthetic commitments of the younger generation that was no longer convinced by the government of the Partido Revolucionario Institucional."[7]

Arnaldo, Laurette, and I remained close throughout the decade I lived in Mexico and beyond. They hid me and my then partner, Robert Cohen, when the repression of 1969 forced us from our home, and our deep friendship continued after I went on to Cuba and Nicaragua, through the years of my return to the United States and the painful deportation case that followed, and until Laurette's death, in 2003. Our correspondence began in the early 1960s but dates mostly from the 1970s, when I was experiencing those first heady decades of Cuban revolutionary

7. The Partido Revolucionario Institucional, or PRI, was the political party that emerged triumphant after the Mexican Revolution of 1910. It retained power for decades, becoming increasingly entrenched. At midtwentieth century, many intellectuals and others were beginning to challenge its predominance.

social change, and the 1980s. They exposed me to ideas and challenged my thinking far beyond anyone I'd known previously.

Susan Sherman (1939) is a U.S. author, poet, playwright, and cofounder of *IKON* magazine, arguably one of the finest literary journals of the 1960s and again of the 1980s, when it had its second, woman-only, run. Both series were "dedicated to creativity and social change." Susan was born to a first-generation Jewish American mother and was raised by her and a Jewish immigrant stepfather who was a Hollywood film agent with clients such as Abbott and Costello. She grew up in Los Angeles and graduated from the University of California, Berkeley in 1961 with a degree in philosophy and English. She began writing poetry during the San Francisco Renaissance and became politically active at that time as well, demonstrating against the violence perpetrated upon students during the House Committee on Un-American Activities police riots of 1960. After graduating from Berkeley, she moved to New York City, where she received a master's degree in philosophy from Hunter College in 1967.

In New York, Susan was involved in the downtown literary scene at Les Deux Mégots and Le Metro, was poetry editor for *The Nation*, reviewed theatre for *The Village Voice*, and wrote book reviews for *The Women's Review of Books*, *Cineaste* magazine, and *The New York Times Book Review*. In 1965 she taught at the Free University (later renamed the Free School) of New York. She also began writing plays, twelve of which were produced at the Hardware Poets Playhouse and La Mama, among other Off-Off-Broadway theaters. In 1967, she attended the Dialectics of Liberation conference in London, where she was a featured poet. The following year, she traveled to Cuba for the Cultural Congress of Havana. Already in touch because she'd sent poems to *El Corno Emplumado*, she stayed with my family and me in Mexico on her way to the island. I also attended that

Cultural Congress, and we shared a hotel room, deepening a relationship that remains close to this day.

Everything pointed to Susan's becoming a successful poet and a spokesperson for an era rich in political and cultural struggle. But although her poetry collections have won prizes and her memoir was enthusiastically reviewed by *The New York Times*,[8] certain aspects of her life conspired to marginalize her. I believe the main reasons for that marginalization are that she was an out lesbian at a time when the U.S. Left was antagonistic to sexual difference, as well as a declared social activist when the lesbian community eschewed a politics of class. Although Susan acknowledged her lesbian identity more than a decade before most of this community came out, the women also saw Susan as part of the male Left, both politically and artistically. And the very male poetry world of the time didn't take her seriously.

Additionally, covert government repression against people who traveled to Cuba and were politically active in the United States was calculated to ruin lives. People were followed and harassed, visited by the FBI, deemed ineligible for the important grants and honors, fired from their jobs, and punished in other ways. In Susan's case—as she learned many years later, when the Freedom of Information Act allowed her to access her FBI files—paid informants had earned their thirty pieces of silver by telling outrageous lies about her activities. She had quite literally been made seriously physically ill by the repression unleashed against her.

Beginning in the early 1980s and until her retirement in 2023, Susan taught part time at The New School (Parsons

---

8. *America's Child: A Woman's Journey through the Radical Sixties* (Willimantic, Connecticut: Curbstone Press, 2007).

School of Design and Eugene Lang College), where, in line with the school's policy, she never had tenure. There she was also active in union organizing, helping to energize ACT-IAW Local 7902. The union finally succeeded in their negotiations for a first contract in 2004. Union organizers are to institutional administrators as lesbians were to the political Left or social activists to the lesbian feminist community back when Susan could have used their support. As a woman, and although she has made valuable contributions to the field,[9] she has never been called a philosopher (except by me).

Greg Smith was born in Pueblo, Colorado, in 1959 and grew up in a working-class Catholic home. Except for a few brief periods when his family moved elsewhere, he spent his childhood in Pueblo. From a very early age he recognized his queer identity and insisted on respect for it in quiet and not so quiet ways. He has long been equally aware of himself as an artist, moving from poetry into the painting practice that consumes him today.

Greg and his longtime partner, tin artist and painter Rich Gabriel, have made a simple, functional, gracious home for themselves in the Manzanita Mountains southeast of Albuquerque. To achieve the lifestyle they now have, which includes being able to travel often to see exhibitions by artists they love, Greg has worked jobs in bookstores and hotel hospitality, among others. Now he spends each morning in his small wood-heated studio on their land. It is built in the shape of an irregular truncated pyramid laid on its side. There he devotes himself full-time to his art. More than with most visual artists I have known, his life and work seem organically of a piece, each flowing seamlessly from and into the other.

---

9. *The Color of the Heart: Writing from Struggle and Change* (Willimantic, Connecticut: Curbstone Press, 1990).

Greg paints with clear acrylic on large clear acrylic panels. The result is an experience that is simultaneously subtle and powerful. It must be seen to be appreciated. But the paintings, each of which takes him around six months of deeply contemplative work, are almost impossible to photograph. To date, he has not been successful at getting gallery owners to visit his studio, and since most galleries require photos to consider the art they want to show, this hasn't happened for him, either. He believes in his work, though, and its practice has become an integral, ongoing part of his life.

Greg also possesses one of the most inquisitive, widely read, and brilliantly original minds I know. He, Rich, Barbara, and I often meet for conversations that leave us as inspired as we are grateful.

The four of us have also traveled together; they introduced us to Marfa, the small art community in south Texas where Donald Judd bought decommissioned army aircraft sheds in the 1970s and turned them into venues for displaying art the way he felt it should be shown: in permanence, unaffected by market concerns, and in harmonious relationship with its surroundings. As Max Tolleson writes, "Judd believed permanent installations challenged the capitalist imperative to make all things, but especially art, property that can be purchased and traded, because permanently installed art could not be 'conquered,' as he called an artwork's dislocation from its place of origin."[10] Judd was another outrider.

Although we live in the same place but because our talks have been so rich in observations about art and politics, Greg

10. Max Tolleson, "More Than a Museum: The Chinati Foundation, Home of the Brave," *Panorama, Journal of the Association of Historians of American Art* 8, no. 2 (Fall 2022).

and I—the two most loquacious of the four—decided several years ago to write to each other in addition to meeting in person. These letters have given us the opportunity to put our thoughts down on paper, where we can refer to and build upon them. Thus the material that makes it possible for me to include him here.

A brief note about method. I read through each of these epistolary collections several times before deciding which parts I wanted to excerpt. When transcribing fragments, I did so in an order that didn't necessarily follow that of the letters themselves but made sense for an accurate telling of our story and for the book's readability. Occasionally, for clarity, I made small changes in syntax, spelling, and punctuation. My intention has been to re-create conversations rather than copy every comma or dash. I've added footnotes when the issues or people we discussed are no longer familiar to today's reader.

This is a collection of conversations between friends who have traveled on the edge, rejecting the limitations imposed by institutions that would mold us to fit the behavior they need us to exhibit for their control. We are outriders in dangerous times, preferring risk to complacency, creativity and critical thought to a follow-the-leader mentality.

1

WALTER LOWENFELS: A POET WHO LAUGHED AT TIME

> It is not a choice between madness and suicide—that's
> only the way it appears. The real choice, historically,
> is to be heard or not to be heard. To accept the vast silence
> that surrounds us or to scream intelligibly.
>
> —Walter Lowenfels

THE MID-1950S IN THE United States was a time of cruel repression. The Soviet Union had been our ally in World War II, arguably doing more than any other nation to defeat European fascism. The Soviets lost 27 million citizens fighting the Nazis. But the United States, already, albeit unofficially, a Christian nation, feared communism, with its "godless materialism" and, most especially, its goal of class equality. The United States dropped the world's first atomic bombs on the Japanese cities of Hiroshima and Nagasaki, presumably to save American lives and end the war. In retrospect, and because we now know the Japanese were already negotiating their surrender, it's clear that the real reason for that crime against humanity was to intimidate the Soviets with our superior military power. Senator Joseph

McCarthy took the anti-Communist hysteria to dangerous lengths when he began investigating alleged Communist infiltration in the State Department, the CIA, the U.S. Army, and other government institutions. Using similar tactics, the House Committee on Un-American Activities (HUAC) rounded up and interrogated suspected Communists. Those targeted ranged from Party members to anyone on the Left; all were considered un-American.

This rampage affected filmmakers, public intellectuals, artists, university professors and teachers, and librarians in particular. The possibility of a nationwide conversation about diverse ideologies and what they mean was subverted for many years into the future. The 1953 execution of Julius and Ethel Rosenberg seared our consciousness as an example of what could happen to anyone suspected of spying for our new enemy. Intolerance was dubbed a Christian value and mindless patriotism enforced. Right-wing politics hiding behind so-called Christian values would be only more widespread and more extreme in the years to come.

Many were called up before HUAC, attacked for their beliefs, and asked to name others. Some complied, while others refused. In the film industry and education, people were asked to sign loyalty oaths. Many lost jobs and wouldn't work for years. No few went to prison before the country reeled itself back from the brink and McCarthy himself fell into disgrace. But incalculable damage had been done. Even those who hadn't experienced the worst of the witch hunt lived for years with the censorship and self-censorship such a crusade leaves in its wake.

For the nation at large, McCarthyism was a warning and, although few realized it at the time, a precursor of the neofascistic bent U.S. society would take years into the future. For U.S. poets, it shaped our journeys for at least a couple of decades. Fear is a powerful inhibitor. An unwritten code continued to stipulate that it was risky to write about social concerns or align oneself with progressive political positions. This initiated an era of toothless poetic imagery, in which mystical strolls through wooded landscapes and dewdrops glistening on leaves proliferated. Publications shunned those whose work might be suspect. Major honors and grants went to writers whose texts were considered safe. The era of university writing workshops, exemplified by the one at the University of Iowa, began turning out writers whose voices were influenced by white, male, heterosexual, and safely "apolitical minds." The idea that anyone is truly apolitical is a myth; an apparently benign position is itself indicative of where one stands.

Two of those who suffered McCarthy's wrath were Walter and Lillian Lowenfels, he a journalist and poet, she a public school teacher and translator. Both were members of the U.S. Communist Party. Walter describes his arrest:

> *I was sitting at my desk in the enclosed porch of our cottage in the woods, working on a poem. Suddenly floodlights and shouts broke through the darkness and the silence. Eight men pointing revolvers converged on my typewriter as if it were a machine gun emplacement. It was 2 A.M., July 23,1953. It was a most successful raid; I haven't yet recovered from the surprise. In the years that followed, I was never even able to figure out what the FBI expected to find. If they were arresting me for my sonnets, I might have understood, and so might others. But for editing* The Pennsylvania Worker? *For sitting through hundreds of meetings? The Department of Justice should have advanced bearing medals, not guns.*
>
> *Under steely-eyed surveillance I was told to put my clothes on. Lillian, in a state of shock, handed me shorts and socks and*

> *insisted over and over again she must make some coffee. She was to be left alone to live out this nightmare with the deer and the rabbits—the only fellow conspirators in our immediate neighborhood. They let me bring one book with me.* Leaves of Grass *kept my mind off the proceedings that followed. I was taken to a building in Philadelphia that houses the FBI along with other Philadelphians under similar custody. About 6 A.M. six of us were taken before a commissioner and each held on $100,000 bail. Never before or since in the United States have I been held in such esteem.*"[11]

Walter was tried under the Smith Act and sentenced to two years in prison. His trial, based on testimony from former Communists who had turned FBI informants, lasted four months, during which time he was incarcerated. Eventually, his sentence was overturned for lack of evidence. Lillian lost her teaching job as a result of the anti-Communist purge. And she suffered a stroke, which left her partially paralyzed for the rest of her life.

Hundreds of public intellectuals, writers, progressive writers' organizations, and others showed support for Walter during his trial: Norman Cousins, the editorial board of the monthly magazine *Jewish Life*, the United Mine Workers of America, the artist Elizabeth Catlett, sociologist W. E. B. Du Bois, and poet William Carlos Williams, to name just a few.

Poet Howard Fast wrote, "As a fellow writer, fellow poet, at least of sorts, and as one who like yourself found art only where freedom lies, I take this opportunity to greet you and embrace you. In you as in other great men of letters in various parts of the world, art reaches its fulfillment in the total identification

11. Walter Lowenfels, "On Trial," *The Portable Walter: From the Prose and Poetry of Walter Lowenfels* (New York: International Publishers, 1968), 34–54.

of a man with his work. You stand now as a soldier enlisted in defense of his country and all that he holds dear. I know that you will stand on your line, bowing to no threat, to no intimidation until the final victory is won."

Painter and children's book author Alvina Sečkar wrote, "I see by the paper that your trial is to begin March 15th—I grit my teeth and curse the way I did when I reached the heights of San Francisco. At one moment I was caught with the beautiful panoramic beauty of the hills. Then I looked out toward the waters and saw Alcatraz and I cursed with my teeth grating. There resided Morton Sobell and I thought I was so close but unable to go to that accursed place to let him know that I was there near him with my immobile sympathy. . . ."

Cedric Belfrage, journalist, Eduardo Galeano's translator, cofounder of the *National Guardian,* and British double agent, himself under political scrutiny, wrote, "I certainly hope there will be some opportunity for us to meet and talk. I would greatly enjoy it. I am somewhat limited in these matters as the powers do not permit me to go outside the New York area."

I was a little too young to have personally experienced the egregious acts or repressive atmosphere that gripped the country at the peak of McCarthyism, yet I came up in its still powerful aftermath. Had I remained in the United States, I am sure my trajectory as a poet would have been different from what it has been. I might have been radicalized earlier, forsaking poetry altogether or producing overly propagandistic screeds. Or I might have gone the way of so many poets of the era whose work was bland and acceptable to editors and publishers.

Because I relocated to Mexico in the fall of 1961, my work took a different turn. I met and became familiar with Mexican and Latin American poets who wrote about everything: love, death, fear, violence, nature, social issues, and, yes, outright political themes. They showed me that our craft could be organic and fearless, reflecting every aspect of our lives.

At the beginning of 1962, Mexican poet Sergio Mondragón and I cofounded and coedited *El Corno Emplumado/The Plumed Horn.* All evidence indicates that Walter Lowenfels first contacted the journal in 1964. By this time, it had reached poetry communities throughout Latin America, the United States, Canada, and, albeit more sparsely, much of the rest of the world. I no longer remember if our initial connection was epistolary or if he and Lillian showed up at our home in Mexico City; artists and writers from across the globe often dropped in on us, drawn by reading the journal. We had an extra bed in our living room and gladly received new friends, who might stay for a few days or even weeks. Evenings were spent reading poems to one another, and of course we also enlisted those visitors to help with whatever issue of the magazine we were working on at the time. They read proof or sat on the floor with us, wrapping packages of copies to be mailed off to bookstores in Buenos Aires, San Francisco, even Mumbai (which we knew as Bombay back then).

Networking was always important: introducing visiting writers and artists to their contemporaries. I have a vivid memory of taking Walter and Lillian to meet Agustí and Anna Bartra, Catalán refugees who—like so many—had immigrated to Mexico after the Spanish Civil War. *El Corno Emplumado*'s fourth issue was Agustí's *Marsias y Adila*, a book-length poem my mother had translated and that we'd produced in a bilingual edition.[12] Walter and Agustí had a lot to talk about: Both were given to writing epic poems, and each had a very different history of struggle in support of the same progressive ideals. I loved bringing people with similar interests together, and still do. The

12. *Marsias y Adila*, *El Corno Emplumado* 4 (October 1962).

Bartras lived in an old building in one of the city's central neighborhoods. I can still see Walter and Sergio struggling to carry Lillian up the several flights of narrow stairs to their apartment.

Another image I retain—this one more of a body memory—is of my sweat-soaked skin imprinted with the large and colorful floral pattern from a rayon housecoat Lillian gave me to go to the hospital to deliver my third child, Ximena. I wore that garment giving birth, and it took several days for the cheap dye to fade.

The Lowenfels were energetic, enthusiastic about life, about Mexico, and about *El Corno*'s efforts to bridge continents. Walter, who had rejected his family's successful butter business for poetry, had an active sense of humor. I remember him laughing a lot. Lillian was more serious, but equally caring. They may have been the first U.S Communists I knew who proudly proclaimed their Party membership. Members of Communist parties south of the border weren't shy about declaring their affiliation, but most U.S. members, still fearful in McCarthyism's wake, wouldn't do so for decades. Walter and Lillian were open and unapologetic.

Before leaving my country, I had known poets and writers who were progressive in their worldviews but wouldn't reveal Party affiliation if they were members. In Mexico, I met many who casually spoke of such affiliation. Walter and Lillian were a revelation in this respect. Consequently, they also introduced me to a whole group of great U.S. poets with whom I was entirely unfamiliar, poets who wrote out of a tradition of struggle they shared with Bertolt Brecht, Pablo Neruda, César Vallejo, and Mikis Theodorakis, among others. None of them was being published in the United States at that time.

One of these was Arturo Giovannitti, an Italian Socialist who immigrated to the United States at the age of twenty-one and was a leader in the Lawrence, Massachusetts, textile workers strike of 1912.[13] In 1966, *El Corno Emplumado* published a bilingual edition by Giovannitti titled simply *Poems/Poemas.* Agustí Bartra made the Spanish translations. We loved introducing the world to work by important writers who had been relegated to obscurity for whatever reason. We also got great pleasure from connecting living poets who might not otherwise have met.

Because the earliest letter between us that I accessed in the Beinecke collection is from Sergio and me to Walter and Lillian, dated January 4th, 1964, and discusses in some detail our dealings concerning the bilingual edition of Walter's long poem, *Land of Roseberries/Tierra de moras,* we must have made contact in 1963. Ximena wouldn't be born until June 1964. Walter must have mailed us the English original of that poem and we accepted it as one of the books we were beginning to produce in addition to the magazine. We translated the poem and obtained a series of original drawings made for it by the great Mexican muralist David Alfaro Siqueiros. Managing the translation through the slow postal system of those years and securing those drawings were both major accomplishments undertaken in difficult circumstances.

Mexico City—January 4th, 1964

Dearest both:

Here is the bill, marked paid . . . I hope it serves for income tax purposes. If not, let me know and I'll make it out in any way necessary. Thanks for the last check. We'll try to get your $500 back, though I wouldn't count on it soon as it will depend on a) when bookstores start coming through, and b) when the special edition sells out and checks come in . . . will send as soon as we can, of course. Will send your 250 copies as requested, and

13. Also known as the Bread and Roses Strike.

many thanks—the arrangements make it easier for us too. We're beset with problems on every side, but much faith. Siqueiros has had the manuscript a week and a half now, but during this time he has been in and out of the hospital, seems to be alright (according to Angélica, with whom we speak almost daily by phone), but so far, no drawings. Sergio was to call again at three this afternoon. We are just waiting on these in order to go to press. We can't print more than 1,000 since the printers here charge for each thousand or fraction thereof. They do extras, of course, to allow for dirty pages, discards, etc., but usually only come out about five under or over. Sending 250 to you and distributing about 200 free among key critics and columnists and various others on our list, leaves us 550 to sell. Orders are coming in daily from individuals and bookstores. About 150 accounted for so far of the regular edition, 20 of the deluxe limited one.

I sent a big batch of flyers off to you the other day, regular mail. Also, a man from Philly (a bookseller who says he is a friend of yours) sent us a huge order and requested 100 flyers to make a mailing of his own in the Pennsylvania area. I sent him 50 because that only leaves us with about 30 here in English (60 or 70 in Spanish) and we want to enclose them ourselves in letters when it seems appropriate.

HOW WE HOPE YOUR TRIP WILL WORK OUT AND BE TO MEXICO INSTEAD OF GREECE!!!!! If only you could be here to sign the special edition! You'd have no expenses once here, stay with us (downstairs bed, so Lillian wouldn't have to climb stairs; downstairs bath), eat with us, only cost would be plane tickets and the umpteen baskets you'll want to buy!

I also enclosed a copy of our new (only) catalogue with ROSEBERRIES listed. I've included this in much of the huge mailing . . . so far, we've sent out about 700 in Spanish and 700 in

> English of the ROSEBERRIES flyer and some of these. And the response is beginning . . . I'm sure this book will be a prepublication sellout.

The letter is heavy on publishing details. It helps me remember the terms under which we accepted manuscripts. Our decisions were based on loving the work, but our precarious monetary situation required that we ask authors to lay out the money for their books, with the promise that we would reimburse them as copies sold. I have no idea how often we were able to make good on that promise. The same letter also includes a paragraph about family issues that surprises me; I have no memory of these events.

> Minor family crisis: my 94-year-old grandfather just had a bad fall, other relatives in the northwest lost their home and all they possessed from the recent storm floods, our maid's baby just got the measles so it looks like our kids will follow, etc. etc. But we finally have #13 bailed out of the bindery and yesterday took care of distribution . . . will be interested in hearing your opinions.

I am curious as to why I would have mentioned my grandfather, with whom I had almost no relationship. And I have no idea what relatives I was referring to in the northwest. But these references were typical of the times; our work on the magazine and our personal lives were of a piece.

> 1/7/64
>
> Dear Ones- I'm trying to help from far off—a hard thing to do—for one thing, I'm responding to your January 4th letter and it will be at least the 11th before you get this—anyway—about the Siqueiros drawings—I suggest you use the one you used on the folder (Angélica can give you another copy like the

one I sent). Also—some of those (for which there are drawings) enclosed. Please send my copies back someday! In addition, there is his painting THE ECHO OF A SCREAM for which there may be a drawing. Angélica would know. This painting is reproduced—#60—in his big book published 1951 by Bellas Artes: *SIQUEIROS: El Eco Del Llanto.*

Nothing else for the moment—except we would like to see English page proofs.

Will write about other things separately—I exhausted myself finding the pictures.

Love and everything. xxxx

Re money, bookkeeping etc.—you keep the books about our $500. And put down you have already paid us $25.00. The Feinberg check we used right away in the A & P![14]

xxx

Walter often ended his letters with a series of *x*'s, the symbol for kisses. He almost always signed with a hand-penned "C." I have no idea what that stood for.

Getting the drawings for *Land of Roseberries* turned into an agonizing ordeal. Siqueiros had just been released after four years in prison for his long history of leftist activity, considered disruptive by the Mexican government. As an example, twenty years earlier he and another comrade, both supporters of Stalin, had managed to enter the exiled revolutionary leader's home and machine-gun the bed where he and his wife were sleeping. It was May 1940. Trotsky and his wife, Natalia Sedova, must have heard them approach and escaped harm by hiding beneath the bed. Trotsky was assassinated a few months later by Ramón Mercader, an attacker who wielded an ice ax in August of that year.

14. A popular supermarket chain.

When Sergio and I asked Siqueiros if he would make a series of drawings for Lowenfel's book, he immediately said yes. But obtaining them entailed months of telephone calls, visits, unfulfilled promises, and inexhaustible patience. This is documented in several of the letters between us. Siqueiros's health had suffered in prison, and he was ill on and off over the next months. But both men were Communists, and the muralist and poet knew and admired each other's work, so we were eventually able to overcome these difficulties.

Following the above note, chronologically, are several handwritten drafts of a letter written on the letterhead of the Hotel Versalles, at General Prim and Versalles, in Mexico City. The stationery advertises the hotel's features, such as the fact that it has one hundred rooms, five telephone lines, and air-conditioning. The Lowenfels were in Mexico City but weren't staying with us. From this letter, dated 5/30/64:

> Dear Margaret:
>
> The rain god Tlaloc was moved from his thousand-year-old home in the mountains to Mexico City the other day. A crowd of thousands was on hand to welcome him to Chapultepec—in the rain, of course. That was the only way Tlaloc could say how he feels at being moved suddenly from his temple in the past to the city a thousand years ahead. He rained.
>
> What will you rain on the typewriter—a young modern moved suddenly a thousand years backward, as you told us you were when you walked with your children over the mountains (from the last road where you had to leave the car) into the past—that four-hour walk with your maid to her tribal home (saying always "it's just over the next mountain") took you to a time scheme and previous life unknown in Mexico City to anyone except Tlaloc?

The people who live in the hovel that you finally reached—they don't have the experience you had—watching Tlaloc move in four hours from his original home to Chapultepec. When Tlaloc weeps his tears of rain for the past, you and Sergio, by singing elegies for the future, will inform others who will not know how our generation was dying with Tlaloc and living with your children in two different memories at once.

We need your "Elegy for Tlaloc" and for the walk always to the next mountain ahead that is taking you into 1970 as you crossed in four hours into 1070.

Best, Walter

"Elegy for Tlaloc" was the title of a poem I had written and sent to my friend. Walter had a poet's mystical sensibility, which was very tuned in to the way time shifts backward and forward in Mexico. This was one of the few letters he wrote to us that he signed with his full first name. Also, one of very few not written on a typewriter. In the archive there are two different drafts, and I had to make an educated guess about some of the words as I transcribed them. In a letter or in person, I must have told Walter about a trip we made into the mountains of the state of Puebla to spend several days with the family of our maid, Ermelinda. We'd traveled as far as possible by car, then continued by horseback and on foot. My daughter Sarah was about six months old at the time and I was still nursing her. It was on that trip, when the milk I was giving her older sister suddenly dried up, that I discovered I was pregnant with Ximena. I believe it was on this trip to Mexico that Walter, Lillian, Sergio, and I first met.

Mexico City—June 1st, 1964

Dearest Walter and Lillian:

Just a short note to let you know how much it meant to us knowing both of you . . . a fine few days, short as they were, and

> we hope you had the simplest of trips back—baskets not withstanding!
>
> This morning, we mailed your books registered and you should have the package in three weeks or a month. Let me know if you don't receive them in a reasonable amount of time and I'll check with the stub on this end.
>
> Still no baby—though I've a feeling it won't be long now! The other two are great! And Juanita is fine with her handsome little boy . . . and very, very, grateful for your kindness in remembering her with something for the baby.
>
> If you'd ever like us to send anything from here . . . books, drawings, or anything else that could get away with being called "educational materials," let us know and we'll be glad to do it.
>
> And don't forget to send us material for the magazine: poems, translations, what you will.
>
> Love, Meg and Sergio

As I read the letters in this archive in the order in which they are dated, I am troubled by the sequencing. They begin with a note bearing a date in October 1954, which I am sure is a mistake; it's from Walter to me and I think he must have meant to write 1964. In 1954, I was just graduating from high school in Albuquerque, New Mexico. But the confusion continues. The content of letters dated earlier, from which I have just excerpted passages, suggests that we are already involved in the project of translating, securing the art for, and publishing *Land of Roseberries,* while the content of those dated later speaks first of reading the book and our desire to produce it in bilingual format. As Walter is long gone, I can only guess at these letters' proper order.

The Beinecke Rare Book & Manuscript Library at Yale University is where these letters reside. The Beinecke is surely one of the best-endowed, best-organized, and most helpful libraries from which I've requested materials. I have dealt with it while working on several book projects and am always amazed at how attentive the staff is. Walter's and my correspondence is in pristine condition and cataloged according to date. But it would have taken a much more in-depth assessment of the letters to have discovered these discrepancies between dates and content. Perhaps this will be one of the benefits of this book.

The following letter, from us to Walter and Lillian, would seem to include our first excited response at receiving the manuscript. I transcribe it in full.

Mexico City—June 12th, 1964

Dearest Lowenfels:

We miss you. This is getting ridiculous, this baby business, since I'm still carrying it around inside and getting bigger and bulkier by the minute. We imagine you as new grandparents (for the 11*th* time?!) and I'm envious. Yesterday afternoon wasted with the doctor, whose only comment was: "Well, any minute now, I'm surprised you're still around." So, the waiting continues, but meanwhile much work. El Corno #11 is finally at press (although for the first time in El Corno's history on borrowed money for the paper) and so we're working day and night reading last-minute proofs, trying once and for all to cut the many errors this time by a simple method of reading and re-reading and re-re-reading. And simultaneously hunt for new patrons and advertisers now that the government here is collapsing about us. And the Ludovico Silva book, Tenebra, makes its appearance tonight which means a weekend of preparing packages, stuffing envelopes, etc. Meanwhile, Sergio and I spend sleepless nights hoping for some sign we can take off for the hospital. The children carry on through it all with their usual aplomb and good spirits.

About your book/poem, Land of Roseberries, wow!!!! Most of the delay in writing this letter has been due to my reading and rereading and absorbing and falling in love with the whole thing. What a book this would make in Spanish and English. That leaves the following possibilities, which I put to you bluntly: 1) A book in our Acuario Series, translated by us and printed bilingually with drawings by someone of your or our choice—but these books, so far, are being paid for by their authors, and as yet we have no money to put into them except for the vague promise that returns may or may not eventually exceed outlay. 2) That we do it as our last issue of each year with us paying, but the fly in that ointment is that this year's goes to Raquel Jodorowsky (already in translation), next year's has been promised to a young Canadian poet, and that takes us to 1966 which is too damned far away. And 3) That I simply excerpt parts—with your permission—for publication in English in El Corno. This last option is probably the most plausible although to my mind also the least reasonable since in three readings I haven't been able to decide on a single part I would choose. The whole thing is such a unit and such a forceful one, even though any section could stand alone. So, please come back at us with suggestions of your own. Is there a chance that somehow money would be available for option number one, or is that too ridiculous a proposal to make to someone like yourself who can get what he writes printed by any number of big houses where you would be paid? And if not, what about excerpts? Are there any sections you personally favor?

We haven't forgotten your copies of Siempre! (re: Siqueiros) or the Indian drawings[15] you ask for, all of which we'll hunt

15. The Indian paintings were images of birds and flowers painted on bark paper by Indigenous people in the state of Guerrero and sold in markets in Mexico City and elsewhere.

> down and send together sometime next week when the baby pressure and other things calm down a bit. For the time being, here are the pictures we took. As you can see, we didn't turn out to be such hot photographers, but at least they can serve as a "recuerdo."
>
> Love from us all, Meg, Sergio, Goyo,
> Sarah Dhyana, and "10/9".

Rereading this letter all these years later and knowing that Walter decided to publish *Land of Roseberries* with us raises some questions in my mind. Perhaps I was naïve to imagine his work was so readily accepted by major publishers; the campaign against leftist writers was still in full swing. Or maybe he admired our work, wanted to be part of it, and liked the idea of the book appearing in a bilingual edition. And how I would love to see the photographs I mentioned, now lost to time.

The following note from Walter, written the day after my letter to him, must have crossed ours in the mail.

> 6/13/64
>
> Dear Margaret & Sergio—The beautifully packed bundle of books arrived in perfect shape. Thanks. I enclose ten bucks in case you get a chance to pick up more of the Indian paintings at the Sunday market.
>
> After a month away from this desk, I find it hard to do jobs I'm committed to. Leafing through folders I find a verselet that may suit your new arrival:
>
> FOR MY 10TH GRANDCHILD
>
> Don't stop the scream you got here with.
> Resist, resist, and then resist.
> And keep up that occasional smile
> that lights your crib.

You can grow as old as Doctor Du Bois
but follow your scream
and your smile
and you'll reach the Himalayas
of eternal unrest.

Best, C

The next letter in the archive is from us to Walter, dated June 21st, 1964. We must have received one from him telling us he wanted us to translate and produce *Land of Roseberries,* because I present him with our estimate of cost. My daughter Ximena arrived on June 17. There was a seamlessness between our family life, work, garden, neighborhood, and the magazine.

Mexico City—June 21st, 1964

Dear Lowenfels:

Here we are, home . . . all went as planned at the hospital. They only kept us a day and a half, and we've never had "complete" possession of any of our babies so quickly. Sort of a strange feeling. Ximena is round and fine and hungry, so all is well. And we're deep in the family again, Prado Churubusco, our garden, the magazine, books, work, children.

We've looked over the manuscript of *Land of Roseberries* and come up with the following sad financial estimate: a thousand copies of the book, in both languages, with 20 drawings, 10 pages of odds and ends (index, title page, notes, etc.) on the paper we use for *El Corno* and with the same or better cover stock, would cost $1,000.00 U.S. This includes the following:

Printing and binding of the book itself
Cost of paper and engravings

Cost of all that goes into distribution of the book to 250 bookstores in 23 countries (stamps, packaging materials, etc.)

Cost of sending out a printed mailing in hope of receiving orders for the book—1,000 flyers, envelopes, etc.

In making this estimate I figured the 64-page manuscript doubled to 138 pages by the Spanish translation, 20 full-page drawings, 10 pages of odds and ends, and it comes to a book of roughly 168 pages. I don't know if it would be possible for you to raise this $1,000, or if you want to. If it sounds plausible to you, I'll gladly write a passionate letter to your brother—just send us his address and some suggestions as to what to stress. Or any other passionate letters to other brothers, cousins, uncles, aunts, etc., if you just give us the word. Raising the money on this end seems impossible. At the moment, our government patronage for the magazine itself is rapidly falling down around our ears and we are up to those same ears in that problem.

As for when we'd need to have the manuscript, that's pretty much up to you. We could do the book anytime and would go at it enthusiastically (the translation, that is) as soon as we were assured the money would be available. I think the translation would take us approximately three months (since we're also busy with other things, simultaneously) and allowing a month after that for us to send you galleys and page proofs for your corrections, and another month for printing and binding, we should have the final book in our hands in, say, five months from the time we begin.

So, let us know what you think, and what possibilities are open to us. And we have our fingers crossed, for we think the book a really beautiful and important contribution.

Love, Meg, Sergio, Gregory, Sarah Dhyana and Ximena

Walter responded quickly.

6/26/64

Dear Margaret & Sergio & Co:

"We must be lovers and at once the impossible becomes possible." I was wondering how you could keep on creating children and poems and books in one continuous childbirth, when I thought of the Emerson quote.

So, it's 3:30 AM. I just finished rewriting a brief foreword to Lillian and Nan's *Modern Poems from the Spanish.* The hardest thing I do is introductions, forewords, etc. So, your June 21*st* letter: Lillian said money from my brother is pure fantasy on my part, and that we will raise it. She is going to write you—so this is just a quickie that it's OK to go ahead with the book. We are happy to be producing children with you. When do you need to have the first $500? Give us a date.

One of our twins, Judy, is here with her three children, the youngest two months old—so it's very Churubusco[16] here. Only not so roomy. We have more ground than you—five acres, but the cottage is tiny: bedroom where Lillian is asleep, living room where sister-in-law Nan is asleep, enclosed porch where Judy and Co are asleep, and my little shack adjoining.

This is all for the moment. Lillian will write soon.

xxxx

C

Writing the letter in which I explained the three ways I thought we could publish all or part of Walter's book, I had no idea of the obstacles we would encounter throughout its translation and production processes. When we charged an author to publish a book, we never figured in the cost of our own time; we always

16. "Very Churubusco" refers to Prado Churubusco, our neighborhood in Mexico City. Our home was always filled with sleepover guests on their way from one part of the world to another.

felt that was a labor of love and part of our commitment. This letter also reveals aspects of our publishing venture that I have long forgotten and haven't come across in texts written by anyone else who would have known what our printing and binding costs were in 1960s Mexico, the time frame in which we worked, the sort of publicity we did for each book, and so much else.

El Corno Emplumado/The Plumed Horn was a project that transcended its almost eight-year life. Its power and influence are reflected today in dozens of independent magazines, literary bridges, and translation ventures. Many people have written about the journal, including me. Several doctoral dissertations and master's theses focus on it, and others refer to it in a variety of contexts. When I have written on, or been interviewed about, it, I've always expressed my amazement that two young people—Sergio was twenty-six, I twenty-five—could have undertaken such a project and kept it going for as long as we did. The 1960s was a decade of rebellion and creativity. It was also a difficult time. We did everything in so much more of an artisanal way than how we are able to do the same things now, using hot lead and big old flatbed presses to print, having to depend on an old-fashioned mail system for communication, constantly begging for enough money to keep going.

Sergio and I conceived of the project together. We complimented each other, with his knowledge of Latin American poetry, my contacts with poets north of the border and my "can do" spirit. At a certain point in the magazine's history our visions began to diverge, and our marriage fell apart. In 1968, he relinquished his editorship and Robert Cohen and I put out the last two issues. But as I look back all these years later, I am overwhelmed by Sergio's and my ability to create something so powerful and long-lasting. *El Corno* was, above all, the product of two young people with a dream and the enormous energy required to make it happen.

We collaborated on important translations, among them *Land of Roseberries/ Tierra de moras.* It's only fitting that I include the letter Sergio wrote to Walter after we'd completed that task. He wrote it in Spanish and Lillian made the translation:

Mexico, October 14th, 1964

The Year of the Winged Head

My dear Lowenfels:

Here it is midnight in my Aztec land. I am listening to a four-violin concerto. Meg is cooking some supper for us. We have just finished a long day, the last day of translating *Land of Roseberries.* Dear Walter, your poem is a shining jewel that will live forever in my heart, and which has done so much for Meg and me. In the book I came across quite a few lines that were the most direct and practical (concrete) teaching I have ever gotten in my life. Thanks, with all my heart. I do not exaggerate in saying that *Land of Roseberries* is the poem the world has been waiting to receive. It is of course the poem that I myself would have wanted to write and one of the most beautiful examples that man is capable of producing when his life is based on love and honor. Certainly, you and your beautiful Lillian are the highest human ideal it has been my good fortune to know. Excuse this cataract of poor words that can hardly express what I feel. I only wanted to let you and Lillian know how happy and proud I am to have worked translating and publishing, together with Meg, this most beautiful poem that sings so perfectly. I am very much moved.

Today our son Gregory was four years old. We took him and five of his closest friends to the cartoon movies and afterwards to the park where we played and laughed with them. Our son was very happy. Now he is sleeping in the other room with his two little sisters, and Meg's voice comes to me from the kitchen telling me supper is ready. I want to deserve this happiness. And I assure you that your poem has shown me a road through which I can deserve it and increase it and be able to extend it to others.

The Mexican night is cool, and a lively wind is blowing on my head and the stars are far away and the murmur of the trees in our garden helps me to send you flowers and kisses.

Sergio Mondragón

7/29/64

Dear M&S&Co: Just read your poem, and it made me dizzy. ("The Glass Shatters") It's beautiful. Someday I feel I'll read a whole book of them. Nothing else, just love. No time for others, no space, no type. Like the father of us all said: "The strongest and sweetest songs yet remain to be sung."

One great advantage we have over Whitman—he could only guess or hope that others would come along. We live it, encompass the continuity of the poem in our own lifetimes. Williams had a strong sense of that.

To get back to your poem, when I read it the second time it made me think of Donne. Be careful of copyright, acknowledgements, etc., and remember someday someone will be copying you.

Well, will write later, this is just hello.

Although money was a concern, our greatest struggle with *Land of Roseberries* was the translation, discussing it long-distance, going over it again and again until we got it right. We constantly hosted poets traveling south to north and north to south or coming to Mexico from Europe. The Chilean "antipoet" Nicanor Parra spent a few days with us during the months we worked on turning *Land of Roseberries* into *Tierra de moras*, and

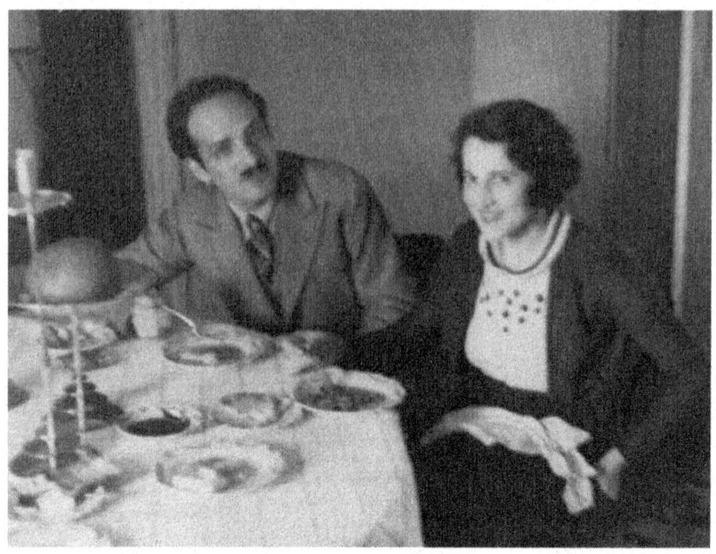

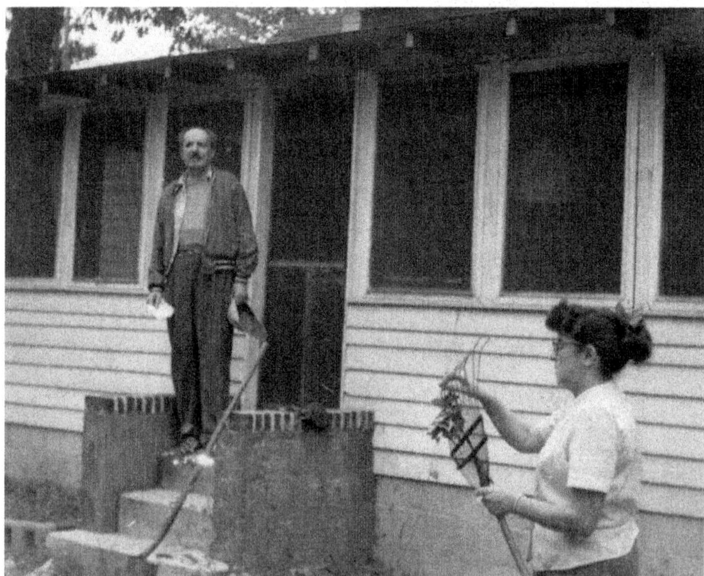

Above: Walter and Lillian Lowenfels at home in 1940s and 1950s.
Right: Walter in 1970s. Courtesy family archive.

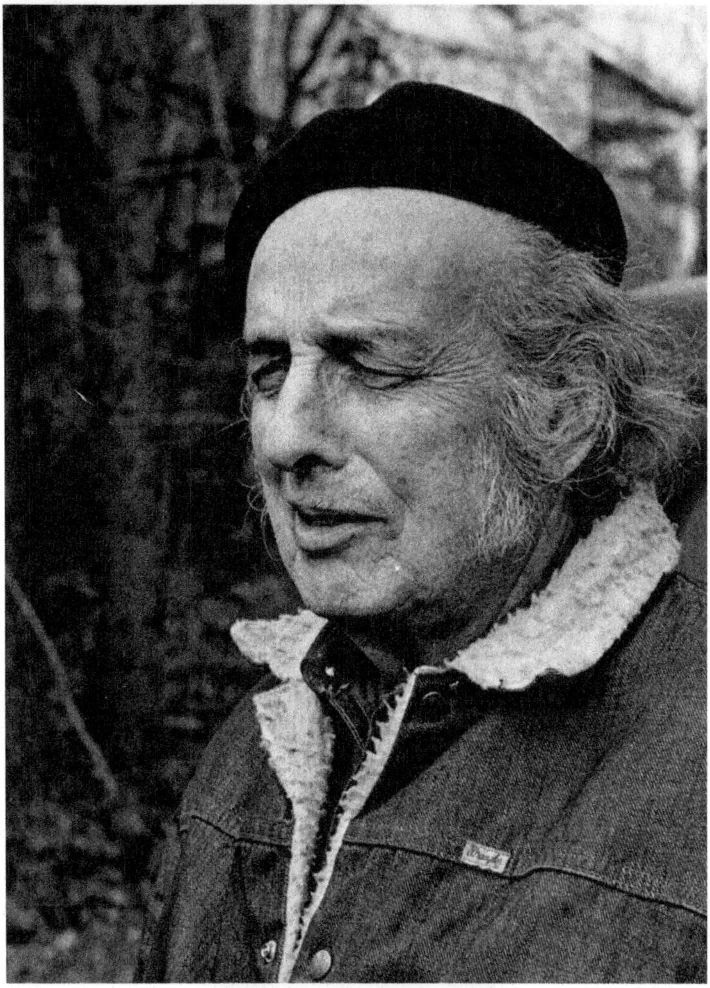

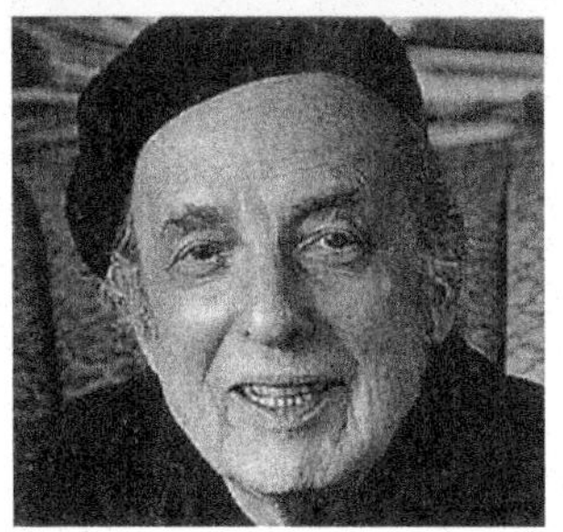

he helped us with several rough spots.[17] Here are fragments of one of many letters in which I asked Walter for help in deciphering lines we didn't understand:

Mexico City—August 20th, 1964

Dear Peoples:

The translation continues, but today in a mad fit of depression we hit a snag, a verse which to us was unintelligible. These things happen sometimes in translation, as you know, and after it's explained will probably look embarrassingly clear. But meanwhile, please explain (word for word, if possible) the following which appears in [the section] THE SUICIDE:

Oral to stercoral (What does stercoral mean?
Who is they?)
brackish dill they swill
the darkness rolls
over the hovels, (What hovels?)
three fathom deep
the Enormous Ma (Who or what is the Enormous Ma?)
mills them like pods, (Again, who are "them"?)
puppets sing,
larvae suckle,
nymphs rehearse,
in the beginning
in the beginning.

And a bit further down the same page:

one wave length (Is this one wave length out
from a myth of a myth or away from being a
one dial twist from myth? Same for dial, etc.?)
a story of men—

17. Nicanor Parra (1914–2018), Chilean poet and physicist.

> Please explain the above as soon as possible. Naturally we'll just continue along but it's depressing and perplexing to leave a hole in the thing. Thanks. Perhaps you could write Siqueiros too. That might help. I see the mural idea, as a marvelous foldout between the English and Spanish sections of the book.
>
> Love from us all, Meg and Sergio

Those of us old enough to have used manual typewriters remember that their inked ribbons were divided horizontally into two strips, one black, the other red. Normally, the keys struck the paper through the black portion, resulting in black print. But one could raise the carriage and strike through the red for emphasis. We used this feature to ask our questions; the bulk of the letter is typed in black, with our queries in red. As we translated, we were also trying hard to get Siqueiros to make good on his promise to provide drawings for the book. At this point we were calling or visiting him every few days. Not long after our letter asking Walter to explain these lines, we received one from him with his answers.

> 8/24/64
>
> Dear Two's: Been wanting to write you a letter—but now I must answer yours of 8/20 so the letter will have to wait. (I mean, this is a telegram):
>
> Re the passage, here is the French:

oral to stercoral	Bucchal excrementiel
brackish dill they swill	ils avalent le jus
the darkness rolls	saumatre de l'aneth
over the hovels	tenebres roulent
three fathoms deep	sur les masures
the Enormous Ma	et l'Enorme Mater
mills them like pods	les moulins comme gousses

> (This French not so good, I think)

The French is an old typescript—may have been corrected. Done by Francois Hugot, whom I hope you'll meet some day.

Now, for what it means—of course, if I knew I wouldn't have written the poem. Anyhow, stercoral has to do with [ineligible word, typed over] of the ass. From Latin "excrement," "dung." As I recall, the passage has an ant reference, and oral to sterocoral is the way they feed, or lick each other—so "they" is the ants, "hovels" the antheaps. The Enormous Ma the Queen ant who lays the eggs, and then again, ants.

one wavelength from a myth
one dial twist from a story of men

The French: une longeur d'onde vouse isole d'un myths
Un petit tour du cadrab vouse separe du radioreportage de l'histoire des hommes.
i.e. away from being a myth—and away from being a story of men.

I will write Siqueiros and send copy of *Land of Roseberries.* Follow up from your end. More later, will have to get the copy from Nan.

Want to catch mail with this—and let Lillian see it, too.

xx xxx
C

I just came across, yesterday, an unmailed letter I wrote last January to Francois Hugot, who has translated me into French. I hope it won't discourage you:

Dear Francois: One of my objects is, of course, to be untranslatable—i.e., human. This includes the hairline between verse and prose poem (as in *Letters to an Imaginary Daughter*) and between prose poem and prose. To be human: to be undefinable. Socialism is one stage but that is just the beginning. In the end we are all poets, all human, all undefinable.

That is, in 1964!
Tomorrow is something else.
See you there,
Etc.

Lillian will try to help & will write separately. I have gotten a Xerox copy of *Land of Roseberries* which I will mail to Madame Angélica. You will love her. She does all the writing.

Mexico City—August 30th, 1964

Dear ones:

Many thanks for the quick answer, explanation, etc. Can't say it's completely clear, even now, but it helps. Lillian, could you perhaps, being a translator yourself, put that one verse into Spanish (any kind of Spanish)? That might help us a lot. And here are a few more questions, re: the same "Suicide":

your page 23:	For the many,	who are the many?
	just that remains	
	of what your Christ is oblivious;	
	just that escapes	
	that makes his dream.	who is his?
	So his acts of revelation . . .	again, who is his?
	. . . .	
	. . . .	
	. . . .	
	. . . .	
	. . . .	
	. . . .	
	. . . .	
	among the rising to no ends.	What does this line mean?

and on the following page, your 24:

His straw was in the wind   In this instance, what is straw, literally, metaphorically, or otherwise?

I don't think we will be having this much trouble with the rest of the poem. Perhaps in places, but looking over the whole thing, I think "Suicide" is throwing us for a strange loop and the rest will be much smoother going.

No reply from Siqueiros, as yet. Will find time to call and ask if we can come to see them as soon as *El Corno* #12 is out . . . these days we are spending long nights at the print shop, days frantic for money to get the issue out, mornings consumed with addressing envelopes, in short, the usual grind that goes with the last few weeks of getting each issue out. This should ease off in a matter of two weeks and then complete dedication to *Land of Roseberries.*

Did you write to Siqueiros yourself yet?

My parents are coming for a week or so on the 8*th* of September. The children are fine. Miguel Grinberg (Argentine poet and editor) is here with us. And a girl from Colombia, alone, who is having a baby in a matter of days . . .

Love from us all, Meg and Sergio.

9/4/64

Dear Margaret & Sergio: (I'm spelling out your names today to be closer to you). Isn't there an Indian belief that if you take away a person's name you are killing him, that is, without his name, and his poem that goes with it, he is nothing?

Yours on hand -8/30- asking questions . . . we will work together . . .

"Many are called but few are chosen." -Mathew, 22, 13. That's who the "many" are on page 23. "His dream," the reference to this is to Christ—that is, the prophet's dream. "His acts of revelation"—again, the prophet's acts. "Among the rising to no ends." You really have me there. Some thoughts occur. It's not the end point, for example, it may be that you die, but look how beautiful you were enroute. "His straw was in the wind." You ask what is straw- literally, metaphorically, or otherwise? Certainly not literally. Perhaps it is a sort of image of a man, desperate, with some odd pieces of straw in his hair, "running like an idiot." Straw can also be not just one straw, but stems or stalks of grain, collectively. Yes, it is a metaphor, sort of his destiny, the way he is heading. At the same time, it's a man with a face because he has moss in his ears.

Some passages like those you'll have to recreate when you are in the mood. I know what you are up against. I had it with Eluard's long *Poésie ininterrompue*, much of which, particularly the opening, I had to get by osmosis. Also, a good deal of Luis Cardoza y Aragón's long poem about Guatemala.

Mexico City—September 15th, 1964

Dear Peoples:

This morning, after much trying, we finally secured a date with Siqueiros. Went to his house at nine o'clock accompanied by our friend Joaquín Sánchez Macgregor who is an old friend of his. It was an incredible experience, especially for me since I had never met the man, and what was promised as a ten-minute interview turned into a two-and-a-half-hour animated conversation over breakfast in a small room adjoining the kitchen in their lovely home.

Siqueiros spoke of many things, mostly painting and our reactions to his current show of more than 200 small paintings from the four-year prison period along with some retrospective work. Afterwards we accompanied him to watch awhile as he worked on his unfinished mural of the revolution in the castle at Chapultepec. The president who set him free to "continue painting for Mexico" apparently forgot about budget approval for his murals in progress, and Siqueiros has been footing the bills for this one which in the past month alone has cost him 80,000 pesos! It is a magnificent work of art!

After much explanation of the enormous amount of work he has (answering thousands of letters from all over the world, to say nothing of his painting and other activities—the man received 20,000 cards from children in East Germany alone), Siqueiros consented to do some drawings for *Land of Roseberries*. We weren't able to pin him down as to whether it will be a series (what we are hoping for) or one mural-type foldout. He says he has never illustrated a book before. He received the copy of the manuscript from you but is faced with the problem of not being able to read English. Do you by any chance have a copy of the French translation? He reads French and that would help. We brought him several copies of the magazine and he seemed pleased . . .

Love, Meg and Sergio.

9/21/64

Dear Ones—The Siqueiros news is great, and you are great in getting that far. Let's hope now he has time to do it. The signed copies project, wonderful. We'd like to make another trip to Mexico and if the money permits we will.

Do you know Luis & Leah Cardoza y Aragón, Callejon de la s Flores 1, esquina con Calle San Francisco, Coyocan, Mexico DF 21. (Tel. 49-04-21)? If not, you will, I hope, get in touch with them. We are brothers, you will find him wonderful. And he could be very helpful on the translations. He has a little English and fluent French. Leah is multi-lingual—English, French, etc. He knows Eluard.

Love

xxxxx

C

Mexico City—October 11th, 1964

Dearest Lowenfels:

It's Sunday. Sergio and I have been working since early morning on *Roseberries*. We've a long hard day tomorrow dedicated to distributing #12 of *El Corno* to all the bookstores in the city, some 40. Usually, Sergio and I do it together, one of us driving the car around the block while the other jumps out with readied package of magazines, pen in hand, order pad open.

Although #12 turned out beautifully printing-wise, we've decided finally to change printers with #13. We are keeping this news from our current man since we are doing *Roseberries* with him (have already given him a considerable amount of the money). Reason for the change: we run ourselves ragged and feel more and more limited by his aging machines and typefaces. Although the price couldn't be beat, the relationship has long strained our nerves. Hundreds of unnecessary trips, things we must do ourselves, etc. We always put up with it for the price. Now we've found another printer, one of the finest in Mexico, unlimited plant, fonts, machinery, enormous, the opposite in every way of our present setup. The kind of place we used our first year (our first four issues) but—and this is the incredible surprise—at the same price we are now paying. We can hardly believe it. The owner, a Spanish refugee, seems to sympathize with us and has cut his estimate to the core to make us his clients. We are excited. All sorts of long-dreamed ideas which had been shelved as impossible now surface again. And perhaps less work, at least once we get through the initial issue on which they'll be learning our needs. We're only sorry we can't do *Roseberries* there, because of having already given money to our current guy.

Meg and Sergio

Mexico City—2.11.65

Dearest Lowenfels,

Please don't worry. Nothing is on our minds but getting the book out. The past two weeks re: telephone calls to Siqueiros had yielded nothing. And then, not wanting to make pests of ourselves, we held off for a few days while he was in the hospital. During that time, we finally met and were invited to the home of your friend Cardoza y Aragón, with whom we had a lovely few hours. He suggested that we call a doctor here who has a huge collection of original Siqueiros work. Sergio called and the man was very sweet. After long explanations on Sergio's part, he said he had three original unpublished line drawings which he thought would work for the book. He will give us photos of them on Saturday, from which we can have engravings made. Then Sergio, in a last attempt, called Siqueiros again. He had left a message for us (first time he's done that—a good sign!) saying he will definitely have a drawing for us on Monday. So, it looks like we may have four or more instead of the one we were resigned to or the very bad alternative of having to use known work when we'd advertised originals. Things may be working out better than we'd dreamed. If so, it will have been worth the wait. If indeed all goes well and we have the promised drawings on Saturday and Monday, we'll go into page proofs early next week, send them to you, and be at press within two weeks at the latest.

Love, Meg and Sergio

Mexico City—2.22.65

Dearest beautiful Lowenfels:

Book has gone into page proofs (as soon as they're ready we'll send your set on to you) with six beautiful and original drawings by Siqueiros.

Have called Mircea Eliade many times at Colegio de México and will try at his hotel this afternoon. We'd love meeting them.

Love, Meg, Sergio, Goyo, Sarah Dhyana, & Ximena

3/28/65

Dear Ones:

Think so of you—a great impulse to rush down and do it all over again, starting with Mérida!

Could we all meet again for the first time? The fresh human touch? Always new? (Whitman's ever-recurring spring)?

Love,
C

Mexico City—4.13.65

Dearest Lowenfels:

We want you to know that *Roseberries* will begin to breathe on the presses early next week. It seems that despite all desire and effort, these mañanas always take place in Mexico. This latest is Holy Week during which everything, including the paper houses, close for seven days. The book should have gone to press yesterday, final corrections are checked, paper chosen, etc., but no one to work on it. So now it will be Monday. But the printer tells us it will definitely be Monday. He is as anxious as we are since he needs the lead.

Meg

Mexico City—5.26.65

Dearest Lowenfels:

Today at last the distribution of Roseberries is complete. A friend helped me in the car, and we painted the town red with the book. So, it's now in every decent bookstore (and some not so decent) in the city, plus in packages and envelopes on its way to bookstores, critics, poets, magazines, reviewers, and those who placed orders from all over the world.

Our friends and some critics have already commented with enthusiasm, and the day after the volume hit the mails one review (short but very complimentary) had already appeared in El Dia.[18] I'll collect all reviews and send them to you soon. We got your card from Germany at least a week and a half ago. The books should have reached you in plenty of time. To your house in New Jersey, we sent 200 paperback copies plus 12 of the deluxe editions, which came out very nicely by the way.

The book is great. Sometimes when one translates a book this long, reads galleys and page proofs, works on all sorts of other aspects of the project, etc., one loses sight of what a great thing it is. Sergio and I are rediscovering the book now.

We both send all our love, Meg and Sergio

Sergio and I finally finished translating *Land of Roseberries/ Tierra de moras.* Siqueiros finally came through with the drawings he'd promised. The book went to press, came out in mid-1965, and sold out quickly, as did the fifty copies of the signed special edition. We had learned a great deal from Walter and Lillian and had grown as poets and translators. But the trials and tribulations connected to running a project like ours on a shoestring continued. The bookstore in Philadelphia where the owner had

18. The most progressive of Mexico City's daily newspapers at the time.

placed a large order neither paid us nor returned the books. Despite the robust sales, we were never able to reimburse the Lowenfels their outlay of one thousand dollars.

And so the long saga of producing *Land of Roseberries/ Tierra de moras* finally came to an end. All the problems connected with the project faded. Our deepening relationships with Walter and Lillian, and the book itself, were all that remained.

Mexico City—6.28.65

Dear Walter:

Did you ever see the review of Lillian and Nan's book of translations that I did for KULCHUR? It appeared in the last issue. It has caused a break in relations between Clayton Eshleman and me. He seems to think anyone liking those translations couldn't or shouldn't like his. He withdrew all work from *El Corno.* I don't agree, think he is acting like a big child, no offense to children.

I had to go to visit Siqueiros the other day because the Bemis Street Property Group sent their limited edition back to us saying they didn't want it unless it was signed by the artist. So, I took it to his house, having spoken with Angélica the day before. When I arrived, I couldn't see Siqueiros who spends most of his time in bed now. He happily signed the book and sent it down, saying he had liked it very much. I have a feeling the man is failing. He hasn't worked on the mural for months and has been in trouble ever since that first fall. It's so sad to think of someone with such energy and direction in that condition.

Love, Meg and Sergio.

David Alfaro Siqueiros would live another eight and a half years, dying on January 6, 1974. But he did slow down, and we felt privileged to have been able to pair drawings by him with Walter's poem. I thought the long story of how we collaborated on *Land of Roseberries/Tierra de moras* was complete, but a letter from Walter later in 1965 added an unexpected postscript.

7/15/65

Did we ever tell you how *Roseberries* was actually financed? Around 1948 or so, when Lee Hays, my best friend at the time, was living with us in Philly, we wrote some songs together, including "Wasn't that a Time" and "Lonesome Traveler." Some years later, middle 50's, tiny royalty checks began straggling in. I got so annoyed about it, not wanting my relations with Lee to be $$$ relations on such a lousy little basis. I turned my royalties over to *Sing Out*, the folksong mag which was struggling to stay alive. And to make sure I would never be touched by the cash nexus of songs, I did it absolutely legally, lawyers, documents, et al. Finish.

We now skip ten years to last November. Scene: Pete Seeger's cabin on top of the Hudson. Toshi asks me about the songs. Don't I need the money, why don't I abrogate the agreement? *Sing Out*, she says is now a money-making business, circulation over 15,000. The song royalties should be going to me. What do I do? I ask. Just tell them, there won't be any trouble or difficulty. I could never do such a thing, could you help? In a minute Toshi was on the phone with Hal, their agent, and Lee's. All you have to do is write two letters. What kind of letters, would you write them? She did, I signed them, and that was it.

Starting last December we began to get twice a year royalty checks—pennies from "Wasn't that a Time" but hundreds from "Lonesome Traveler." So, we figure, everything averages out. And "Lonesome Traveler" became *Land of Roseberries*.

Love, Walt

Walter Lowenfels continued to be an enthusiastic collaborator of the magazine. In our #17, which appeared in January 1966, we published a prose piece by him:

HOW IT STARTED

Paul Bunyan was born one day in the Gitchee Gumee woods in the great Tahquamenon swamp in Delta County, Michigan, USA. And his father was Ilya Murometz of Moscow, Russia and his mother was Fleet Footed Deer of the Ojibwe Nation. He nursed on the waters of Lake Superior, and when he drank the big lake dry, he started screaming for more. That blew up a range of mountains on the north shore, bringing the Nipogon's flow into Lake Superior. The blast of Paul's first cry shook the Upper Peninsula and rocked the country as far as the Everglades which never got over it and are swamps to this day.

Still Paul was thirsty, and he got real angry. He hitched Babe, the Big Blue Ox, to the primeval spigot and yanked out the Atlantic Ocean. The rest of the oceans trickled out when he fell asleep and left the tap dripping. And the Big Auger River squirted 77 barrels of water into his eye before he woke up.

Then the squirrels started complaining to Paul that the nights were too cold and the days too hot. He hitched Babe, the Blue-Eyed Ox, to a big Sequoia Forest on the coast, threw out the Canadian Rockies for an anchor, and yanked. That slowed down the earth until it got to be 24 hours a day, and the little ants began crawling out of the Archeozoic stew.

But still, it didn't have the modern orbit. Paul threw a lariat over the Milky Way, tightened the noose around the spiral nebulas in Andromeda, and got the orbital eccentricity low enough for the bumble bees to molt and the algae to sprout.

This was all before Adam and Eve, when the chemical content of the air, ocean, and land surfaces was polluted with dirt

> *from the original dust, making it inimical to biological operations. Paul ran his whiskers through the Saragossa Sea, churned up enough soap suds to wash up the air and got 140 million whales to blow the dirt off the face of the globe. The first baby was a whale that gave birth to Jonah, and the human race began.*

This was an era in which some poets as well as historians were beginning to realize that we couldn't depend on the history books to tell us our true history. Epic poets such as Ernesto Cardenal were writing poems that told parts of our human narrative from the point of view of Indigenous peoples, the poor, and other previously unheard groups. Lowenfels wrote in this tradition, but his work was often infused with a sort of whimsy.

Over the next few years, my life would take some surprising turns. Sergio and I met and fell in love at a very particular moment in Latin and North American literary history. Poets on both sides of the border had previously looked to Europe for inspiration; now we were beginning to realize there was a rich legacy in our own countries. Only good translation was lacking. We undertook the creation of *El Corno Emplumado* to fill that need.

In 1967, Sergio and I separated, and the following year he left the magazine. Two trips to Cuba, one at the beginning of 1967 and the other a year later, made deep impressions on me. I had never seen socialism in action, and it brought me even closer to the Lowenfels. I also became a Mexican citizen in 1966, inadvertently losing my U.S. citizenship as a result. People assumed I had done this for political reasons, but that wasn't the case. I simply wanted to be able to support my family, and acquiring Mexican citizenship made that a lot easier.

In 1968, as in so many other parts of the world, young people were rebelling.[19] The Mexican student movement suddenly surged and gripped us all. It began in July with a march in honor of the Cuban Revolution. The government cracked down on the marchers and a student was killed. Students took to the streets throughout the country, eventually joined by intellectuals, farmers, and workers.

The fervor might have subsided, and everything gone back to normal, had it not been for the fact that Mexico was preparing to host the 1968 Summer Olympics. A great deal of money had been invested in new sports installations, hotels, and other venues. Prospective visitors began canceling, and the government panicked. The Olympics were due to begin on October 12. On October 2, military and paramilitary forces attacked a peaceful demonstration at a place called the Plaza of the Three Cultures. Some estimates put the death toll at more than one thousand. Many of the survivors were imprisoned. Some managed to leave the country. Like thousands of others, I'd taken part in the movement. My life changed radically as I saw for the first time what a government was willing to do to its citizenry when it felt threatened.

A year later, as we were preparing to commemorate the first anniversary of our struggle, I was hit with a political repression that sent me underground, and we made the painful decision to send our four young children to Cuba until I could find a way out of the country and join them. By then I was living with a young U.S. poet named Robert Cohen and with him had recently

19. In France, they called it "the Paris May." Columbia University was shut down by a student strike. Struggles came to a head in South Africa, among other places.

had a daughter named Ana. Robert helped me edit *El Corno*'s last two issues, after Sergio relinquished his coeditorship. But the repression finally made further publication impossible.

I believe the Mexican and U.S. governments had their eye on me long before this, however. A foreigner involving herself in leftist politics was probably suspect. My two trips to Cuba also brought unwelcome attention from the powers that be. And, for the United States, adopting Mexican citizenship also put me in a bad light.

Just after changing my citizenship and before we separated, Sergio and I had plans to do a reading tour of U.S. universities, take the children, and spend Christmas with my parents in New Mexico. No longer a citizen, I had to apply for a visa. Our plans were jeopardized by my being denied the right to visit the country where I was born. In a letter to the Lowenfels, I described a week of interrogation at the U.S. consulate in Mexico City.

November 15th, 1966

Dearest Walter and Lillian:

This has been a grim week. I received my Mexican citizenship last Tuesday and on Wednesday went to the American consulate for my visa. They denied it, accusing me of being a member of the Communist Party. I am not and never have been, but almost all week (Wednesday through the following Monday) was spent at the consulate. About half that time I was shifted from office to office, the other half locked in a tiny room with a man I assume to be FBI. He carried out a prolonged and repetitive interrogation that went something like this:

You are.

I'm not.

You are. We know. Admit it.

I'm not. I never have been.

(Shuffling of papers and five minutes of silence)

Okay, ready to admit it now.

No.

We have proof.

What proof?

Can't say.

May I have a cigarette?

No.

May I go to the bathroom?

No.

How can I prove something I'm not? You should prove I am, no?

No. We can't disclose our sources. It might compromise them.

Well, you're compromising me with false accusations.

(This conversation repeated ad infinitum)

At night they would let me go, in the morning I would have to come back. I thought it had something to do with the magazine until they cleared Sergio and issued him a visa. So, the scary part is not knowing what this is about. I called Rafael Squirru in Washington, and he promised to do everything in his power to help.[20] This morning the consulate sent a wire (which I had to pay for) to the State Department for its decision. The reply should come by Friday. If they grant the visa, we will leave as planned, just a few days late. If not, Sergio will go alone, read

20. Rafael Squirru, an Argentine poet, was head of the Pan-American Union, the cultural arm of the Organization of American States (OAS). We had published him in *El Corno,* and he got the Union to purchase five hundred subscriptions, which would have paid for an entire issue. But when he said we shouldn't publish work by Cubans, we refused, and he canceled the subscriptions. Nevertheless, faced with the refusal to issue me a visa, I called on him for help.

my poems along with his, and at each university explain why I couldn't be there.

When I was in that little room, I kept thinking of you, Lillian, and you, Walter, Miguel Donoso Pareja and Judith Gutiérrez,[21] and countless others. I realize what they put me through is minimal in comparison, yet it shook me to my core.

Love to you both from us all, Meg.

11/19/66

Dear Margaret:

Re your visa experience, I hope you write it up. Like I wrote Cubby (Hubert Selby): Don't waste time being crazy in the Institution. Get a typewriter and get it all down. They must want something from you. Remember, everything is bugged so they have a complete record of the conversation.

Love, Walt

I was finally granted a temporary travel document that allowed me to make that trip to the States, but I had to keep a list of every place I visited and what I did there. It was a good trip. Soon after our return to Mexico, Sergio and I traveled to Cuba for the Encuentro con Rubén Darío, an event hosted by Casa de las Américas to honor the one-hundreth anniversary of the great Nicaraguan modernist poet.[22] Cuba impressed me profoundly, and I wrote a series of poems about the experience. I called the series *So Many Rooms Has a House but One Roof.* I

21. Miguel Donoso Pareja and Judith Gutiérrez, he a poet and she a painter, were victims of repression in Ecuador who took refuge in Mexico and were friends. Judith helped us with *El Corno* for a time.

22. Rubén Darío (1867–1916) was a Nicaraguan poet who initiated the Spanish-language literary movement known as modernism that flourished at the end of the nineteenth century.

sent those poems to Walter, and he wrote, "The Cuban series arrived. I read it once and it brought tears to my eyes. What that means I don't know. Will read more and write you again." These poems were published as a small book by New Rivers Press in Minneapolis. Felipe Ehrenberg, a Mexican artist who did several covers for *El Corno,* designed the cover.

Shortly after that first trip to Cuba, I went to the post office one morning, as I did every day, to retrieve the contents of our postal box. I parked in front, which wasn't legal, but I was just running in and out, so I chanced it. As I was exiting the driver's side, the corner of my door caught a passing cyclist, tore up his leg, and threw him from his bike. He was nine years old. Passersby urged me to flee the scene, but I couldn't leave the kid alone in the road, so I reentered the post office and called an ambulance. This resulted in an ordeal for me, as well. As I wrote in a letter to the Lowenfels dated 2.22.68:

> Jail for the traffic offense was in line with how such things are handled here. There were no fines involved and, strangely enough, the bribes I offered weren't accepted, making me wonder if this wasn't political. The problem was, I stayed with the boy who was hurt, called an ambulance, and waited for it to come instead of fleeing. The police came and took me to a nearby police station. I told the truth, that I was briefly parked illegally when the boy hit my car. For telling the truth, they threw the book at me. I spent the night in a small cell at the precinct and was transferred to prison the next day. Anyway, it's all over with now. What remains are the faces of my cellmates who don't have the influence I have and will probably rot there. Love, Meg

One of the most popular features of the magazine was a section of letters at the back of each issue. Poets and artist wrote to us from across the globe, describing their lives, their work, and the various situations they faced. In our issue #28, we published a letter from Walter:

Peekskill, New York—7/20/68

I've read your plastic age poem and I wish I had time to find the relevant pages in my autobiography that I want to send you—about how to grow old. It boils down to this: we are surrounded by barrages of what to do to stay young. But the problem nobody seems to write about or teach us about, is how to grow old, how to wage daily battles against nostalgia (ou sont les neiges d'antan?) I think I indicate some of that in *Imaginary Daughter . . .*

For poets and editors, it is a very practical affair: how to keep up with tomorrow. Among the 90,000 "best poets of our generation" that throng the publishing highways of the USA, there are innumerable circles, few of which are aware of the others. To the Lowell-Auden-Kunitz circle, the Sonia Sanchez-Olga Cabral-Clarence Major circle doesn't exist.

The poetry upsurge continues. And Alice would have a hard time keeping up with the Red Queen of poems.

That's where the age problem arises. How fresh and useful is your ear? Can you still hear tomorrow's poems today? (We can all hear our own poem; the youth problem is to be able to continue to hear the other new poem.)

Critics don't have this problem. Their job seems to be to bury yesterday's poem. To hear Dante the minute Dante writes it—that's the eternal youth of the ear that can't be stopped.

Apollinaire said it years ago:

"Pitie pour nous qui combattons toujours aux frontieres
De l'illimite et de l'avenir."

And yet—why pity? What other life is there?
See you there!—

Love, WALTER LOWENFELS

Life in Mexico rapidly deteriorated for me. I must have sent Walter and Lillian news of what was happening, at least in telegraphic form, because on September 1, 1969, Walter wrote.

> Your autobiography I raced through to find out what had happened to you recently. I am bewildered; please give ordinary facts. There is in general a lack of news here about events below the border, so we are completely in the dark.

On September 5, I wrote to them.

> It's a long story. We were a happy family with a new baby and marvelous plans to finally take the Cubans up on job offers there in September, after the children saw their father for the summer. So, we were slowly making plans to rent the house, leave *El Corno* in the hands of a good administrator who would take care of the secretarial and distribution ends here, and set off. All this when, on July 7*th*, two agents came to our house and by means of a clever ruse we fell right into, stole my passport. I had no choice but to denounce the theft and apply for a replacement. The government refused to issue a new passport, and police harassment at the house got heavy. We were forced into hiding and had to send all four children (including Ana who was born in March 1969) to Havana for their safety and our mobility. For about a month, I didn't show my face. Robert was forced to go around more or less in the open, although he, too, lost his job when all this began. Gradually, I've begun to go out more, that is to say I'm not completely in hiding, but we haven't been able to go back to the house. It's up for sale (friends are

helping), and we've given everything else away: furniture, books . . .

The repression seems to center on *El Corno*. We can never do the magazine again in Mexico, and we managed to get an article into one of the daily papers to the effect that the magazine is dead. (That's why I'm returning your subscription check.) But the government won't give in. We got a lawyer, and while there doesn't seem to be an official charge against me, they simply refuse to issue a passport. I went to the American consulate in an effort to get my US citizenship back (I'd been called in earlier to sign an affidavit regarding the Afroyim decision, which affected loss of nationality, so there was a precedent for my showing up there) but while they, for once, treated me with polite civility, the answer was no, direct from Washington. It could well be the Americans are behind this whole thing, as you might imagine.

Meanwhile, we wait. The children's absence is like an open wound, although we know they are being well cared for. The news we get from and of them proves beyond a doubt that children are really the "privileged class" in the revolution. But it's been almost two months now without them, almost a third of the baby's life.

Meanwhile, we float. Friends have been terrific, and we've been living with one, then another. We certainly don't have much to complain about in comparison to so many brothers and sisters suffering torture, imprisonment, and other hardships everywhere, to say nothing of the vast majority of the world's oppressed. But it's the uncertainty of the situation that's so disconcerting.

We've thought of trying to make an international scandal but have been advised to hold back until we've exhausted all possible influences here first. The Mexican government doesn't

> seem to respond well to outside protest. I remind myself I haven't been hit as hard as many, including both of you, but can't help falling into periodic depression when everything seems very dim. Anyway, I'll keep you informed.

A few days after writing this letter, I was able to make my way out of the country. A friend got the promise of a false passport if I could manage to get to the northern city of Chihuahua. I went to a beauty parlor in a part of vast Mexico City where I knew no one and got a complete makeover: my hair dyed and teased, eyebrows plucked. I don't think my own mother would have recognized me if she'd passed me on the street. I dressed very traditionally, and Robert and I flew to Chihuahua under assumed names. The passport arrangement fell through, but the person charged with obtaining it for me got me out of the country in the back of a refrigerated meat truck.

Robert flew to New York to spend a week with his parents, then went on to Cuba via Madrid. Without legal papers, I had to use a different route: a Greyhound bus from El Paso to Toronto—crossing the border with an old birth certificate—a flight to Paris, where I managed to avoid immigration officials, and then on to Prague. There the Cubans received me and put me in a hotel for nineteen days, while I waited for a seat on a once-weekly flight to the island. Elsewhere I've told the story of meeting the Cuban airline pilot who had flown my children from Mexico City to Havana. He was in Prague, waiting for a replacement part for his decades-old Soviet plane. Magic realism exists even in such crises.

I had been ill since Ana's birth. In fact, I was in bed when the paramilitary agents came to my house and took my passport at gunpoint. Unable to see a doctor, I didn't know what was wrong. Periodic high fevers and chills accompanied me on that dramatic journey from Mexico through the United States and Canada to Paris, Prague, and then Havana. It wasn't until I arrived in Cuba and reunited with Robert and the children that I was able to seek medical attention. Doctors removed my left kidney in December 1969. I wrote to the Lowenfels shortly after I got out of the hospital.

La Habana, Cuba—12.4.69

Year of the Decisive Effort

Dearest Walter and Lillian:

Just back from the hospital. Feeling better but still have to take it easy.

I hardly know where to begin—suddenly realizing you aren't up to date on all that's happened. Briefly, we did get out of Mexico. I had to go halfway around the world, but finally managed to get to Havana October 12th. Robert had arrived on the 4th. The children are great, real little revolutionaries already. The older three are "becados," in school during the week and with us on weekends. The baby is in a casa de cuna until we are assigned housing; we visit her every day. I'm working at the Instituto del Libro, translating Martí into English. Robert may have a job at Radio Havana; he'll know for sure this week. We're still living in a hotel but happy, together, relieved. Over these last months and especially during the repression, I began having increasingly serious kidney attacks and so was finally operated on last Thursday. They removed my left kidney. So, I'm not 100% right now, but hopefully things should go well from here on out. There's so much work I want to do . . .

Much love to you all, Meg.

All of us, to various degrees, adapted to life in Cuba. Participating in a society aimed at establishing social justice for all its citizens was a continuous lesson—in ingenuity, creativity, sacrifice, and human frailty. The Lowenfels and I continued to correspond regularly. Although I never saw them again, I felt closer than ever because I understood more fully what they had been fighting for their entire adult lives.

The revolution marked my life profoundly; I've always considered it my great good fortune and a privilege to have lived in Cuba eleven years, juggling the enormous problems that come with social change of such magnitude and experiencing on the ground how constant imperialist attacks impede progress. I've always wondered what Cuba might have achieved had the United States left it alone. Those eleven years also taught me that revolutionary societies, too, make mistakes. I often ask myself what Walter and Lillian would have made of the developments—good and bad—that accompanied "real socialism's" successes and eventual failure. Would they have remained in the U.S. Communist Party or left, as so many did?

On June 27, 1975, I wrote:

> Dear Walter:
>
> Last night, eating dinner with a Canadian friend, Robert Davies, the conversation turned to you, our mutual friend. Suddenly, I learned that Lillian died. Somehow it was more of a shock than similar news about much younger, apparently healthy, friends. Certainly, these years have been filled with a great deal of death: Chileans, Vietnamese, Africans, and the deaths of friends. Hearing about Lillian leaving brought to my racing mind so many scenes: of her giving us all her constant energy, her endless courage, her lasting lessons of strength.
>
> I wish I could be there with you now, to share her absence, what must be hard times for you, my dear friend. The same enemy that tried to diminish Lillian's energy (but couldn't) keeps us apart. Perhaps that enemy will continue to keep us

apart so that we won't see each other again. But I am with you. You have my love and solidarity . . .

Much love, Margaret.

In a letter I can no longer find, I remember Walter's telling me that the night before she died, Lillian asked him to make sure to pay her Party dues. She didn't want to go with that debt on her mind. In an undated letter, written I believe sometime later,[23] Walter wrote, "Have decided not to publish any more short books, but concentrate on getting out my *Later Collected Poems.* Do you think the time is ripe? Or shall I wait for my 100th birthday which I will celebrate next year. I was born in 1897 but can't wait until 1997."

Walter didn't make it to one hundred in Earth-year terms. He died at the age of seventy-nine in 1976, not long after Lillian. He'd done enough in the time he had to render the actual years irrelevant. And inspired by his ability to read time backward and forward, we must judge his life span by a different standard.

23. The correspondence at the Beinecke has several letters from each of us that are undated.

11

LAURETTE SÉJOURNÉ: COMPASS, MENTOR, FRIEND; ARNALDO ORFILA: A MAN WHO FILLED A CENTURY

These walls that crumble in peasant hands
contain the key to the Mesoamerican spiritual edifice.[24]

—Laurette Séjourné

Arnaldo Orfila not only lived for a century but filled it.[25]

—Carlos Fuentes

FALL 1961. A YOUNG single mother of twenty-five, I'd recently arrived in Mexico City with my ten-month-old son, Gregory. Four years living and learning among the Abstract Expressionist painters and Beat poets of New York City had helped me embark upon my own journey as a poet, but now I needed a

24. Laurette Séjourné, *Pensamiento y religion en México antiguo*, chapter 3, "El lenguaje simbólico nahuatl." The original Spanish reads: *"Estos muros que se deshacen entre las manos de los campesinos encierran la clave de la estructura spiritual mesoamericana."* English translation M.R.

25. Attributed to the Mexican novelist Carlos Fuentes, in "La revolución editorial de Arnaldo Orfila Reynal," by Víctor Irwin Nova Ramírez. The Spanish reads: *"Orfila Reynal no solo vivió un siglo, lo llenó."* English translation M.R.

change of scene. In New York at that time there were few social services for mothers with small children, and I had to work so hard to support the two of us that I rarely had time to spend with my son. New York had given me a lot and now it was time to go elsewhere. I had visited Mexico previously and believed its slower pace and more humanistic approach to life would enable me to spend more time with Gregory and connect to some ancient mystery I only vaguely intuited. We boarded a Greyhound bus and headed south, stopping to visit for a week with my parents in Albuquerque.

In New York, I worked with Nancy Macdonald at Spanish Refugee Aid, a hand-to-mouth endeavor established to help the survivors of Spain's Civil War who, following their tragic defeat, had escaped to camps in southern France and North Africa. When I told Nancy I was going to Mexico, she gave me a list of friends she thought I should look up; the list included such illustrious names as Lázaro Cárdenas and Erich Fromm. I was much too shy to call on an ex-president or world-renown psychoanalyst. The only names on that list that didn't scare me off were those of Laurette Séjourné and Arnaldo Orfila Reynal, probably because I didn't know who they were. Had I known, I might have been intimidated by them, as well.

It took me a few weeks to find a small apartment in the modest middle-class neighborhood of Colonia Narvarte, hire a young woman to help with the baby, and start looking for work. I occasionally glanced wistfully at the list Nancy had given me. There was no phone number for Laurette and Arnaldo, but I noticed that their address, on Avenida Universidad, wasn't far from my new home. One day I wrapped Gregory in a rebozo—Mexico's Indigenous version of the canvas sling I'd used in New York—and walked to their apartment. They weren't home, but

I left a note with Isabela, the quiet but gracious Indian maid who answered the door.

Nancy Macdonald and her brother, Selden Rodman, had spent much of their considerable family fortune rescuing intellectuals and artists fleeing mid-twentieth-century European fascism. They posted the financial bonds required for them to take refuge in the United States or Mexico and often also paid for their transatlantic passage. They had helped Laurette and her second husband, Victor Serge, escape France. Perhaps this was why the brief note I left for Laurette and Arnaldo moved them to respond so quickly. We'd been back home only an hour or so when I heard a knock on my door and opened it, to see them standing there with warm smiles and a box of chocolates in hand.

I no longer remember those initial visits that brought us close, because it soon felt as if we'd always been friends. As with so many artists and writers in New York—the majority much older and more established than I—I think back with astonishment that Laurette and Arnaldo would take an interest in someone like me, a young, inexperienced woman just starting out on her creative journey. But for whatever reason, and despite the vast difference in our ages, we soon enjoyed a deep friendship, one that would last until their deaths many years later.

Laurette was the quintessential outrider, a brilliantly fearless thinker, and a rebel in every area in which she engaged. She rejected her father's fascist leanings, left home to escape them, and gravitated toward intellectuals and artists, such as André Breton, Henri Cartier-Bresson, Victor Serge, and Claude Lévi-Strauss, who were politically progressive and breaking with convention in their fields. She married powerful men but never subsumed herself to them, keeping her own name and making contributions in professions in which few women excelled at the time. Like most Western intellectuals, she had a strong foundation in Marxism but took what she considered valuable and discarded what she didn't. She consistently imbued her work with her own vision, even when it was at odds with what the experts were saying.

Laurette always felt like an older sister to me, although her vast knowledge, consciousness, depth, and willingness to transmit what she knew without ever making me feel ignorant or inadequate made her unusual in that regard. Rare in many, she trusted her intellect and her intuition, allowing them to feed each other. She told me fascinating stories about trips she'd made entirely alone to sites of ancient Mexican life, sometimes spending hours sitting quietly as evening closed in, simply absorbing the descending light, temperature, and feel of the land those people she was trying to understand had inhabited before her.

In the early 1960s, Laurette was working on a dig at Teotihuacán she called the "Palace of the Butterflies." This was a residential area for those who'd built the imposing pyramids. She would drive out there once a week—her back straight and her small gloved hands on the steering wheel of their gray Peugeot—to evaluate what her on-site workers had unearthed, decide what she wanted to take back to the city for further study, and instruct them on how to proceed until her next visit. She often invited me and my son to accompany her. She would prepare our lunch in a beautiful wicker basket—roasted chicken, fine pâtés, several different cheeses, and fruits—and we would picnic surrounded by the unknown meaning of ancient pyramids and the secrets of barely revealed artifacts. Gregory would play happily in the dirt while she introduced me to a history that fascinated as it seduced. On other occasions, Arnaldo would join us and we'd make short trips to Amecameca or to other nearby villages with strong Indigenous legacies.

This was our introduction to a world about which I knew nothing but which exerted an attraction I found impossible to resist. I am sure it was the beginning of my fascination with ancient sites throughout the world. Young as he was at the time, Gregory says the same about himself; when they were young, he told his own children stories of ancient peoples. I've since traveled to, written about, and photographed the great Incan and pre-Incan cities, Greek and Roman ruins such as Carthage, Delphi, and Ephesus, Nabataean Petra, Butrint in previously inaccessible Albania, and many Ancestral Puebloan sites in my own U.S. Southwest.

I soon began to understand that the vestiges of Mesoamerica's ancient cultures so fascinating to Laurette weren't simply romantic holdovers from some distant and so-called primitive past. They were evidence of complex sociocultural and spiritual systems that the anthropological and archaeological establishments were trying to decipher. Theories abounded, generally tainted by the filters imposed by "experts" unable to shed their modern-day biases. The code underlying the early language of the Maya wouldn't be fully broken until the 1980s. I began to understand that Laurette was developing ideas that often found themselves in contradiction with the male-dominated xenophobic status quo of Mexico's elite.

The mid-twentieth century was not an easy time for smart, assertive, courageous, and independent women whose thinking differed from that of their male colleagues. Although a great deal has changed, it's not nearly enough. Laurette was a freethinker capable of testing her intuition with meticulous research. She'd acquired vast cultural knowledge in Europe, equal, if not superior, to that possessed by many in the establishment that she had the audacity to try to join. Many of her Mexican contemporaries were intimidated by her brilliance. They tried with every weapon in their arsenal to discredit her. Arnaldo, then the director of El Fondo de Cultura Económica, believed in her work and published splendid lavishly illustrated editions of her early books, thus angering her detractors even more.

Laurette's conclusions emerged from her refusal to accept any sort of dogma—historical, economic, political, psychological, or religious. She was a Marxist who was more interested in the practical problems of social change than in competing party lines. She wasn't religious but understood that systems of belief developed by cosmological observation and ritualistic stories created to explain natural phenomenon shaped the way the Nahua and Maya lived. Throughout her career, whether in her archaeological work, later investigations of popular theater in Cuba, or oral history work with Cuban women, she asked questions, listened intently, and followed her own extraordinary mind. Eventually, she won respect from those who matter, but not without enormous personal cost.

There are so many strong, independent, and brilliant women in every field who suffer marginalization and must learn to resist the temptation to give up. Laurette was certainly not alone in this. But she was the victim of particularly egregious treatment along the way. Mexican scholar Tatiana Coll has written about some of this: attacks by establishment figures and even the mysterious disappearance of every copy of one of her books.[26] Her

26. The book was *Un palacio en la ciudad de los dioses: Teotihuacan*. This book contained the only evidence of the existence of a series of extraordinary murals that Laurette had discovered in the 1950s at Zacuala. The murals had been removed from the site, to prevent them from being damaged, and taken to the National Institute of Anthropology and History for safekeeping. But they disappeared from its warehouses and were never seen

response was always to immerse herself more deeply in the exploration of her ideas and keep working.

Laurette married three times, but, except in the case of her first husband, Bernard Séjourné, kept her own surname. Bernard introduced her to the world of cinema, where, as a very young woman, she excelled as the editor of several important films. Her second husband, the Belgian revolutionary and novelist Victor Serge, expanded her political horizons at a time when communism was attempting to transform societies through class struggle and its goal of greater equality and social justice. It was with him that she came to Mexico.

When Serge died, in 1947, leaving her to rear his two children, Vlady[27] and Jeannine, Laurette was already studying anthropology. A few short years later, she married her third husband, the Argentine public intellectual and publisher Arnaldo Orfila. Their marriage would last for the duration. The scholar and essayist Víctor Erwin Nova Ramírez said of them, "It's difficult to know where their work life ended, and their personal life began." They were a couple who complemented and supported one another. I remember observing them and wondering if I would ever be fortunate enough to have such a relationship myself. But Laurette was never subordinate to any man. She came up in an era before the articulation of second-wave feminism, and never that I knew of described herself as a feminist. But she possessed all the qualities of one: a commitment to

---

again. Laurette's book was published by the INAH in 1959 and then the entire edition mysteriously disappeared from bookstores and libraries, only to be republished by El Fondo de Cultura Económica in 2002. See "Laurette Séjourné Una Mujer Libre, de Pico y Pala," by Tatiana Coll, Mexico City 2024.

27. Vladimir Victorovich Kibbalchich Rusakov (1920–2005) was a Russian-Mexican painter known simply as "Vlady" in Mexico.

gender equality, independence and individuality, the conviction that she had the right to demand the time and space necessary to do her work, the assumption that she would be able to accomplish whatever she set out to do, and a fierce sense of purpose. She had many important friendships with women. I always felt privileged to be one of them.

Arnaldo Orfila had his own history of struggle. Born in La Plata, Argentina, in 1897, he earned a doctorate in chemistry from that city's university, was one of the student leaders of the University Reform Movement that exploded in Córdoba, Argentina, in 1918, and was a member of Argentina's Socialist Party from 1930 to 1948. In 1937, he traveled to Spain as a correspondent during that country's Civil War. He founded the Alejandro Korn People's University in 1938 and was its director until 1947, but eventually he went into publishing, where he had a stellar career.

Argentina had few book publishers at that time, and Orfila immigrated to Mexico in 1947. El Fondo de Cultura Económica, a continentally known publishing house founded in 1934, was already an influential institution. Arnaldo became its director in 1948 and led it in the acquisition of important titles in history, economics, sociology, psychology, and literature. But FCE was partially funded by the Mexican government, and when it released *Listen, Yankee!*, by C. Wright Mills, and *The Children of Sánchez*, by Oscar Lewis—two books that the powers that be felt showed the country in a bad light—the government fired Orfila, giving him and Laurette seventeen hours to vacate their home, which was situated above the publishing house's offices. It was 1965.

Authors who had been published by Orfila, as well as intellectuals and artists generally, were outraged and immediately came to his defense. I was one of them. Rarely had these extremely competitive personalities agreed so overwhelmingly about anything. A group of us hosted a dinner—at Mexico City's Swiss Club, if I remember correctly—with more than fifty in attendance. Our goal was to sell bonds to help Arnaldo establish his own publishing house, free from censorship. I remember Elena Poniatowska[28] rising from her seat at the table to offer her home as its physical site. Arnaldo accepted on the condition that it not be a donation but, rather, in trade for shares in the new venture.

That evening, Siglo XXI was born. Over the next few years, I would publish often under its imprint. Two of my books came out in the popular Colección Mínima series, small, inexpensive books with a wide circulation. The first was called *Los hippies.* It was an introduction to the origins and impact of the countercultural youth movement then sweeping the United States. The second, *Las mujeres,* was a small anthology of texts from diverse sectors of the burgeoning feminist movement that would profoundly change the world and my life. I remember that Arnaldo wisely suggested that we keep the word *feminist* out of the title so that the book would make it past the censorship then rampant throughout Latin America.[29] All these years later, both books remain in print, and I still occasionally receive letters from grateful readers. Many of the letters I reprint here detail aspects of our collaboration.

---

28. Elena Poniatowska (1932) is a French-Mexican journalist and author who has written fearlessly about taboo subjects. Her book *The Night of Tlatelolco,* an exposé of the Mexican government's brutal repression of the 1968 student movement, was censored for thirty years before being available in Mexico.

29. Writers were proud of their books being excluded by censorship. On the other hand, Friedrich Engels and Karl Marx's pivotal work, *The Holy Family,* made it past the censors because they thought it was a religious book.

In Mexico, as discussed at length in the previous chapter, I would launch my own publishing venture with poet Sergio Mondragón. We called it *El Corno Emplumado.* Laurette was one of the witnesses to Sergio's and my marriage in Tepotzlán. Years later, divorced from Sergio and living with U.S. poet Robert Cohen, I named my fourth daughter Ana Laurette. Arnaldo was an important mentor to my son, Gregory. The couple had a central presence in our family's life.

Living in Mexico and reading its contemporary literature had made me aware of the vibrant poetry being written throughout the Spanish-speaking world, and the urgent need for good translations.[30] Poets in the global North had little knowledge of what our contemporaries south of the border were writing, and those throughout Mexico and Latin America were equally ignorant of what was being produced in the United States and Canada. Few in one language were being published in the other and, when they were, the translations were usually atrocious.

Sergio and I cofounded and coedited *El Corno Emplumado/The Plumed Horn* to try to remedy this situation. We were young and inexperienced, and I still look back in awe at what we were able to accomplish. We published Ernesto Cardenal for the first time in English and Allen Ginsberg for the first time in Spanish, among many others. We may have been the last to publish a poem by Hermann Hesse, as he sent it to us weeks before his death. We also produced a series of bilingual books, such as Walter Lowenfels's *Land of Roseberries/Tierra de moras.* We were able to sustain the venture for almost eight years, producing

30. The need for a venue such as *El Corno Emplumado* emerged at the nightly salon held by U.S. Surrealist poet Philip Lamantia and his wife, Lucille. I frequented that salon during my first months in Mexico. I met Sergio there, and together we took on the challenge.

quarterly issues of between 100 and 250 pages each. We distributed them around the world, albeit in small quantities. The magazine was forced to stop publishing in 1969 as a result of the editorial stance we took in defense of the 1968 student movement.

Arnaldo was one of our first and most faithful supporters, providing us with lists of potential patrons and placing ads for his publishing house in several issues. Laurette was equally enthusiastic. *El Corno* #1 opened with her beautiful essay "El culto mágico de una virgen" ("A Virgin's Magic Cult").[31] The following year, our issue #5 featured another text by Laurette, "En busca de la cultura perdida ("In Search of the Lost Culture").[32] And that whole issue was illustrated by Laurette's longtime collaborator Abel Mendoza, with his wonderful drawings from pre-Columbian codices, artifacts, and tombs.

Laurette and Arnaldo helped us with contacts, financial aid, and intellectual input throughout the magazine's life. They were among our most assiduous supporters. Following the Mexican student movement of 1968, when I was hit with the repression that forced me into hiding and eventually out of the country, they hid us for several weeks at their home adjacent to Siglo XXI. From those fraught evenings, I retain the comforting taste of vegetable soup sprinkled with grated Parmesan; that must have been my introduction to soup served in that way. After I managed to take refuge in Cuba, we continued to see one another when they visited the island and sustained a rich correspondence for many years.

31. *El Corno Emplumado* 1 (January 1962).
32. *El Corno Emplumado* 5, (January 1963).

In 1983, Mexico recognized Orfila with its prestigious Order of the Aztec Eagle, the country's highest honor. Jesús Silva Herzog, in his presentation, made it clear that this was the government's way of apologizing for its earlier treatment of a man who contributed so much, not only to Mexico's cultural life but to Latin American culture, as well.

I can't remember the year in which I saw Laurette and Arnaldo for the last time. By then, I was back in the United States after almost a quarter of a century in Latin America: eight years in Mexico, eleven in Cuba, and four in Nicaragua. I had survived five years of deportation proceedings by the U.S. government because of the content of some of my books, had won my case, and was finally able to travel again. I was visiting my two adult daughters, who had chosen to make Mexico their home, and my son, Gregory, was also visiting from Uruguay.

Gregory suggested we pay Laurette and Arnaldo a visit. This must not have been long before Arnaldo's death, because I remember him sitting almost motionless, strapped into a high-backed chair, barely able to speak, but I had the feeling he knew who we were. Laurette, still active but plagued by a heart problem that affected her breathing and impeded the fluidity of her speech, received us warmly. I had trouble holding back my tears in the presence of two people whose friendships had impacted my own life so profoundly and who were now so fragile.

A few years after Laurette's death, I visited Mexico again. This time I had lunch with her stepdaughter, Jeannine. We talked about the woman who raised her and who had been my closest friend for so long. Unexpectedly, Jeannine told me that a few years prior she'd discovered Laurette unconscious after a suicide attempt. She seemed proud of herself as she said that she'd acted quickly to save her. I was appalled. I couldn't imagine anyone interfering with the will and desire of a woman who so clearly lived unapologetically and according to her own beliefs and needs. I remember leaving that lunch outraged.

I've since learned that Jeannine also prevented Laurette's ashes from being buried where she wished. It is sad that a woman so independent in thought and action had to put up with such lack of understanding and support from the broader community and even members of her own family. Her life included a great deal of tragedy, which I believe made her stronger and more determined to be the person she was.

Laurette once told me about her only son, who was lost to her at the end of World War II. She was living in Paris and had sent the child to her mother in the French countryside to keep him safe, with the promise that he be returned after the fighting ceased. Her mother didn't keep that promise, and Laurette had to reconcile herself to life without him until many years later, when her son, now an adult and at his wife's urging, consented to a reunion. They reconnected, but their relationship remained difficult. To this day, I retain an image of a mother standing alone on a railway platform, waiting for a son who never appeared. I think Laurette tried to re-create those years she'd lost with her only child by being a devoted grandmother to Jeannine's eldest son, Santiaguito. I remember, during my years in Mexico, her joy when she was able to take her first grandson to interesting places and delight him with one experience or another.

Laurette and Arnaldo were risk takers, a quality I believe all outriders possess. There seemed to be no limit to how far Laurette would go in support of the people and ideas about which she was passionate. And passion was also something of which she possessed a great deal and which she indulged fully.

During the time I was briefly in hiding at their home, I met Rodrigo Asturias,[33] the son of the Nobel Prize–winning Guatemalan novelist Miguel Angel Asturias.[34] Rodrigo, who had worked with Arnaldo at Siglo XXI as well as El Fondo de Cultura Económica, founded the Organización del Pueblo in Armas (ORPA), one of the guerrilla movements fighting to overthrow the Guatemalan dictatorship of those years. When she was seventy and he eighty-three, Laurette and Arnaldo traveled clandestinely to meet him there. Throughout her adult life, Laurette also frequently traveled alone deep into the Mexican countryside to small villages and ancient sites. She braved whatever discomfort or danger to experience the physical landscape and intimate customs of those whose lives she studied.

I saw this fearlessness again in Cuba when Laurette, intrigued by an experiment in popular theater taking place in the Escambray Mountains, spent several months living with and observing those taking the project to that remote part of the island. At the time the Escambray, which had been a focal point of counterrevolutionary activity, was still plagued by residual bands of armed bandits. Living and working there wasn't an experience most visitors to Cuba would have risked.[35]

Soon after I went to live in Cuba, in 1970 I was invited to be part of the poetry panel for that year's Casa de las Américas literary contest. Laurette was also invited, to judge the newly

33. Rodrigo Asturias (1939–2005) was a Guatemalan guerilla leader and politician.

34. Miguel Angel Asturias (1899–1974) was a Guatemalan poet, novelist, playwright, and journalist. He also served in his country's diplomatic corps. In 1967, he won the Nobel Prize in Literature. His work helped bring attention to the importance of Indigenous cultures, especially those of his native Guatemala.

35. This experience resulted in Laurette's book *El Teatro del Escambray: Una experiencia*, published in Havana in 1977.

established category of testimony. I have a photograph of the judges sitting around a long table. We are in the company of the great Argentine journalist and writer Rodolfo Walsh, who within a few years would be hunted down and murdered by his country's dictatorship; the brilliant director of Cuba's film industry, Alfredo Guevara; the writer and Guatemala's ex-minister of state Manuel Galich; Cuban revolutionary heroine Haydée Santamaría, who headed Casa and imbued it with her singular spirit; and Raúl Roa, Cuba's foreign minister, who has often been called "the minister of dignity." I look at their faces now and realize, with a certain sadness, that I am the only one of the group still alive.[36]

I've known a number of people who have changed me, and I've tried to take their gifts and pass them on to those coming up. Laurette was such a person for me; Arnaldo, too. There was no difference between the impact of what each of them gave to the world and what they gave me personally. I was privileged to know and love them.

Our correspondence resides in several different archives in two countries. I copied all our letters, selected those I wanted to include here, translated them from the original Spanish to English, and have arranged them mostly chronologically so as

36. Rodolfo Walsh (1927–1977) was assassinated by Argentinian paramilitary forces after writing a public letter denouncing the disappearance of his daughter Patricia. Alfredo Guevara (1925–2013) was the founder and for many years director of Cuba's film industry. Manuel Galich (1913–1984) was a Guatemalan playwright who served as his country's minister of foreign affairs and minister of education until a dictatorship forced him into exile. Haydée Santamaría (1922–1980) was a Cuban revolutionary who founded and until her death directed Casa de las Américas, one of Latin America's preeminent cultural institutions. Rául Roa (1907–1982) was a Cuban intellectual, politician, and diplomat. He was his country's foreign minister from 1959 to 1976.

to give a sense of the journey our relationship took. I offer them here as they are; additional commentary would be redundant.

Mexico—August 18th, 1962

Dear Laurette:

Just a few lines to tell you how grateful we are for your marvelous gift. The book is a gem and promises many hours of pleasure. Sergio just finished the introduction and I've read fragments here and there. But together we've looked at the splendid drawings and full-color plates: extraordinary. In them we've been able to revisit that world that still vibrates through the culture and thought of a people rich in the divine. In time, between work, we will read the whole book, trying to understand it fully. Laurette, you can be sure of the great gift you've given the world, a gift that is carefully structured, beautifully presented, and filled with inspiration. These days, when there are so many archeologists and historians whose words go no further than dry facts, it's rare that anyone looks beneath the surface at that which is poetic and evocative. This is why your work has such value.

We are genuinely happy and honored to know you and your books.

Thank you again for the book and for everything. Come to see us as soon as you can. We love you, Meg, Sergio and Gregory.

A TOLTEC DISH

for Laurette

filling the palms of both hands
flat & open, a palm across
at the joining of base and wall
tiny chisel lines

that look of use or finding
:two parts of the same act

second or third century
the colors a small dish
black into brown into gray
into cream, smoke into clay
of days & later called
the shape of elegance

by clean-browed designers
with no visible past.
hands that made & shaped
& filled and used this vessel
bowl arrived to me

complete from eighteen
centuries of stillness.
if there are words contained
can only be   :listen,
the stillness of wind
and time speaks out of time.

MR Mexico 9/12/63

(Handwritten, I added at the bottom of the page: *I wrote this poem looking at the dish you gave us. It's for you—I hope you like it. Hugs, Meg.*)

Mexico, August 1st, 1968

Dear Arnaldo and Laurette:

I miss you a lot. I love you a lot. You are real friends. I think about you all the time. Today we got news of the children. They're at a kind of camp/recreational facility in Santa Maria del Mar. I don't know if you've been there. It's outside Havana. I went when I was at the Congress. It's very beautiful, by the sea. They're studying five days a week and on weekends our friends take them to see family people they know. We haven't yet received a letter from Gregory and I'm really eager to get one, to find out how he feels. I think this separation is worse for Robert and me than for the children.[37]

There's been no change, Robert will have told you that.

I want to propose a concrete idea, Arnaldo, a similar book to the one I did about the Hippies but about women's liberation. I don't know if you're aware that in the United States there is a powerful movement that grows more so by the day. Women have different ideas of what women's liberation means; there are conflicting opinions. They mostly base their ideas on their own experience, and this has important implications for the revolution. Most see women's oppression as something that is 2,000 years old, emerging long before class struggle, and that it continues to exist even in nations that have been liberated. They read Engels' *Origins of the Family, Private Property, and the State* and other texts. There are many different groups, throughout the whole country. They have consciousness-raising groups where they discuss these issues. Many have carried out actions designed to unmask the consumer society, the laws that control abortion, the draft, etc. They mock the superficiality of contests such as Miss America and Miss Universe. There are many different factions, ranging from the most radical to the most liberal. I've been collecting relevant materials for more than a year now, and one of the things I managed to take with me when we

---

37. Due to the repression launched against me after my participation in the Mexican student movement, I was forced underground, and we sent our four children to Cuba for their safety and our mobility. In this letter I was speaking about this. "Our friends" refers to the Cuban government officials.

were forced to leave our home was the folder containing them all, because I've known for a while that I want to write about the phenomenon.

What I have most of right now is time. I try to keep working so as not to feel the frustration of this situation. I want to put a book together, more or less the same length as the one on the Hippies. I would choose the most interesting texts and write an introduction. I know that this issue doesn't yet have the impact in Latin America that it does in the US or Europe, but I don't think it will be long before it does. And I think it's important not only for women but for justice-loving people in general. If you agree, tell Robert and I will have a manuscript to you soon.

Again, I love you a lot. I hope we can see one another before long. A big hug, Meg.

p.s. Arnaldo, if you don't agree that a book about women's liberation is important, I will assume that your critical sense is overshadowed by your male chauvinism(!)

Air Canada—enroute
Afternoon of September 22nd, 1969

Dear Ones:

How I've thought about you both! I'm finally on my way from Toronto to Paris and then on to Prague. I've sent a few telegrams along the way. What a trip! We got to Chihuahua and thought all was lost. But through the efforts of some real comrades and after paying $2,500 pesos I managed to acquire a very provisional document that was nothing like what I'd been promised. I got across the border in the back of a refrigerated meat truck. With luck, I made it into the States, met up with Robert, and we traveled together as far as Dallas. He then flew to New York and I to Chicago. I continued by bus, into Canada. Despite my exhaustion and state of mind, I had some great experiences with people. All my connections were closely timed. I hardly had a chance to eat, much less sleep. Tall imposing Black men, a young white kid reading the apostles (the Bible, not our Martí)[38], grumpy old women, in short, everyone with whom I came in contact. I really love observing people, no matter the circumstance.

So far, it's all gone as planned. I hope it continues to. I'll mail this from Paris. I love you like you have no idea. You are real comrades. I can't thank you enough for everything. You know how we feel.

I spoke with Robert by phone an hour ago. He's good, with his family. He'll be there for a few days, a week at the most, and then continue his own journey. In Chicago, in a taxi on my way from the airport to the bus station, we went along freeways named after the great criminals: Eisenhower, Lodge, etc. In Canada passed many US factories. On the bus an elderly woman refused to let a young hippie occupy the seat next to hers. There are so many experiences I'd love to share with you. Well, not the horrible ones. I'll send you another telegram from Prague or from my final destination.

I hug you both with all my love, Meg.

Havana, Cuba—November 27th, 1970

"Year of the Ten Million Tons"

Dearest Laurette and Arnaldo—

The letters on this typewriter remind me of the letters on yours, Arnaldo, in your red velvet studio (where I wrote so much

38. In Latin America, they refer to the nineteenth-century Cuban revolutionary José Martí as the Apostle.

and dreamed so much)![39] The folks at Monthly Review sent the typewriter with Robert, who just came back from New York. I love using it. Now I can write better in Spanish with the appropriate accents and ñ. I gave my English-only typewriter to a comrade here who didn't have one.

Roque Dalton[40] has written what I think is an extraordinary book. It's very long, around a thousand pages. It is the testimony of Miguel Mármol,[41] an old member of the Central Committee of El Salvador's Communist Party. The man has lived the entire Salvadoran revolutionary process, and his story doesn't only reflect that country's struggle but the struggle throughout Central America. The book will be published by Masperó in France and in Italy by Feltrinelli. I don't know, Arnaldo, if you'd be interested in reading a copy (I ask because it is so long). I've been helping to type it, which is why I know how good it is. Meanwhile, Roque told me he'd give you a copy of his book on Debray, the one published by Casa.[42] I'm sending

---

39. During the months of hiding following the 1969 repression, Robert and I spent several weeks at Laurette and Arnaldo's home adjacent to Siglo XXI, the publishing company Arnaldo ran. During the day, we had to be quiet, for fear our voices would be heard on the other side of the wall. In the evenings, after the workers had gone home, we could gather with our friends for dinner and to talk. Arnaldo let me use the typewriter in his home study.

40. Roque Dalton (1935–1975), Salvadoran revolutionary, poet, essayist, and novelist, who spent much of his exile in Cuba before returning to El Salvador to fight. He was murdered by members of the ERP, his own revolutionary organization.

41. Miguel Mármol (1905–1993).

42. Régis Debray (1940) is a French philosopher, journalist, former government official, and academic. He traveled to Bolivia to interview Che Guevara when the latter was fighting his final battle there, was captured by the Bolivian army and imprisoned for several years. His theory of armed struggle provoked passionate discussion among Latin American revolutionaries in the 1970s.

it separately but in this same mail. He's also going to write to you about the Mármol book.

I hope you are both well. Big hugs, for our other friends as well, Meg.

Havana, January 14th, 1971
"Year of Productivity"

Dear Laurette and Arnaldo:

I want you both to read a story Gregory wrote the other day. He spent the entire day writing on Robert's typewriter. Then I made a copy. I only corrected his spelling a little, the rest is his. You'll see that it is "fiction and reality," as he says. He also said: "I included a lot of information because I want it to be didactic." I know you'll understand it because there's so much there of who he is, and he is so connected to you both.

Everything is good here. We had a marvelous week of vacation with the three older children. We went all over and enjoyed ourselves a lot. They are such great kids. Right now, the lawyer who may take my case in the United States is here; he'll be coming to dinner tonight. We'll see what he says.

We are so eager for your visit, Laurette.

Big hugs to both of you and all our friends, Meg.

Havana—April 29th, 1972
"Year of Socialist Emulation"

Dear Laurette:

Goyo and Sarah were so enraged by the recent bombing [of Vietnam by the US] that they made some drawings and took them to the North Vietnamese Embassy across the street; they wanted them to be sent to Vietnam as examples of their solidarity. They made friends with two comrades at the embassy and now they're studying Vietnamese four hours a day! Of course, as they are at boarding school, this is only on weekends. Over the summer they plan on having daily lessons. The comrades say that Sarah, especially, has a great vocation for the Vietnamese language.

Havana, February 6th, 1979

My dear Laurette and Arnaldo:

I'm so perplexed. I feel like there's some sort of conspiracy against your receiving my letters. I wrote several times from the US. I can't remember right now how many but I'm sure at least three. Then, when I got home, I wrote you again. And just the other day I sent a long card with Gracia Canclini. Yesterday Goyo got the book you sent—very useful for him, by the way, I'm sure he'll write soon—with a note from you, Laurette, saying again that you haven't heard from me in a while, and telling him that in December you got a letter he sent in September! My parents just wrote to tell me they received the fourth edition of *Women in the Revolution* (I was thrilled because I only realized there was a third edition when someone showed me a copy one day in New York. Now the existence of a fourth shows the book keeps selling—always encouraging).

I'd like to have 20 copies of this fourth edition. If you need payment first (I know my credit is exhausted!), let me know and I'll have my father send a check. If you can send these copies with someone who's traveling even better, maybe Eugenia Meyer or Thelma Nava. I also need to know if you've gotten copies of my recent books: *No se puede hacer la revolución sin nosotras* (Casa de las Américas), *Estos cantos habitados* (new Cuban poetry in a bilingual edition published in Colorado), *We y Carolota* (two poetry books in English), and the Canadian edition of my book about Doris Tijerino in English translation by my mother. Since my letters seem to be getting lost, I'm worried about the books. If you haven't received them, I'll send more with some traveler.

I'm also very interested in having news about a manuscript of mine I sent just before my trip, *Sueños y realidades de un guajiricantor.* I'm hoping it can be published there, but since I know I've mentioned it in previous letters I won't repeat myself now and try to wait patiently.

Laurette and Arnaldo, from the card you sent to Goyo, I know you've been in Europe, at least you, Laurette. Where did you go? Was it for work or just a visit?

All is well here, except for my asthma. It's been bad since my return. I have a new treatment now that consists of gradually increased doses of what produces the allergy, in my case house dust or, more specifically, a certain fungus that lives in Cuban house dust. I've just begun the treatment and each time I must go for the injection I get a lot worse. But fingers crossed. I'm hopeful. And I also have a lot of solidarity here at the house, at work, everywhere so I shouldn't complain.

The problems I've had these past few years now seem like a nightmare that's passed. Even—although this may seem strange to you—like some sort of test. The children are fine. Ana is bright as always, happier than she's been and doing excellently at school. Ximena's had some trouble with her grades, nothing serious but it's pressuring her to work hard to get into high school. On the other hand, she seems happy and is planning her 15*th* birthday party, much more modest than Sarah's. Sarah, as always, doing very well at school and talking about going into some field of engineering. Here at home, with me and with everyone, she is more loving and communicative. It seems as if her difficult years are over. And Goyo, what can I say? He's magnificent, growing in every way. In his first semester at university, he got five 5's and two 4's, excellent grades. Now he's working at a radio assembly factory from three in the afternoon to eleven at night as part of the work/study plan. The books you've sent have been extremely useful to him.

Nothing more right now. I need news of you, how you are. Although our communication is sporadic, I know the love we have for each other doesn't depend on that.

All my love, M.

Mexico, March 2nd, 1979

Dear, dear Margaret:

I know our correspondence has been difficult. Some letters take a long time to reach their destination. I think this is mainly due to the Mexican mail system being overloaded because it also happens with letters sent to France and other countries throughout the Americas. Despite this obstacle to our communication that can leave things up in the air since one never knows where the conversation is—either physically or internally—and the fact that this intensified during your recent very fruitful trip to the United States, it's true that "something" paralyzed me in my relationship with you. Perhaps the changes in your life. I know that Antonio[43] IS magnificent, but I do love Robert so . . . The years of anguish that you endured and during which I felt so impotent to help (your sense that those years were a sort of initiation seems supremely just to me), your new tasks to which I didn't feel I had access, my lack of knowledge about those closest to you and those you love, beyond our usual orbit, this combination of elements or perhaps something I'm not seeing, provoked this state that I can't even define. Because

43. Sometime after Robert and I separated, I began a relationship with a Colombian comrade named Antonio Castro. It lasted for about five years.

I never really felt distant from you. I've always loved and admired you from the moment of that historic meeting at our home in El Fondo . . .

It may be that the deepest reason for my feeling this way was helplessly contemplating a suffering I felt in the most profound part of my being. It seemed to translate the enormous difficulty that, despite your insuperable worth and vital energy, represents true integration into a world turned upside down: a nation that has achieved a revolution such as Cuba has. I felt so small at your side . . . It's easy to admire you for a few weeks and then depart, to observe the existence of certain painful mechanisms but ones that scarcely touch me. I who am barely affected by them. All that is NATURAL, yes, but one still needs to have an incredible inner strength to resist. And you never gave up, you never just decided to leave, you always sought the truth about what was happening to you. Again and again, you hit walls the origins of which you didn't understand. And always with that passion, with that capacity for suffering that comes from your enormously generous and creative nature.[44]

I believe those years may have been necessary for you to fully commit, as you've always done, to that unknown reality. I

---

44. Laurette refers here to the painful situation I endured during my last few years in Cuba. I lost my job without being told why, and clearly became a persona non grata in the eyes of certain government officials. Friends were warned about visiting my home and some took that warning to heart. At the same time, I continued to receive my salary, and my work continued to appear in the country's press. Try as I did, I couldn't find out why this was happening. Some people close to me suggested I simply leave the country. But I knew I had done nothing wrong and refused to do so until I received an explanation. This prolonged situation was very difficult for me. When I finally had the answers I needed, I did leave Cuba and moved on to Nicaragua. It seemed I had been too much of a feminist for the Revolution at that time and had entertained people of various leftist persuasions at my home, something frowned upon back then.

think this in particular because of the essay you wrote for CASA magazine.[45] I found it to be not only beautifully written and well-constructed, but a precise expression of your process, from the moment of your departure from our house on Mancera street to embark on what at that point was simply a dangerous unknown, to who you are today. From the woman who rejects a society made up of values based on the things that society has given you to the woman who accepts a community of different interests and struggles. It's extraordinary how that whole path is reflected in those pages. And I ask myself, as I tell you this, if others have felt the same as I. For me, those pages are worth the entire issue of the magazine because all the rest, valuable as it is—and I admit I haven't read the whole thing—seem superficial, created from afar, something I might have written. What can I say about that experience in comparison with someone like you who has lived it in the core of your being and have taken it on completely?

And, curiously, that text has allowed me to dissipate all the cobwebs that were hiding you from my eyes. Suddenly I saw you as I did that first day, entirely different but nevertheless completely natural for someone of your impulse and energy. And, despite the fact that I don't know much more about the circumstances than I did when I watched you struggle with that horrible situation, now I understand exactly where you are. In short, I didn't know how to accompany you when you needed me. I only know how to feel close to you, really close to you, when you are yourself, like you were before and are now. I know this isn't brilliant on my part, but I must recognize that it's the truth. The only thing I can say in my defense is that I

45. I have no idea what essay Laurette is referring to here. Over the years, I published often in Casa and continue to do so.

was always sure I would find you again. I've always known that, and it's precisely what I told Maru so many years ago when you spoke to me about the sacrifice you were making as a poet.[46] You will always be a poet, you had to endure real pain to discover a way to express this new reality. You first had to internalize it to the point where you could own it. (If this all seems boring or ridiculous to you, forgive me. You have no idea how I needed to get close to you again without that screen. And I can do nothing but write these poor lines to reflect on the path I followed to understand what happened in our relationship.)

Speaking of Maru, I saw her by chance for a moment when she came back from Havana. I would have loved to have understood what she said to me back then, or for her to have said it now. She was brimming with energy and decision.

Your books, Margaret. The only one that didn't arrive was your mother's translation of the one about Doris Tijerino. The others we have. I read several times, as I could, both We and *Carlota*. The one Casa published I'd already read in English (and afterwards passed the manuscript on to Nuestro Tiempo publishers by way of Alonso Aguilar's wife. She is an American and a good friend of mine. She seemed very interested. I told her that Casa should publish it and, if she agreed, she should get in touch with Roberto. I didn't hear anything further. It appears she did nothing. I really love *Sueños y realidades de un guajiricantor* and several times recommended to Arnaldo that he do it. Another reader was equally enthusiastic about the book. But my lord husband says it's not possible, that it just doesn't fit in his plan of books that have already been accepted or are awaiting a decision (it's true that Siglo XXI receives more and more

46. Maru Uthoff (1937–2017), Mexican Communist and English teacher at my children's school in Mexico, was a dear friend of Laurette's and mine.

manuscripts, many of them now from Mexico too, and that he's really upset about having to reject so many in which he's interested. He says it's the only bad thing about a profession he adores.) I don't know if he might change his mind, but considering the continuous avalanche, I'm afraid he won't. In that case, would you like me to send it to Extemporaneos? How was your experience with them? Are you still in touch? Do they tell you how your book is doing?[47] I don't know who else might be interested in the subject, despite it being so attractive, so new, in terms of transmitting the reality of the revolution.

Useless to speak of that which has us all so distraught, China's attack on Vietnam. Despite all evidence to the contrary, I still refuse to believe in the failure of the revolution in that country and each morning I find myself hoping that the newspaper will wake me from the nightmare. I imagine how people there must be following the news and how you must feel, you who in addition to all we can imagine, have physically visited that country.

I received Goyo's most recent letter. You don't know how happy I am—and proud—that he writes us once in a while. And you also can't know what I feel, the frustration of not being able to admire and love the lives of all your marvelous children, all of them. Oh, I know . . . but I always feel it as a loss, as something . . . well, it's hard to explain. I'll leave it for another time, along with our trip to Europe (which was important for my work, I promise to catch you up).

My best to Antonio, all my love to the children, and big, big hugs to you, my friend, Laurette

Mexico DF, March 2nd, 1978

---

47. Editorial Extemporáneos was another Mexican publishing house. It brought out my book *Somos millones* in 1977.

My dear Margaret:

Laurette and I received your recent letters that Thelma Nava had the kindness to deliver.

We know that correspondence is difficult or at least very slow, particularly for understandable reasons in terms of the restrictions on the "free flow of mail." We understand this is true for everyone.

I waited until now to respond to your dear letter. I wanted to have more concrete news about your book. At last, I learned that it did come out and that Thelma sent you the copies you requested. Extemporáneos promised to send over a copy this afternoon, which makes us very happy.

It's very opportune that the book is appearing at this critical moment for Nicaragua, in which once again the empire is launching its barbarism against that impoverished and unfortunate nation. We hope Nicaragua will manage to liberate itself. Just one more of the dramas that from my own country extend themselves the length of the Continent.

It was wonderful to have the good family news you sent and we're happy to know that you are working enthusiastically. We are hoping to visit you soon; Laurette needs to be there to complete some tasks in connection with the book she's working on. I hope it will be soon. We just need to resolve some difficulties that have come up.

Receive the love you know lives in us for you and your whole family. This letter goes out with a big collective hug. Arnaldo

(undated handwritten postcard)

My very dear Margaret,

I brought your long, beautiful and generous letters with me so I would be able to speak at length with you. I find that I can't even indulge my desire to visit places I love. As always, there are rushed visits to publishers, friends, and family. There's also the fact that one of my sisters has been operated on and is gravely ill in the hospital. So, for the moment I can do no more than send you my enduring friendship and profound love. Laurette.

East Lansing, Michigan—October 7th, 1978

Dear Laurette and Arnaldo:

It's strange writing to you from this cold and interesting place, so far from where we are used to being. I've hope you've received the two or three cards I've sent from spots along the way. This trip came up almost spontaneously: 20 cities in three months. I've been lecturing about Cuban women and reading poetry (mine and that of others traditionally silenced across our Continent). I can't remember if I told you that it all began with an invitation to The Berkshire Women's Conference, a gathering of historians who work on women's issues and which, this year, was held at Mount Holyoke College in Massachusetts. My original plan was to attend the conference and spend a few days with my parents. I spoke to the Cubans about extending the trip to several weeks and they were enthusiastic. They suggested I try to line up other events that would allow me to cover the cost of the trip and make for a more complete itinerary. Before I knew it, I had a great many invitations to speak. I also obtained a US visa without difficulty. That's how it all started. Among other thing, I'll be giving a minicourse at Oberlin College based on five lectures I'd already prepared. I'm about at the halfway point and, so far, it's been an excellent experience. A few days ago, I spoke on the phone with Antonio. The children were in bed, but he tells me they are all well. As you know, Gregory is at the university now, in electrical engineering, Sarah is in tenth grade, Ximena in nineth, and little Ana in fourth.

Arnaldo, here in East Lansing, at the house where I'm staying, I saw a copy of the third edition of Women in the Revolution. I was thrilled to see it, since I didn't think a third edition would be possible. And it's the most complete version of that book, since the postscript is included. Would you send 20 copies to me in Cuba? I'll be back at the end of November. You can send the bill to my father. I'm earning more money now and promise to pay it promptly.

My love to you both, Meg.

Havana—March 12th, 1979

Dearest Laurette and Arnaldo:

I cried when I got your letter dated the 2nd. This morning Tatiana's mother called to say I had a letter. I went right over, and the temptation was too great: as soon as I got to the street, walking to the bus stop, I began to read. I kept reading and didn't even board the bus when it came. I just kept walking along Línea, reading and crying, tears of relief and joy. I've never really felt you absent, all through these recent times that have been so difficult for me here. And over the past few months, when our letters were so delayed . . . well, you know all this.

The truth is the nightmare is beginning to fade now. I say beginning, because there are always reminders: a few people who clearly still feel cautious around me, even though the revolution has assured me that my problems are a thing of the past. I can see now that the whole thing was a test of some kind, although it didn't feel like it at the time. Not that it was intentionally set up as such, but that's how it feels. But I never wanted to give up, I was never inclined to leave the country. I was always sure of my commitment and that one day the situation would be explained. Anyway, enough of this. There's so much to do. Love, Meg.

Mexico, DF, May 9th, 1979

Dear Margaret:

I'm surprised not to have received a response to the cable we sent you on April 5*th*, which said: "WE AGREE TO PUBLISH SUEÑOS REAIDADES WE THINK IT BEST TO BEGIN BOOK ON PAGE 29 ELIMINATING INTRODUCTION (STOP) CABLE ME IF YOU AGREE. HUGS."

What happened is the following: When I received the book I was interested of course, inspired by Laurette's enthusiasm. She read and recommended its publication. But as I have often repeated, I am living the drama of an editor who can't do everything he wants, not even everything he should.

The problems of a catalog that features 32 collections, each of which must grow equally, makes for difficult moments that force us, me in particular, to sacrifice my taste and desire to the necessities. This is what happened with this recent book of yours.

Upon receiving your letter in which you lament the fact that this book, the "one you love best," won't be published, I felt moved again (even though I'm sure you say that each book you write is the "one you love best"). Laurette insisted, and I sought the opinion of a writer who works at Siglo XXI, and interest in the book intensified after the glowing report she sent in (which I attach).

In the end, overcoming these difficulties, and once again making an exception, I told you we would publish the book, at the same time suggesting the deletion of those first 28 pages of introduction, because we don't believe they are necessary. The book reads well without the introduction; it might even take away from its unity (both aforementioned readers agree).

And so, I reiterate my offer: We will publish it without those 28 initial pages. If you agree, you can send a cable that simply says "I agree" or "I don't agree," and we can settle the matter.

I am hoping Adelaida, Roberto, or Mario can give you this letter. They will be here at the house tonight. If they can't, I will look for another way of getting it to you.

Nothing left but to reiterate our loving wishes for your beautiful family and for you. A big hug, Arnaldo

Havana, May 14th, 1979

"Year of the Twentieth Anniversary"

Dearest Arnaldo and Laurette:

Today—a few minutes ago—I received your letter, Arnaldo, written on the 9th. A comrade who works at Casa brought it. She is Silvia Gil who lives in our building on the 10th floor and is Ambrosio Fornet's wife. The first thing I did was cry a bit, with happiness. Then I raged a bit at a telegraph system incapable of dealing with underdevelopment! After that I dictated two telegrams: one for you with the single phrase: "We accept." And one for Moreno, who now works at the cultural department in the city of Matanzas and who will be as happy as I am. After writing to you, I plan on getting in touch with "Che." He was here at our house three days ago. He had just won a décima contest held by ANAP, which was why he came to Havana.[48] Between one thing and another he made time for a visit and from the worn black bag he always carries took out three or four kilos of black beans, a bit of fresh garlic, and some onions "to brighten the mind" as he said. He talked to me about the book, then was on his way.

48. The *décima* is a form of traditional poetry popular among Cuban farmers. The book in question is *Sueños y realidades de un guajiricantor*, the story of the peasant poet "Che Carballo," written by Angel Antonio Moreno and me, with photographs by Grandal. The ANAP is Cuba's National Peasant Association.

I know the publishing house is facing big problems, and that I have been immeasurably favored by our Siglo XXI! I'm happy . . . for "Che" Carballo, for Moreno, for me . . . but most of all because I sincerely believe that this book offers a look at what poor Cuban farmers were and are, and a sense of the popular culture that is the result of the power and reality of revolution. That is to say, I think it is a useful book. I don't know if I told you that we sent it to the Casa de las Américas contest this year, in the testimony category. The category remained deserted. The same thing happened in 1976 when I submitted my book about Doris Tijerino. That year the prize was supposed to have been given to a book about the struggle of Latin American women, and that year it was also deserted. This year, after the prizes were announced, I asked one of the judges—Federico Álvarez from Spain—what he'd thought of the book. He told me, textually: "Look, it's a good book. It should be published. But, you know, Casa can't award a prize to a book like that. They need to give it to a book about Latin American women in general, a book about torture, etc." I almost responded: "Well, I guess I mistook the year!" Because I believe that one can feel the revolution through its culture. Not everything must be about torture.

Of course you can eliminate the introduction. I thought it would be useful, especially outside Cuba, but if you think it's all explained in the body of the book, that's fine with me. As far as the photographs are concerned, if the cost leads you to limit the number, that's fine as well. If, on the other hand, you decide to use them all, they should appear in the order I've indicated. In short, I leave it to Siglo XXI. Your design and production are always very fine.

I'm working a lot. Along with the magazine, I'm putting together an anthology of poetry by Cuban women: from Mirta

Aguirre to now.[49] It will have an ample introduction that covers the history of women in Cuban poetry, and I'll do all the translations so it can be published in the US. I'm also putting the finishing touches on a book of the lectures on Cuban women I gave in the fall, incorporating some of the questions and criticisms I received along the way. I wrote an additional lecture, or chapter, on women in the countryside. I think it will be a useful book. It's turning out to be something of a sequel to *Cuban Women* Now, but with a very different structure.[50]

We're all well. Gregory is studying a lot. So far, he enjoys his major. He's also very happy with his partner, a Uruguayan woman who studies architecture. Ximena just returned from a stint in the tobacco fields. She's so beautiful. Sarah is a woman now. She is happy and much more animated than before. Ana has been writing some great poems; I'll include a few for you to see. Antonio is also studying and doing well health-wise. He hasn't found a job yet, though, and is a bit depressed because of that. That's hard on us all, but the most important thing is that we're all well.

I don't have much more time now. It's 11 p.m. and I've been working since 6 this morning. I promise a better letter soon. Until then, I love you and send big hugs to all, Margaret.

Havana, June 4th, 1979

Dearest friends:

Maybe you could send me a cable to tell me if you've received my recent letters. Since I sent them with different

---

49. This became *Breaking the Silences: Poems by 25 Cuban Women Poets* (Vancouver: Pulp Press, 1982). Photographs by the author.

50. *Cuban Women: Twenty Years Later* (New York: Smyrna Press, 1981). Cover and photographs by Judy Janda.

people, that would put my mind at ease as to whether they arrived.

The Federation of Cuban Women has asked me to write and deliver one of the organization's papers at a seminar of women leaders in the Caribbean that is taking place in July. So, I've put aside all my other work to take on that task. Of course I'm honored, but it's also challenging because it will be the first time I've done something like that.

The kids are doing well. I'm sending a photo of Gregory with his partner (another Laura!) and others of the rest of the family.

Lots of love. Write when you can. M.

Mexico, DF, July 25th, 1979

My dear Margaret:

I hope you received the cable I sent on July 13*th* that said: "ON OUR RETURN WE FOUND ALL LETTERS POEMS PHOTOS BOOK WILL WRITE LOVE."

To reiterate, your book is in process, and we think it will go to press next week. Our technical department has some question which I will include here.

I hope you can respond in brief via the postal service you maintain with your innumerable friends. You mail always reaches us, but it often takes a while.

Laurette is also very happy with this latest book of yours. She was the first to sing its praises and insist that we publish it. She sends her great love.

We received Goyo's warm letter and were delighted to have it. Also, the beautiful, truly incredible poems by Ana.

I hope you can respond quickly to the questions we have. Meanwhile, our love to your entire family and a big hug for you,
Arnaldo

Moscow, August 7th, 1979

Dear Margaret:

We are so happy to be able to send you our love and ask that you share it with your beautiful family from this extraordinary country we are visiting for two weeks at the end of our trip through Europe. This has been a touristic journey that has surprisingly transcended that to produce some new realizations and necessary revisions that have helped us understand the historic importance. This is a people who have been able to carry out and continue to carry out a change no other people—with the exception of Cuba—has even been able to try. We think of you all the time, with much love for you all. And before leaving for Mexico tomorrow we want to send this off. Laurette thinks about you often, she loves you so much, and asked me to write these few lines dictated by our memories. For you all, kisses and hugs, Laurette and Arnaldo.

p.s. We want to send our best to Robert. Will you send it on? Thanks.

Mexico, DF, August 15th, 1979

My dear Margaret:

I don't know if in this complex exchange of letters we've been able to give one another the latest news and opinions.

We just received yours of August 2*nd* that your girls mailed from the United States. It came in plenty of time to clear up the vocabulary issues about which we had doubts. Although we still have a few, their implications are less important. I'm also accepting your suggestion that we use the introduction we'd thought about eliminating.

To that point, we've reduced the introduction, correctly I believe, so that it still presents the protagonist and the book. I'm confident you'll be happy with how it reads now.

We await a call from the girls. According to Sergio, who we ran into in the street, they will be here soon. We are eager to see them; it's a way for us to feel closer to you and to the whole family, with whom we are linked by such deep affection.

The book is at the printer, and we are confident we'll have it in circulation in the first half of December along with a novel and a collection of stories by Latin American writers. I think it will be in good company because they're all excellent.

I'm writing today hoping to give this letter to the beautiful messengers, and as always, I send Laurette's and my love and a big hug, Arnaldo

Havana, August 18th, 1979

Dearest Laurette and Arnaldo:

I don't know if I've told you, I have something new and very beautiful in my life: photography. I don't really understand how I came to it, nor how it is that I didn't come to it sooner. Sometimes I think 42 is too old to try to learn something like this, not only in the aesthetic sense but in terms of all its technical aspects. Anyway, I've created a small darkroom here at the house, in what used to be the servant's bathroom that is next to Sarah's bedroom. It's very minimal. The truth is, to do something like this in Cuba is hard, even for a professional. Finding what I need, even the smallest item, has been quite a challenge. In any case, it's all set up now, at least enough for me to learn. It would be great to have a system to filter the chemicals from the air, but I'm working well with what I have. I often go to bed at 10 or 11 and get up around 2 or 3 in the morning to work. The sun rises and finds me still there: practicing, learning. A friend who works at the magazine has been teaching me the basics, but I find that I learn best of all from my own trial and error. We're lacking everything here: paper, film, chemicals, so it's all on a very small scale.

It's possible that one of the things that's motivated me to try photography has been my frustration living for so many years in countries where my language isn't present. For example, I write my poetry in English and not many people know or can appreciate that. Translations, at least of my poetry, have so far been very deficient. And I haven't been able to write poetry in Spanish. Of course I'm not saying I'm going to stop writing. But photography is a more universal language, and I find that satisfying.

I want to send you a tiny gift: I can't call it a portfolio, that would be a presumption on my part. These are the first photos I took, developed, and printed on my own. I'm sending them to you until I can share something better.

I love you a lot and need to hear how you are. All my love, M.

Mexico, DF, January 14th, 1980

My dear Margaret:

We've received beautiful news from you, first in your December 1*st* letter that reached us on the 26*th* and then in the copies of the letters you sent to your children in Havana.

I am hoping these lines of greetings and love will reach you, despite the usual problems with the postal services in all our countries.

I also hope you've received the 20 copies of Sueños y realidades de un guajircantor as well as a duplicate for the copy that was damaged. We sent another five to Havana in response to your airmail request. We'd sent 100 copies to you in Havana, also by airmail.

The letters we've received from you have been very moving and, as always, we admire your marvelous capacity for carrying out those tasks.

I'm already concerned because when you finish the book, I'll already have committed to publishing two others at the same time. I contracted them before you went to live in Nicaragua. On the one hand, Alma Guillermoprieto's book, which was recommended by Tomás Borge with the support of the Ministry. Hers is also a book of interviews. And previously, at the very beginning of the Revolution, I accepted two other texts on Nicaragua that I will also have to publish.

All this concerns me because as usual we are going through a difficult situation in terms of production, not only in the area of publishing but in general. The excessive number of books contracted and the incredible rise in the costs of production are creating difficult situations I don't know how I will be able to handle.

In any case, I know that your book will be saleable and that in Cuba they will publish it because of their interest in contributing to an examination of the passionate reality you are living.

Nothing more for the moment except to wish you happiness and the very best in all your endeavors on the part of Laurette and myself. A big hug, Arnaldo

Havana, March 29th, 1980

Dearest Laurette and Arnaldo:

I take the opportunity to get this note to you. I was so moved by your lines to Goyo, Laurette, on the backside of the beautiful calendar that he and I received from our Siglo XXI. Aside from thanking you for the gift, I want to say that from that moment you have been with me very especially, Laurette. I want you to know that you have my love and solidarity for what it's worth, my commitment and my "understanding." I put "understanding" in quotes because I know we can never completely understand what another experiences. For each of us pain surfaces differently. I love you, both of you, so much, and hope you can feel that.

I'm sending these little cards, photos I took in Nicaragua. I like some especially, which is why I printed them small so I could send them to friends. The first was taken in a poor neighborhood of Managua called San Judas. The inscription on the wall is one seen often in that country. The second was taken in the countryside near León, the third in the same peasant home. The fourth I made on a street in Diriamba, and the last in the mountains north of Estelí, far in the mountains (several hours' walk) at another peasant home.

I'm working hard on the book.[51] I've finished six chapters which I like a lot. And I'm trying to do something new: to combine the testimonies with more analysis. This is more difficult for me but I'm pushing myself and think I'm succeeding to some extent. When I have more, I'll send you a chapter or two to see what you think.

The family is good. Gregory is doing well in his second year at university. Recently he was among approximately 50 students who earned maximum grades in all their classes for the semester (out of a total of 800 students). He's also been working as a student aide, meaning he's been giving classes to others, in his case teaching physics. His students are adults and he's happy when he gives a good class. Sarah just took second place in a provincial chemistry contest; she's training now for the national. She's doing well, more communicative than she was, more integrated. Ximena has made a leap as well. Suddenly she's loving to read, something she didn't care for before. She goes to museums and to the theatre. She's discovering a world of culture, and loves it. Ana has some problems. Lately she hasn't wanted to go

51. This would be *Sandino's Daughters,* for which I did the fieldwork in Nicaragua at the end of 1979 and beginning of 1980 and then came back to Cuba to process the material and write.

to school, seems fearful, etc. She is an exception child and also problematic, which doesn't surprise me. I'm trying to spend more time with her, give her more attention and a chance to talk about what's bothering her. I've been feeling bad: the old problems which have been resolved at the official level but continue like some gray cloud and seem interminable at times. But I'm sure I'll emerge eventually. My parents are coming down in May.

Well, dear friends, that's it for now. When are we going to see each other again? M.

March 31st, 1980

Dearest Margaret:

We are in your debt for not having responded sooner to all your beautiful letters, materials, poems, photos and stories . . . I answered some to you in Nicaragua and see that you received those.

We now have your lines of February 17*th*. A month and a half isn't bad for communication between our two worlds.

We are happy to hear that you are doing well, satisfied with the beautiful jobs you each have.

The photographs are very fine. They transmit a very fresh image of Nicaragua.

We are living the dramatic process of Central America with anxiety and hope. You must have an enormous number of experiences and impressions. How I wish we could talk!

Laurette sends this book we just published, a result of the work she did in Cuba. It was a labor of love, and she hopes it will be useful for understanding certain aspects of the Revolution.

I have been overwhelmed by affectionate attention because the president of the country presented me with the "Condecoración del Águila Azteca" in a somber ceremony that I found very moving. It was held at the president's home with the attendance of hundreds of friends and an exaggerated speech by don Jesús Silva Herzog in representation of the authorities who—they said—recognize my efforts in favor of Mexican culture and also in the way of an apology.[52]

Nothing more except for big hugs from Laurette and Arnaldo

Havana, May 2nd, 1980

Dear friends:

How I long to hear from you! You are always in my thoughts. I hope you, Arnaldo, received the telegram I sent when I learned about your well-earned tribute by the Cuban government.[53] I just learned from a friend here that your book, Laurette, about Cuban women just came out. I think someone saw a copy that Alejandro Alonso had. Would you send me one? You can imagine how eager I am to read it. Thanks.

As Goyo said in his letter, the atmosphere here is one of enthusiasm, so much energy on every front. The revolution is at a complex stage, both externally and internally, but as usual Fidel and the Party are managing things with extraordinary brilliance. And people are responding. One can learn a lot at this stage of new complexity and contradictions. I continue to feel privileged to be here.

I finished my book about Nicaraguan women. In Spanish I'm calling it *Las compas*, at least provisionally. The manuscript

---

52. Arnaldo refers here to the fact that the Mexican government ousted him from the directorship of El Fondo de Cultura Económica after he published *The Children of Sánchez*, by Oscar Lewis and *Listen, Yankee!*, by C. Wright Mills. With the support of many intellectuals, he then founded his own publishing house, Siglo XXI, where he continued to publish important books.

53. Arnaldo was awarded the Felix Varela Medal, Cuba's greatest honor bestowed on a foreigner.

has 350 pages: ten chapters and an introduction in which I quote you, Laurette, quite often. I like how it turned out. I wonder if one is always most satisfied by one's most recent work, or if this has to do with trying to improve on what one's done previously. Right now, I'm typing up a clean copy, which is made more difficult by the fact that I'm out of onion skin paper and so must type the whole thing twice. Then I plan on doing the English translation myself because I want it to be perfect. I don't yet have a Spanish-language publisher, although of course I plan on sending it to Ernesto,[54] which was our agreement from the beginning. But I don't think it likely that the Ministry will be able to publish it, at least not soon, because it has such shortages of paper, ink, everything. Doris Tijerino was here last week, and we spoke at length. The FSLN's propaganda department is very interested in its release and promised to read it. So, we'll see. I still maintain the hope that something will happen and Siglo XXI will be able to do it. I love the publishing house too much, or maybe I'm just very obstinate.[55]

Here at home things are okay. Ana was adversely affected by Robert remarrying and that they are expecting a baby. I imagine she'll eventually get used to it.

I love you more than you know, M.

Mexico DF, June 11th, 1980

Dear Margaret:

I received your book about Nicaraguan women that you sent with Gustavo Esteva.

54. My old friend Ernesto Cardenal was now Nicaragua's first minister of culture. He invited me to write the book and arranged for me to do the necessary fieldwork.

55. Siglo XXI did publish this book in 1980 as *Todas estamos despiertas.*

I am reading it and of course I like it very much. For this reason, I can tell you that we will publish it. The edition will be 5,000 copies so as to be able to send 3,000 to the Ministry of Culture in Nicaragua.

We received a letter from Ernesto Cardenal dated May 10*th* in which he formalized his commitment to buy those 3,000 copies and we responded immediately agreeing.

They will be sent at cost. I am not sure if you want to perceive royalties for those 3,000 or if you want to cede them as a donation. If that's the case, we would pay you royalties on the 2,000 remaining copies.

I imagine the run will seem small to you but unfortunately books about Nicaragua don't sell very fast. I think this is because many have appeared in recent months. We ourselves have also contracted Alma Guillermoprieto's book that has a prologue by Sergio Ramírez and another by Melba Castillo, as well as a study of Sandino that Gregorio Selser has promised.

I'll send you a contract as soon as you give me your decision with regard to the books for Nicaragua.

I can't promise to include more than eight photographs in the book, despite how splendid those you sent are. You know about the difficult situation all publishing houses are facing. This is due to the high cost of materials which results in the books costing more and selling less.

Laurette asks me to send you her love and assure Goyo that we received his letter.

Many and big hugs, Arnaldo

Mexico DF, September 19th, 1980

Dearest Margaret:

I believe I am in your debt because this answer to your many packages has taken so long.

I hope Sarah and Ximena have given you the latest news that I asked them to write down: that the translation of your book is finished and we made the corrections you asked for; we sent fragments to FEM and they promised to publish them; we'll send fragments to other magazines although most resist publishing selections from forthcoming books; your piece on Cuba women was sent to UNO MAS UNO but hasn't come out yet; the book is at press and I am confident it will appear in November.

You can imagine the grief with which we accompany all of you, all the Cuban people, for Haydée's death.[56] I was finally able to see her on Saturday the 19*th*. She was very animated, I would say almost joyous, as she dedicated one of the photographs you so generously gave us. Laurette couldn't go but I shared the happiness of that memory with her. We are so sad to have lost her.

Good wishes for all of you from Laurette and me,
and a big hug, Arnaldo

Havana, October 14th, 1980

Dearest Laurette and Arnaldo:

This long 11-year-long nightmare of living as a person without a country has finally ended. The new Mexican ambassador to Cuba is the same who represented Mexico in Chile in 1973 and acted with such courage and dignity in aiding the victims of the coup.[57] I made an appointment to see him and tell him about my problem. You may remember that I did that

56. Haydée Santamaría, Cuban revolutionary hero, founder and director of Casa de las Américas, and a personal friend of Arnaldo's, Laurette's, and mine, committed suicide in July 1980.

57. Gonzalo Martínez Corbalá (1928–2017) was an exceptional human being. He was as incensed as I was about the repression I had suffered in

with the previous ambassador, but this time the results were different. I now have my passport in hand! One of the first things that occurred to me was going to see you. I don't think it will be possible, though. I'm still trying to put my life back together here, looking for work and so forth. But once I have resolved these issues, I'm thinking a trip might be possible—not for work but just to relax, something I realize I desperately need. I'd love to rediscover the Mexico it feels I left so long ago. I love you a lot and wanted you to be among the first to hear my good news.

We thought you might be coming this month. Is that still a possibility? A few days ago, Gregory received your wonderful birthday present. Someone brought it to the house personally, but I wasn't here so didn't meet him. Goyo is delighted; I know he'll write to you soon.

Much love, M.

Havana, November 20th, 1980

Dearest Laurette and Arnaldo:

Today I received two letters from you, Arnaldo, one sent September 19*th* and the other October 29*th* that included a check in Canadian dollars.[58] I've noticed that this often happens. My mail must be held up somewhere and then all delivered at once.

Yes, Sarah and Ximena told me about my book; I imagine it will be out soon and I'm very anxious to see it. At least one of my letters must not have reached you, in which I said that of

---

Mexico and the fact that I hadn't been able to get a new passport and issued me one immediately.

58. In Cuba, because the country had no relations with the United States, we couldn't cash American dollars or checks in U.S. currency.

course I don't want royalties on any of my books that you distribute in Nicaragua because I want the Sandinistas to be able to buy them at the greatest possible discount.

I do hope you've received the letter in which I wrote about the big change in our lives. I finally decided to accept the offer of a job in Nicaragua, and I'll be leaving in a few days. I'll be working at the Sandinista Women's Association and possibly also at the Ministry of Culture. As you can imagine, I'm both excited and nostalgic. I asked each of the children what they want to do. Gregory, Sarah, and Ximena chose to stay in Cuba, at least until they finish their studies. I think it's the right choice for them, but of course I'll miss them terribly. Antonio will also remain, at least until he finishes university which will be at the end of this year. Ana will come with me. These past few weeks have been busy. I've sold many things in order to leave money for the kids. I've packed what I want to take with me. The Cubans have been wonderful, helping in any way they can. I will be leaving this Island with sadness, and of course I won't be leaving it for good. But you more than most others know the details of my situation here and how rough the last few years have been.

I am eager to receive you both at my new home in Managua. It would be wonderful to see you there. As I've been sorting things these past few weeks, I've experienced a sort of revision of my life. In considering what to take and what to leave for the children, what to give away or sell, each object evokes memories. Among the thousand or so books I'm taking with me (I've sent many already with friends traveling), are of course all yours, Laurette. I'm leaving almost all household items for the children, but among the very few going with me are the beautiful salad spoon and fork you gave us. Each object contains a memory of someone I love or of some important event, and I'm choosing with great care.

How are both of you? How is Siglo XXI and your work, Laurette? Write when you can. Much love, Margaret.

Mexico, January 26th, 1981

Dear Margaret:

We've been so happy in recent days to have your dear letters, allowing us to follow your decisions over the past few months. And we're delighted you've been able to accommodate yourself in that comradely country.

As I mentioned, the book came out and 3,000 copies are already packed and ready to be sent to the Ministry of Culture, as well as 100 for you.[59] We are currently in communication with the Nicaraguan Embassy here, that requested authorization from the Ministry for LANICA to bring them cargo to be paid for upon arrival. I'm confident that in a very few days you'll have the books in your hands.

Responding to a request from the Ministry, we already dispatched three copies by air. I hope you like the edition, and that these formalities will be over soon.

We believe you are doing magnificent work, and that Ana will also benefit from experiencing that beautiful revolution.

In a few days María Dolores de la Peña will arrive in Managua. She has collaborated with the publishing house, and I gave her your telephone number because I'd like you to talk.

---

59. This was *Todas estamos despiertas: Testimonios de la mujer nicaragüense hoy,* my second book about Nicaraguan women (Mexico City: Siglo XXI, 1980).

All that's left is for me to reiterate Laurette's loving memories of you, and I send this off with my own strong embrace, Arnaldo

p.s. I'm enclosing a copy of the invitation we made for the presentation of your book. It was a very lively affair.

Managua, Nicaragua, January 6th, 1981

Dear Arnaldo and Laurette:

Ana and I arrived on Monday the 29*th* in the morning. To begin with, things were difficult because everyone was enjoying a well-earned vacation. For the moment we are staying with Gladys. Do you remember her? In Cuba she went by Ruth and later Sofía.[60] She sends her best. I'll be working at the Ministry of Culture and the Women's Association. I am so eager to see the new book and hope you will send the customary 100 copies. Yesterday Ana began at the Nicaraguan French School. Maybe one day you and she will be able to converse in French, Laurette. Well, we are off to a new beginning. When I'm settled in, I'll write more. Right now, I miss Gregory, Sarah, and Ximena a lot.

I love you a lot. Please write. Margaret.

Managua, February 5th, 1981

Dear Arnaldo and Laurette:

I was very excited yesterday around noon to receive two copies of my beautiful new book. Jaime Labastida brought them down. With this book I was beginning to feel like a pregnant woman who couldn't give birth, so much time had passed

60. Gladys Zalaquett was a friend and member of the FSLN temporarily living, as so many Sandinistas were, in Cuba. She returned to Nicaragua following the victory of July 19, 1979.

without my seeing it but knowing it had come out. The other copies have also arrived but have been in customs for more than a week. Every day the guy in charge tells me: "Soon, soon . . ." In any case, I love having these two copies.

I love the edition! Naturally I haven't yet had the chance to go through it, but it looks very clean (free of errors). I love the selection and distribution of the photos, even when I wish they had printed a little better. (This is almost always the case.) I also like the idea of including the added section before the last chapter instead of after it. That way the book ends with that moving passage about the ex-military man who joined the FSLN. And I love the cover design. Thank you once again for such delight.

I can tell you that Ana and I are doing well. We still haven't found a place to live. This seems to be a common problem here, even worse than in Cuba. Otherwise, I think we've made a lot of progress for only having been here a month. I'm working at the Ministry of Culture (after several brief experiences in other jobs). I'm in the Ministry's cultural outreach department, in charge of contact with the written press. I like the work. It gives me time to write quite a bit and also to use my photographic talents. I earn very little, like everyone here, but I think it will be enough to live. At first, I had Ana at a private school, the Nicaraguan French, that had been recommended by several friends, among them Gladys. Academically it's a good school, but almost all the other students are right-wing or from right-wing families. It was hard on Ana, who they took to calling "a little Cuban Castro-Communist"! And there was no contingent of Sandinista youth at the school. Today I am in the process of changing her to the "Rigoberto López Pérez," a public school, where she may have other problems but not those.

I miss my other children a lot. Ximena may join us here at the end of the year. I've had great letters from them all, showing me that they're taking the separation with enormous maturity. It seems it's also united them more. So, I think our collective decision was the right one.

Please tell me about yourselves. What's going on with the publishing house and in your personal lives. I'll see if I can send this letter back with Jaime. I'm also sending you a photograph of the group of people working at the Ministry, with Daisy Zamora in front. She's the Vice Minister. It was taken last Saturday when we marched to Revolution Square to support the FSLN and government's decision that we should all join the militia. I've been in it since I arrived and have been participating in the first training sessions (Mondays from 6 to 8 p.m., three hours one Saturday a month, and one Sunday out of every four). I'm finding it tough but doing the best I can.

Well, my love as always. You are both very present in our lives. I hope we can see each other soon in this free territory: threatened, suffering, but struggling hard. M.

Managua, March 17th, 1981

Dearest Laurette and Arnaldo:

Just a few lines. In general, things here are going well. It's a privilege to accompany this nation at this time, to share and work and learn. I continue to feel good at the Ministry of Culture. I like the work and learn something new every day. The problem of housing became quite problematic, as it is for many, especially of course the neediest. It was taking a long time, and I finally realized it would be easier to buy than to rent. I asked my parents for help, and they were willing. So, I now have a house and it looks like we'll be able move in a couple of months. It's a simple house, smaller than what we need, but it's pretty and centrally located. It will be a huge relief for Ana and for me to finally be in our own space after such a long time living out of suitcases and bothering others.

Ana is doing splendidly. I think I told you I took her out of the private school and enrolled her in a public one. She is fully integrated there now, in the Sandinista Youth and the militia. She feels good about it all. Of course, she misses her brother and sisters, as I do terribly. But she's growing and having important experiences. Love, Margaret.

Managua, April 29th, 1981

Dear Arnaldo:

Today I received your telegram. I'd known for three days about your generosity regarding a trip to Mexico, had heard it from Margo Glantz and Elena Urrutia. In any case, I'm taking advantage of a friend who is traveling tomorrow to send you this letter in which I can say much more than in a telegram.

I'd like to travel on June 1st and return here on the 8th. Unfortunately, it can't be a longer trip. Work is demanding, and besides, Ana will be leaving on the 12th to visit Robert in New York and I should really be here to help her prepare her trip. The writers' congress is from the 3rd to the 6th, so in any case it will allow me some time to visit with friends. I know I won't be able to really experience Mexico on this trip, just bridge the distance of these past 12 years. I want to see you, visit the publishing house's new quarters, and attend the congress which sounds interesting.

So, if you can arrange for a ticket between those two dates, that is to say leaving here on the 1st and returning on the 8th, that would be wonderful. On this end I am taking care of everything I need to do here: obtaining permission from Immigration and so forth. When you can send me information about the flight, the airline, etc., let me know. Much love, Margaret.

Managua, June 10th, 1981

Arnaldo and Laurette, dear dear friends:

Well, the Mexican experience is now "a thing of the past," even if a very recent past. It was very rich and full for me. Your presence was all that was missing, although of course I felt it there. Of course I would love to have been able to see you, embrace you. I hope you'll come here as promised.

As you can imagine, at Siglo XXI they treated me wonderfully as always. Cocó was there for me every day and others at the publishing house were also very kind. I loved the new building; it really is an important publishing house now. I still miss the incredible garden and warmth of Gabriel Mancera, though.[61] Of course time passes, and worthwhile efforts prosper.

I can't find the words to express how grateful I am to you for making this trip possible. Nothing I can say is enough. So many times, I thought I would never again see that beloved country. This return, although necessarily short, was so intense and important for me. The Congress was disappointing, somewhat incoherent, although there were a few good papers and the chance to meet a few people and reconnect with others. But just being in Mexico was extraordinary.

I walked a lot. I saw old friends. I tried to recognize the city, delight in its great features. I took quite a few photographs. If some of them turn out as I hope, I'll send them. I had experiences as varied as walking through La Merced Market at five in the morning, when that whole world of middlemen and women is just walking up; and driving up to Las Lomas where the new bourgeoisie think the most elegant thing is to build a house that

61. Because I took refuge during the repression at Laurette and Arnaldo's home, which was adjacent to the publishing house, Siglo XXI's first office always had a great deal of meaning for me.

clings to the walls of the ravine and where a single terrace of just one house costs more than a dozen homes for needy families in any of our countries. In short, Mexico in its idiosyncrasy of tremendous contrasts but also filled with the dignity all the conquest in the world hasn't been able to erase.

I told Cocó I wouldn't write a note to you before I left because it would only be one of those obligatory thank yous, but that I would write a real letter when I got home. So, I want to get this off right away. I feel it's still not the letter I wanted to write. I just got home last night and am at the office with a lot of work that piled up while I was away. But I want you to have these lines, filled with love and gratitude for your gift. Please write and tell me how you are, how the trip to Europe was, and when you are coming here.

Ana is doing very well. I think the kids in Cuba are too. You will see them there in August. Love, Margaret.

Mexico, DF July 15th, 1981

My dear Margaret:

I know we are in your debt for not having responded to your letters and the other things you've sent since returning from our trip.

We've been back exactly a month today and as is always the case, there have been urgent tasks to attend to. In addition, I broke my leg in Budapest at the beginning of June, making for some problems with my ability to do everyday things.

I'm emerging from all that now. Yesterday they removed the cast I've had for 45 days but which didn't prevent us from continuing with the restful vacation we'd anticipated and which we were able to complete without further problems.

We're very happy to learn of the important activities of the Writer's Congress. Many people have told us about the role you played as well as of your interviews on television and in the papers. The truth is, several have said that you were the outstanding figure at that gathering.

We were glad to know that you also felt the trip was worthwhile and that you found everything in good shape upon your return.

We received the marvelous photographs you sent, in particular the one of Ana the guerilla fighter. She is beautiful and so is the photo; it's absurd that you still claim you lack skills as a photographer. Of course, we showed them to Concepción, and she loved them as we do.

We are enormously grateful for your invitation to stay with you in the event of a probable visit. We have no plans at the moment, but perhaps in the future.

Here's to everything continuing in the best possible way. Receive all love from Laurette and me, Arnaldo

Mexico—August 24th, 1981

My dearest Margaret:

Day before yesterday we had the pleasure of spending time with Goyo and his compañera and with Ximena. We're always amazed at these extraordinary beings you've given the world.

I'm writing this in longhand because my secretary, Lupita, hasn't come in yet and I want to send you a few lines for them to take to Nicaragua. I'm also sending five copies of the second edition of your book. I think you'll be happy to know the first edition sold out so quickly, something that doesn't often happen.

I'm responding to the question you asked in your last letter. I say the last but that's not correct; later we got yours of August 3rd that Goyo brought.

What you say about your book not being available in bookstores in Mexico City isn't true. What happened is that the first edition sold out and the second is circulating now. As for Nicaragua, I don't know because we don't handle distribution there. It would be the Minister who could tell you. The second edition, as I say, came out very soon after the first.

We appreciate more than you know your invitation to visit you there. At the moment, it doesn't seem possible. But it would be wonderful.

Your children told us about what you and Ana are doing. Laurette sends a book about Mexico for her.

I hope we can see each other soon in whatever part of the world. I'm recuperated now from my accident and Laurette is doing very well. She's awaiting the release of a book she wrote about Nahuatl culture.

Warmest love to you and Ana from us both, and a hug,
Arnaldo

p.s. The Ministry received the 3,000 copies.

Mexico, October 19th, 1981

My dearest Margaret:

I have given this letter to our collaborator Aurora Velasco in order to send you Laurette's and my love.

I hope you've received our answer to your most recent letter, with our news. We sent it with the great Goyo.

The personality of that young man is really extraordinary. He has matured in the best possible way one could hope for. We consider him an exceptional human being and that you are largely responsible for this.

Our representative Aurora is there to handle some business issues in that beautiful nation and, sadly, she must touch on a few "commercial" aspects we cannot avoid, especially now that the economic situation is causing us so many headaches. All Central America is difficult for us and she will be on a trip of inspection throughout the Continent and Caribbean.

You should be happy with your latest book. It sold out very quickly, we reprinted it, and it continues selling.

I hope you and Ana are well and happy. We send big hugs, an expression of our love,

Arnaldo

Managua, October 30th, 1981

Dearest Arnaldo and Laurette:

I have your letter from August, Arnaldo, after you saw the children in Cuba. I'm embarrassed not to have answered sooner. I can only say, in my defense, that these past few months have been exhausting in every way. In the first place, the situation of constant imperialist attack has us in a state of stress. Ana is in an army reserve battalion, the 50-13 out of San Judas, and during the worst moments of "Operation Halcón Vista" she was constantly being called up. The counterrevolution, both inside and out of the country, continues to do great damage as we knew it would—not unlike what Cuba has experienced for all these many years. Despite all this, the process of transformation is going well, with a great deal of effort and quite a few successes.

As for me, I continue to work on my book about religion in Nicaragua.[62] I finally decided to focus on two projects, one here in the city in the El Rigueiro neighborhood where Father

62. This became *Christians in the Nicaraguan Revolution,* which had a number of editions. It came out in English from New Star Books in Vancouver in 1983; in Spanish from Editorial Nueva Nicaragua and Poseidon Editores in Caracas in 1984; and in German from Union Verlag, Berlin, in 1987.

Uriel Molina and some university students formed a community in 1972-73. Those students today are among the leaders of the revolution. Some are even members of the FSLN's National Directorate. The second is the contemplative community that Ernesto Cardenal founded in Solentiname in 1966 and that continued until October of 1977 when Somoza attacked the San Carlos Barracks. I think that through these two experiences—one made up of students and workers and the other composed of poor peasants, I will be able to give an idea of what's happening in the Church, its development and goals in conjunction with the revolution. I think that limiting my story to those two places, I'll be able to focus more deeply.

And so, I've been working every week with Father Molina. A few weeks ago, I was finally able to go to Solentiname with Ernesto. There were a lot of people there to commemorate the fourth anniversary of the attack on San Carlos, so I was able to interview many of the original participants. Ernesto and I stayed an extra week, and I was able to speak with people who'd been in the community for more than ten years. It was a marvelous experience. I took a lot of photographs and filled more than ten cassettes. I'm enclosing some of my personal journal from that time so you will have a more in-depth idea of what I was able to accomplish.

I have good news from the kids in Cuba. Sarah began university and seems to be much happier. She is living at home, which she loves (she's got my old room) and is doing excellently at school. So far, she really likes her major, which is chemical engineering. Goyo is great as always, in his next to last year of university now and with a lot of work. Ximena is in her last year of high school. She seems to be the one who needs me most, but also seems good in her recent letters.

I received a copy of the second edition of Todas estamos despiertas. I'm glad that the book has been selling so well. Here you can't find it anywhere.

Well, I came back from Solentiname with malaria and still don't feel completely well. So, I'll close now with big hugs for the two of you and my hope that we'll see one another soon.

Margaret.

Managua, Nicaragua, December 1, 1981

Arnaldo, comrade:

A while back I wrote to ask if our Siglo XXI would be interested in a book I'm currently working on about the Church in Nicaragua. I have a recent letter from you, but you don't say anything about this so I'm not sure whether you received mine.

Now I'm writing once again with the same question for the following reason. The book is going well, that is I'm still in the phase of conducting the interviews and gathering some really exceptional material. I think this book would be even more important outside of Nicaragua, and that in a certain sense this importance is also particularly timely now. (I don't believe the subject will become less interesting, nor am I writing a book "of the moment," but that the current struggle within the Church is one of the sharpest contradictions between imperialism and revolution).

All of the above in general terms. But there are also a series of more specific considerations. The Ministry of Culture is interested in publishing the book (for distribution exclusively in Nicaragua) in a new series of books about Christianity and Revolution. The series is to be called Monimbó Editions and will be launched jointly by the Ministry and Nueva Nicaragua publishing house. They are trying, and I think particularly with regard to this book, for these texts to appear simultaneously in other languages. The question I'm asking is if Siglo XXI would be interested in producing the book for Latin America (with the exception of Nicaragua). And also, if you would be able to set the type there and photograph it for the local edition.

All of this is particularly urgent now because it turns out that this year, at the Frankfort Book Fair, the event's official theme will be religion. I don't need to point out how interesting it would be for the book, the Revolution, the revolutionary church, and for us to be able to present the book at that fair. For that to happen, the manuscript would have to be here in Nicaragua no later than July. Despite the work it will be, I commit myself to doing everything possible to be able to have it ready by then.

Okay, I await your ideas, comments, response. Later I promise a longer letter with news of us. I hope you and Laurette are doing well. I love you, Margaret.

Mexico, DF—May 10th, 1982

Dear Margaret:

We received your April 16*th* letter at the end of last month. We also loved your last visit here and were sorry you couldn't have stayed longer close to us.

I want to briefly tell you about what's happened with El espíritu de un pueblo.[63] The book has had two editions so far for a total of 4,000 copies. Unfortunately, the printer, for reasons they consider justifiable, destroyed 435 copies. Four hundred three copies were sent to Spain, and we will ask them to return what haven't sold. I'll send you a complete accounting of the edition.

63. Margaret Randall, *El espíritu de un pueblo* (Mexico City: Siglo XXI, 1975).

We continue to follow that great country and its great revolution with the warmest interest. At the moment, we are preparing to publish Omar Cabezas' book. I think it's very beautiful and we'll try to host a launch which he said he would attend.

Laurette has begun to complete her exploration at Teotihuacán, continuing the work she began a decade ago. She asks me to send you and Ana her love along with mine. A hug, Arnaldo

Mexico, November 9th, 1986

My dear Margaret:

You are right to reproach us for not having written you all this time, especially when you've sent us such beautiful messages.

We wanted to write after receiving your last letter and then again when your lawyer visited. And again, when Ximena brought us your most recent note with copies of the documentation around the horrible problem the government of that country has embroiled you in. What's happened is simply incredible, and we continue to hope that we will soon hear that in the end that common sense, justice, and public decency will prevail and give you back your citizenship.

We are happy to know that a Defense Committee has been established on your behalf and are confident that justice and decency will win out.[64]

We continue to be passionately concerned with this political moment, throughout the world and especially in Our

64. I returned to the United States to live in January 1984. Because I had inadvertently lost my citizenship when, married to Sergio, I acquired Mexican citizenship in 1967, I had to apply for residency. The U.S. government denied my request and ordered me deported in 1985. I fought the case, which lasted almost five years, finally winning in August 1989.

America—right now in our Nicaragua where we were supposed to have gone this week invited by our friends in the government to the anniversary so beautifully celebrated yesterday. We couldn't go.

When Sarah and Ximena arrived with your letter, we invited them along with Sergio to come to lunch, but they couldn't—and we didn't see them again. We would have loved to have been able to talk with them since we can no longer do so with you.

We continue with our work: Laurette with her studies and writing. Her books are making their mark. The Ministry of Education recently republished two of them in editions of 50,000 copies—which goes to show that this country cares about its past.

My Siglo XXI just celebrated its 20*th* anniversary with a gathering of more than a thousand people on the terrace of our offices. We continue with the desire to launch new books and bring out new editions of others, although everywhere the economic crisis keeps us from doing as much as we'd like. Still, we are doing what we can.

I know the publishing house is keeping you informed about your books.

We would be so happy to hear that you've resolved your problem and could come to see us and for many many days. Our friendship is as strong as it was the day it was born, when you came to our apartment at El Fondo, the day you arrived with Gregory in your arms. What beautiful memories . . .

Although we don't always write, write to us. We always love hearing from you. And our joy will be complete when we can have you here in person, talking and embracing each other all we desire.

For now, our embrace must go to you in these lines, and our hope that your family is well. Laurette and Arnaldo

Mexico, DF—February 11th, 1987

My dear Margaret:

After all this time we had the joy of receiving your letter of January 20*th* along with some informative material about the adventures and misfortunes you've had in your very complicated country.

The most recent news was what we were able to glean from your daughters. Despite the fact that Ximena is practically a neighbor, we haven't seen her much.

We're pleased at the general response your immigration case has had in your country's intellectual and political circles. And we're distraught at the aggressivity of the absurd and contradictory political problems you've suffered, which that country gives its own citizens as well as so many others throughout the world.

We follow with enormous interest the many problems the US provokes everywhere and, logically, right now we're consumed with Nicaragua where those problems are acquiring a dramatic intensity. We are hopeful that justice and honor will prevail to save our Nicaraguan brothers and sisters.

It makes us very happy to know that you are continuing to work, that you've published new books, and that in this sense you keep going with the same enthusiasm, wisdom, and imagination you've had your whole life. You are a great example for us all.

We had a letter from Gregory in Paris a while back and hope that he received our answer. Please don't stop communicating with us. Keep on sending your poems and news as you have up to now. We really appreciate them.

Despite how hard it is to get things from abroad, we will order a copy of the poster produced by your Defense Committee. Laurette sends you her most affectionate embrace, as do I,

Arnaldo

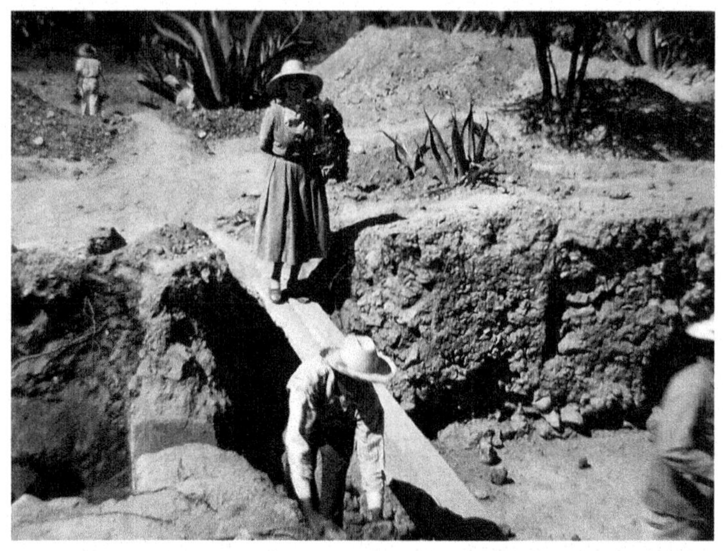

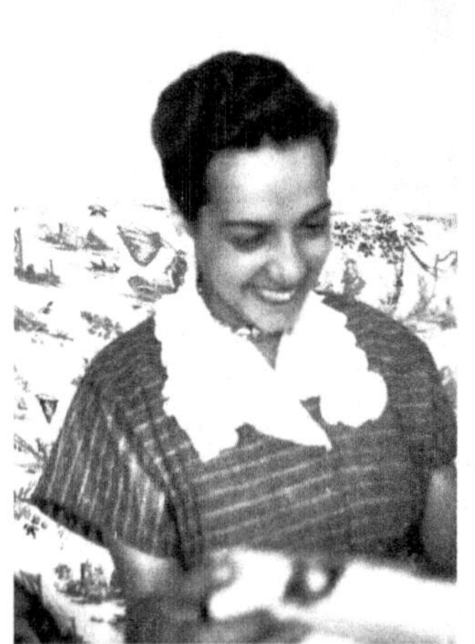

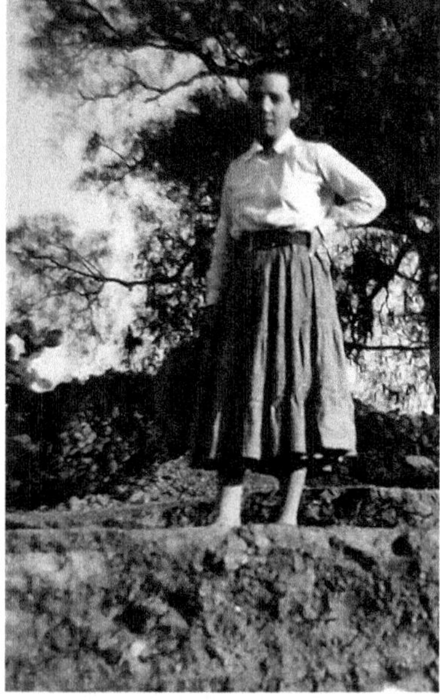

Above: Laurette Sejourné working at Teotihuacán. Courtesy Tatiana Coll. Right top: Arnaldo Orfila courtesy Siglo XXI. Right bottom: Arnaldo and Laurette in 1990s, photo Margaret Randall.

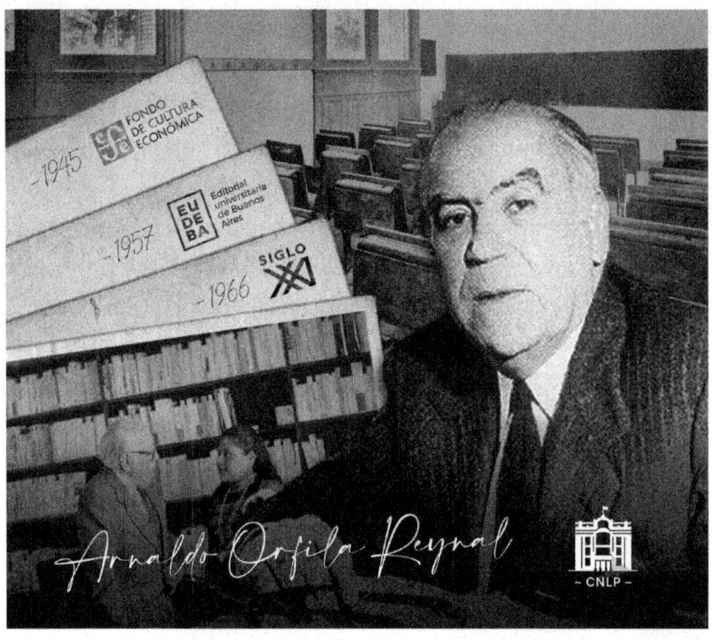
-1945
FONDO DE CULTURA ECONÓMICA
-1957
EU DE BA
Editorial universitaria de Buenos Aires
-1966
SIGLO XXI
Arnaldo Orfila Reynal
- CNLP -

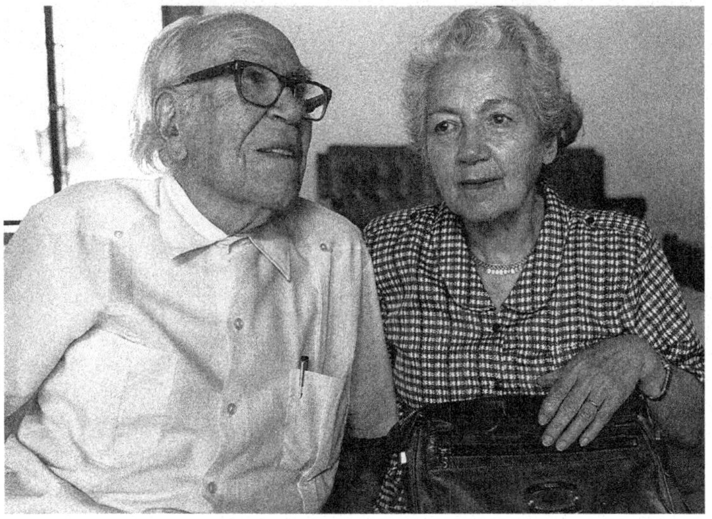

I didn't stop communicating with these two extraordinary people who had been mentors, colleagues, and friends. Nor did they stop communicating with me. Death was the only thing that could interrupt our conversation, although I like to think that it continues as part of the powerful chain of human expression, of memory in action, which links one generation to the next. From Spartacus and even further back, it remains unbroken despite the tremendous forces of reaction that try to impede it in every era. Spain's Civil War embodies so much of the October Revolution, the October Revolution holds so much of the Paris Commune, and back and back. How can we understand the Cuban Revolution without its Spanish predecessor? The colors of Sandino's red-and-black flag reappear in that of the Chilean MIR. This is living hope in an infinite number of tiny streams of memory. Laurette and Arnaldo embodied that hope for me.

III

SUSAN SHERMAN: A WOMAN BEFORE HER TIME

> I think it's coming close to death
>
> that does it
> both others
> & your own
> that magnifies the values
> begins the definitions
> —Susan Sherman[65]

SUSAN SHERMAN CAME OF age in the 1960s and half a century later would write one of the most vivid and accurate accounts of a decade whose rebel spirit extended itself into the mid-1970s.[66] She was born in Philadelphia in 1939 to a first-generation Jewish American mother who soon after divorced her father, a

65. Lines from her poem "Definitions."

66. *America's Child: A Woman's Journey through the Radical Sixties.* The spirit and impact of the 1960s extended to at least halfway through the 1970s, leading many to call the period "the long sixties."

department store furniture salesman, and married a Jewish immigrant Hollywood agent, affording her the glamorous life she wanted. Her mother was quite ill after a difficult cesarean delivery and hired a baby nurse to look after Susan. Since her mother was unprepared to raise a child, she retained the nurse to look after her daughter. Susan described her as more of a mother to her than her biological mother. After the divorce, her mother took Susan to live in Florida, where she worked in a liquor store. When she met the man who would become Susan's stepfather, they moved with him to California.

Susan's stepfather was controlling in the style of that culture and era, the price her mother paid for the life she desired. He played an ambivalent role in Susan's childhood and adolescence. While he was the kinder to her of her parents—supporting her when she won awards and attending school events—he was also sexually and emotionally abusive.

Her mother, whose love she longed for, was incapable of providing it in any meaningful way. An issue as she reached adolescence was Susan's weight. Her mother hounded her about her weight. She once went so far as to take a piece of clothing from her daughter's closet, hold it up, and say, "Look how big this is!" As someone who suffered a similar problem with my own mother, I know the lifelong problems this can cause.

After Susan graduated from college, when it came time for her to leave home to go to New York to join her poet friends, her stepfather had an emotional breakdown. Her mother gave her fifty dollars and told her to leave immediately, without a word of advice, love, or encouragement. Susan didn't return home until her mother had a stroke almost twenty years later.

As was true of many in their culture and time, alcohol played a prominent part in Susan's parents' home life. They had a bar at the house, and Susan blames their alcohol consumption for much of the drama and occasional violence in her childhood home.

Although Susan had a stepbrother and stepsister—children adopted by her stepfather before he and her mother got together—they didn't come into her life until she was four or five. A four- or five-year-old has little in common with kids seven and five years older, respectively, and so her early years resembled those of an only child. She was also ill a great deal, suffering prolonged bouts of measles, scarlet fever, and other diseases. She was an avid book lover from the time she learned to read and devoured books during those periods of enforced bed rest. She says that her mother read a great deal and that there were lots of books in their home. Favorites were all forty of the Oz books; Susan read every one and still treasures them all these years later. She frequented the library and tells a story about when she was in the third grade and the librarian called her mother because Susan had checked out *The Count of Monte Cristo* and *Les Misérables*. She wanted to make sure the little girl would be able to read them.

Because Susan was such a sickly child, when she was about to enter fourth grade her parents enrolled her in a Christian Science school called Berkeley Hall. She credits the school with saving her life. She says it wasn't overtly religious but promoted values that serve her to this day. The teachers were kind and encouraged her interests and talents. The gender distinctions of the times were not as pronounced there as in public school. Susan took shop and played basketball. She started a little magazine and wrote her first poem. But mostly she continued to read, books that were considered those for adults as well as those for children.

Susan herself describes her parents best in two of her poems, the first a portrait of her father, the second of her mother:

WHAT WE SEE

World War II 1940s USA Paranoia permeates
every corner of our Jewish home The visual indicator
of beauty approval acceptance The ability or inability
to hide The length and structure of the nose

Born to blackouts every evening Songs of soldiers
marching from a nearby base at early dawn
I was blessed with a small ski-jump astride my face
My sister not so lucky At eighteen welcomed
a beautiful new appendage from which to breathe

My stepfather behind his back nicknamed "runt"
A cruel caricature Twin brother to the fabled witch
Thick body crooked nose as if pieces of him
had forgotten how to grow

Eleven years old an immigrant fighting
his way up from poverty to a measure of success
he acquired my mother blue-eyed blonde petite
as trophy wife

She could pass where he could not Be accepted in places
that shut him out Appearance denying him an entree
even his newly won riches could not buy

Equal parts caring and abusive Racist to the core
he saw himself reflected looked down upon despised
like hated others They deserved nothing and neither
in his mirrored self did he

My mother oblivious to anything outside
her silhouetted frame had left her own impoverished
past behind turned her back on immigrant parents
Never again to speak their names

Growing into the 1960s   Denying my own parents in turn
Their values   expectations   their past no longer
a conscious part of mine   I recognized
a more dominant oppression   color
A racism endemic to our adopted home

Anger crowding every corner of my mind
in spite of all my poetry soul-searching activism rage
I was also deluded by surface symbols
visual stereotypes of others   and myself

Jewish   Lesbian   Privileged in more ways than one
True daughter of a mother who didn't look the part
I imagined I could hide   Choose when and if and what
I decided to let others see

2019   almost a century has passed   The merciless struggle
to listen   to let others in   to look beneath the surface
remains
To recognize discrete individuals behind coined clichés
To fight the stereotypes that foster hate   The invisible
nose
of childhood still firmly plastered on my face

LONG DIVISION

Nothing ever really seems to add up
My mother aged   frail   at seventy-eight
But I don't feel old   Don't feel any different
than I ever did

No different than fifty long years past
before her marriage drained sustained her
with rings and furs   A crazed husband's
unloaded gun pressed against her willing throat

Another piece of meaningless melodrama
in a world where children starve   old people die
lacking a few dollars to pay their bills

She used her talent looks to marry money
tossed her only daughter aside   A complication
An imagined contender for her throne

I could have loved you forever Mom   if you had let me
As it was I left   gave you hardly a backward glance
kept you from becoming my world

only to find the world becoming you

It's not my childhood that betrays me
I've digested that   Spit out what I couldn't use
It's a world that's taken on your face
the duplicity of your tongue   Your style

Alone at night sensation sinks too deep
In the mind's open cavern language
disappears   Everything is washed away

Even knowing what is real   How righteous anger
saves   Whether I will it or no
Her voice remains

Freedom to be who she is finally began for Susan when she entered the University of California, Berkeley. She moved out of her parental home and shared an apartment with two friends who would become well-known artists, the poet Diane Wakoski and the avant-garde composer and musician La Monte Young. The three took part in the social struggles of the times and explored the worlds of poetry, art, and music. The turbulent and creative 1960s was approaching and, along with it, the Berkeley Free Speech

Movement and West Coast hearings launched by McCarthy's anticommunist crusade. Protest drew Susan to social action.

Joining political struggle distanced Susan even more from her family. She's written:

> One morning I came down to breakfast to find my stepfather sitting at the breakfast table reading a headline that went something like Reds Instigate Berkeley Riot. Slamming the paper down on the table and looking me full in the face, he blurted out angrily: "You're not involved in any of this are you?"
>
> "No," I lied. "Why?"
>
> "Good. Because if I thought you were, even though you're my daughter, I would be the first one to turn you in to the FBI."
>
> I believed him.
>
> I never spoke to my parents about anything that was important to me again.[67]

After graduating with a degree in philosophy and English, in 1961 Susan followed her friends Diane and La Monte to New York City, by then the place where the most exciting experiments in literature, music, and art were taking place. New York became her home. Her friendship with Diane was also significant. The attraction she felt for her—although it never developed into an intimate relationship, was never even spoken of—was her first intimation of her attraction to women.

The lack of comprehension Susan suffered, and its resultant isolation, didn't only come from her parents and the larger society. Sadly, she was also targeted in different ways by a Left that wasn't ready to consider identity issues and a lesbian community that prioritized gender. Many women in the feminist movement and parts of the lesbian community identified her with

67. This and other quotes, unless otherwise noted, are from *America's Child.*

the male Left because of her political activism and failed to understand her friendships with the prominent male poets. It's also important to remember how dangerous it was back then to be an out lesbian in every aspect of life: in terms of jobs, housing, even walking down the street. And there were psychological ramifications as well, no place to turn to, no one with whom she could speak. The two therapists she consulted considered homosexuality a mental disorder. This was a decade before Stonewall and the beginning of the gay rights movement.

In her memoir, Susan writes about an incident that took place shortly after she arrived in New York City. She was beginning to try out her poems at some of the local venues. On this night she had been invited to read at a benefit for the Greenwich Village Peace Center. She describes the scene:

> My hands were perspiring so badly I could hardly hold my poems. I tried to focus on the words and not think about anything else—it wouldn't do to show I was so nervous. Here I was reading with Allen Ginsberg, and I had only been writing for a short time, and the poem I had picked to read was new, untried, and Denise Levertov was there, and reading also. Grace Paley and Bob Nichols had believed in me enough to ask me to read, and I didn't want to let them down. I was excited. I was scared. I wanted to run out of the room. I couldn't wait for my turn.
>
> I would be reading a poem I had written for Norma—without the dedication. Exactly one week before, while we were making love, we had connected in a way that was entirely new to me. For that one moment, the undercurrent of guilt that still plagued me when I made love with a woman had disappeared. Later the same evening, as Norma slept, a poem began to take form. It was that poem, "The Meeting," I was about to read before all these friends and strangers:

To touch your face
To touch your arms
To touch your waist
To touch your thighs

To touch your sex

To hold it soft against my cheek
To breathe it slow against my lips
To hold you close against my breast

My love . . .

An understanding so tenuous, fragile, a connection so easily broken.

I would hold you gently
Throw myself against you as
the rain Talk to you of
small things As you would
touch a child Or yourself
small and vulnerable to even
the slightest breath.

To be able to reach out, to make contact, to open out, to connect.

No longer afraid The touch of you deeper
than any fear Deeper than your naked form
The single syllable of your name

As I touch your body
As I touch the earth
As I touch this paper
As I touch each word

It is everywhere This night and the
outline of our form As we are together
Without boundary Without dimension

As I touch the depth of you
My love

There was loud applause. I sat down relieved, happy to be able to relax and enjoy the rest of the reading, when Denise turned to me with a puzzled look and said, "What strange images for a woman to use."

To which Ginsberg commented wryly, "That's because she's gay."

I was so startled by the unexpectedness of his comment I hardly noticed Denise's reaction, except that she got very quiet. I didn't say anything, neither did she. I knew she believed, like many others, that Ted[68] and I were a couple—a convenient idea I did nothing to dispel. I wasn't even aware that Ginsberg knew about my relationships with women. At the time I was quite friendly with Peter Orlovsky and might have mentioned something to him. Or maybe it was more common knowledge than I thought.

Nothing more was said. The evening went on as if nothing had happened.

A few weeks later when I sent Denise a new batch of poems—I hadn't heard anything from her since the benefit—I got a note back from her that she was disappointed in my work, it seemed to her I was basically always writing about the same

68. Theodore Enslin (1925–2011), an American poet close to Susan at the time. They would remain good friends until his death.

subject. She never mentioned what that "subject" was. I didn't understand.

Or maybe I understood only too well.

Despite such obstacles, her integrity led her to respond by continuing to do her work. There was the war in Vietnam, which Susan protested in action as well as in print. There was the second wave of feminism, which changed her even as it solidified an analysis of society begun years before. She continued to develop as a poet and essayist, founded and edited *IKON,* an important literary magazine,[69] traveled to Mexico, revolutionary Cuba, Salvador Allende's Chile, and Nicaragua during the first years of the Sandinista revolution, in search of truths ignored or misrepresented by the U.S. media. She taught generations of college students, became an active member of her school's labor union, ACT-UAW Local 7902, and grew old, as so many principled people do, with little security and few resources. Her life experiences and her responses to those experiences have made her an outrider in every sense of the term.

Susan's political activities in the 1960s and 1970s cost her a job, brought FBI surveillance, and literally made her ill; an ulcer would plague her until she traveled to Cuba, where the

69. *IKON* magazine had two important series. The first, from 1966 to 1969, was a large-format publication focused on poetry and progressive texts. The second, from 1982 to 1994, was book-sized and published mostly women, with themed issues such as "Asian Women," "Women & Love," "Women and the Computer," "Women in Struggle," "Spotlight on Photography," and "Art Against Apartheid." Both runs were enhanced by Susan's innovative graphic design as well as her acute editorial eye. *IKON*'s press runs were large. For the first series, they ran ten thousand copies, unusual for an independent undertaking. For the second series, they were fifteen hundred copies, except for the "Art Against Apartheid issue," which was five thousand. Raising the money to produce such a publication was always difficult, and a lack of funding eventually caused the magazine's demise.

revolution put her in a hospital without charge and gave her the chance to heal.

Susan and I met because I, too, had a literary magazine, *El Corno Emplumado.* Susan sent me poems for the first time in 1964, and we published three of them in our issue #10, which came out in April of that year.

Susan became one of *El Corno*'s stalwarts. We published her again in our issue #21 in January 1967, in #26 in April 1968, and in #27 in July of the same year. I also published frequently in *IKON*, eventually becoming a contributing editor. We planned on creating a magazine together, one that would continue *El Corno*'s goal as a bridge between North and South, but that never materialized due to our inability to raise the necessary funding.

Thus began our correspondence and a long friendship based on similar political and poetic visions. Susan visited me in Mexico, I later visited her in New York, and we spent time together in Cuba and Nicaragua. We remain close to this day.

We began writing to each other in the mid-1960s and continue to do so—many hundreds of pages filled with an analysis of what was happening where each of us lived and our own struggles to survive and make a difference. For years, this correspondence traveled the uncertain byways of postal services that were too often invaded by governments that eavesdropped on anyone known to be involved in leftist politics. At one point, we tried numbering our letters to make sure we were getting them all, but frenetic times caused us both to lose count and we gave up. We often wrote cryptically, using people's initials rather than their names if we were trying to protect them from scrutiny. Eventually, as the decades passed and we graduated to digital communication, emails replaced letters sent through the mail system.

When I think back to the times Susan and I have shared, intense feelings float to the surface. The energy we expended on projects we knew were important. The constant surveillance—some we were conscious of and some we didn't even notice until years later in the Freedom of Information Act era, when we accessed our files and read what wasn't blacked out—the lies informants told about us to earn their stipends. Our astonishment when we traveled to Cuba and witnessed a society in which people were able to dream of a different social structure, one that encouraged justice. Those years of exuberant hope.

I remember the 1968 Cultural Congress of Havana. Susan and I shared a room at the Habana Libre, formerly the Habana Hilton, a luxury hotel taken over by Castro and his fellow revolutionaries just as it was about to open in 1959. At that Cultural Congress, hundreds of public intellectuals, writers, artists, religious leaders, and philosophers talked about real problems and suggested real solutions. Susan delivered a paper in one of the commissions. It was received enthusiastically. I was embarrassed to admit I didn't understand it all.

The week ended with a gala reception at the presidential palace. My friend and editor Arnaldo Orfila grabbed my hand, saying he wanted me to meet Fidel. I grabbed Susan with my other hand and dragged her along with us. Our conversation with the legendary revolutionary leader surprised us; he seemed so knowledgeable about any subject broached. He referred to a recent issue of *El Corno* we'd dedicated to Cuban poetry and art and said he thought it was excellent. I told Fidel he should check out Susan's *IKON,* said it was a great publication, as well. An aide took notes.

It was a heady experience having those few minutes with Fidel, more so because he seemed so interested in what we were doing, so genuinely eager to be informed. But the person who ended up making an even deeper impression on us both was a tall, white-bearded man named René Vallejo. He was Fidel's close friend, aide, and doctor, a constant presence at his side. The next day, Susan departed to return to New York but left several copies of *IKON* with me in case Vallejo made good on his promise to pick them up.

Around 2:00 A.M. the following night, I was sound asleep when the telephone in my room rang. It was Vallejo. He was in the lobby and had come for Susan's *IKON*s. Could he come up? I said yes, hastily pushed scattered undergarments under the bed, and had just managed to pull on pants and a shirt when I heard his robust knock at the door. Vallejo had trained as a gynecologist, spent several years with the U.S. military treating survivors of the German death camps, and spoke perfect English. We exchanged stories about his doctoring to Cuba's poor and my experiences with midwifery in Mexico. I remember him calling down for a couple of packs of strong Cuban cigarettes–*negritos,* we called them—as the dawn light seeped through the hotel room window looking toward the sea. We talked for hours.

Vallejo and I became good friends that night, as he and Susan also would—through letters and when he invited her down to be admitted to the hospital where she was treated for the severe health problems intensified by the harassment and attacks that were constants in New York after her first trip to the island. He was the one who invited me and my family to spend a couple of years in Cuba—to experience firsthand the struggles and rewards of radical social change. In the summer of 1969, after Mexico's paramilitary repression forced me underground, I was hiding at Laurette and Arnaldo's when the terrible news arrived: Vallejo had suffered a cerebral accident; he lived for more than a month in a vegetative state but died without regaining consciousness. He was forty-nine.

But I digress. What I mean to convey are some of the experiences Susan and I shared, experiences that allowed us to glimpse a different world, one in which the possibility of greater justice was a reality. It wasn't the magic realist, often astonishing aspect of that world that gave us such hope. That was its poetry. It was the fact that we had experienced change on the ground rather than in the competing theories presented in books or manifestos. It was real, palpable, unfolding before our eyes.

This shared experience was the basis for a friendship that is now more than six decades old. Even the word *friendship* doesn't fully describe our relationship. We have known experiences that many today have forgotten or are too young to have known. We speak the same language. And when we see the signs that old dangers are hovering about us again, we understand what their consequences are likely to be. We operate in an outrider terrain difficult to describe if you haven't inhabited it.

Poets express themselves most eloquently through poetry. Susan's poem "Reminiscences" conveys the impact her first visit to Cuba had on her.

REMINISCENCES

for Cuba

& for *Meg*

1

Speaking to you   I was reminded
of those weeks   how far they seem
distant & yet   how strong

speaking to you

words fail me now   often
I sit for hours   without speech
images stray through my mind   songs

as I work a feeling of hunger   and then
of pain

Sometimes   no often it is harder to remember   and then
on the faces   I discover it   in the streets as I walk
learning to look out boldly   into those eyes

it is not despair that turns them away   but hope
you asked why & that is the answer

refusing solace   refusing their dark places
their tombs

I sicken of those eyes their sharp edges   their
wit   I sicken of the sophistication
of those eyes

by their death   they remind me

as those others did
that winter

so few weeks ago (we spoke together then)

as they did

by their life

2

It is the song that has meaning   I heard them
sing   We heard them   in their winter   Their
hands   their voices   the song   as the poem
its words strong

& behind the words   the meaning   the syllables
the depth

There is this pain inside me For years now
I have known it This pain This companion of
mine

It reduces things cleverly this friend

What is greater than I

it croons to me

it sings to me

What is greater than I

There are things greater good good good

good What are they

What is more important than this pain

How cleverly it reduces things this ache
in my side

& those weeks made it deeper I know now

what caused it & that it will never leave

3

It reminded me your voice of those days
The sea outside my window I could never live long
beyond the reach of sea At least sensing it there
around me its song even its silence Always
I have lived near water & there it surrounded me

The East River is not an ocean
Is not beautiful like that sea
Does not break against the streets
furious & then calm

But it is water   & every now and then a boat passes
& the stillness of it   even the darkness
sometimes

& I see into it as one looks into water

with the backs of the eye

4

It is not finished   is never over
Repeating again and again   Each time holding
the balance   tipping it
forward

    The revolution is for people
    they said   but it was not
    their words
                it was them

    the way they were   the way they spoke

It was as hard to carry as water

And now months later   I have begun to
live   to speak   the change

the words written in blood in pain

You could scream it in the streets
and who would listen

But the scream remains   the sound of it
like the sound of your voice   and those
others   like their memory   like water

changing   as it flows

Reporting on Cuba in articles and talks was more difficult. Following her return to New York, Susan began preparing an issue of *IKON* that included, in English translation, some of the more important papers from the Cultural Congress. Our correspondence was mostly concerned with making sure the material from Cuba reached her; by this time, the U.S. postal service couldn't be counted on to deliver mail it labeled as subversive, and Cuba's mail rarely reached the States at all unless it was brought in person or sent through a third party.

On April 5, 1968, Susan attempted to give me a sense of what New York felt like at that point:

> We were afraid there would be a lot of violence in the city yesterday because of Martin Luther King's assassination. The last month has been totally chaotic, with Johnson's "announcement" he would not run and that he would cut back the bombing in Vietnam (which I trust you can imagine how much). And then this, and then the rioting in Washington yesterday. The right wing is pushing for tight restrictions, "law and order" based now on King's death. The kind of law, of course, that would have stopped King, not his assassin. The unfortunate thing in all this is that it is completely without any kind of responsible leadership. Right now, it's just a big mess here. That's one reason I want to get out of the city this summer; it's already started and when it builds it will hit without knowledge or direction. But it is impossible to say what will happen. The mood is ugly on all sides, and anything is possible. They have passed very strong New York state anti-inciting-to-violence laws (whatever that means). I'll write more about things as they come up. Since speculation and analysis are impossible, about all you can do is report. I plan to take part in the April 27*th*

> demonstration—the Chicago demonstrations are fast turning into fiascos because of Johnson's statements and the irresponsibility of the Yippie organizing. The SDS people at this point are telling people to stay away. I'm going to try to get in touch with Dellinger[70] next week and talk to him a little about what is going on and what he thinks is the best course of action. I'm supposed to give a lecture about Cuba on Monday at Day Top (a center for drug addicts). So far, I have given a talk at the Free University which turned out quite well and the first of the month will host an evening of Cuban poetry and music for the Folklore Center.

Susan was disseminating positive information about the Cuban Revolution in every way she could: speaking and writing anywhere that would have her and hosting events at the small neighborhood storefront she'd rented. She was up against a powerful propaganda machine that sought every opportunity to distort and discredit what was happening in that country that had dared escape its radius of control. She published an article in the *Los Angeles Free Press,* only to see an "Editorial Disagreement" appear in the same issue. She responded with a letter of protest, which said, in part:

> [. . .] the last paragraph of your "disagreement" was as inexcusable a misuse of editorial distortion as any I could expect to find in an establishment newspaper. [It] combined just the right amount of truth, half-truth, and lies to completely distort and misrepresent what I was trying to say. Revolutionary thinking does not pretend to be infallible, but yours evidently does. Of course there are problems in Cuba. I stated so myself.

70. David Dellinger (1915–2004) was a U.S. pacifist and activist for nonviolent social change. He reached peak prominence as one of the Chicago Seven, who were put on trial in 1969 for disrupting the Democratic National Convention the year before.

> [. . .] The whole point is that Cuba is doing a beautiful thing in the face of almost overwhelming odds. And in the face, I might add, of prejudices such as yours.

On August 4, 1968, Susan wrote:

> Last week a brick was thrown through the store window. We had the window replaced and will now have to get a gate (about $80) or face the consequences of paying for the next broken window (at least $90). I am just hoping the landlord doesn't kick us out. He hasn't renewed our lease yet so legally he can throw us out if he wishes to.

And on August 31, she sent me news about what had happened at the Democratic National Convention in Chicago:

> Things continue happening so fast and are getting so bad. The mess in Chicago was unbelievable. I see now how people get trapped. They just don't believe what is happening. 20 reporters beaten up. A delegate to the convention dragged off the floor, another beaten and arrested in the hall, not to speak of the brutality to the students and protesters, which was somewhat expected. And Humphrey saying they all deserved it. I saw his speech on TV and the man is not only everything he is accused of; he is also really crazy.

Living where I did, I had the advantage of a milieu that was much more open to what was going on in Cuba. I was freer to speak and write about what I'd experienced. Mexico was the only Latin American country at the time that maintained diplomatic relations with Cuba following its revolutionary victory.[71]

---

71. This was a legitimate show of independence, but also served as a useful point of contact through which Interpol, the CIA, and other U.S. security agencies could get information about what was happening on the island.

In July of 1967, we'd dedicated *El Corno #23* entirely to Cuban writing and art. But as someone born and raised in the United States, with all the biases that carried with it, the revolution had also caused me to question many preconceived notions. Following my first visit to the island, in January 1967,[72] on the third of March of that year, I'd written to Susan:

> The Cuban experience has thrown me back on myself. In fact, we're cutting out publishing all El Corno books, and I'm stopping the midwifery. Just writing for a while and being quiet. I feel like I've stepped out of myself like a skirt falling to the floor and need time to adjust to the new person whose skin I inhabit.

Now another year had passed. Susan and I attended the Cultural Congress, returned to our respective countries, and worked to get the word out that change was not only possible but was happening on that small island only ninety miles from the tip of Florida. The pushback we were experiencing was different depending on where we were. In the United States, the FBI and other repressive forces were in for the long haul: paying informants to report on activists, spreading false accusations that split communities and set comrades against one another, and—when the protests got too forceful—putting them down brutally. In Mexico, there was an additional urgency. The country was scheduled to host the Summer Olympics that fall, and the government knew it had to put an end to a movement that threatened its profit margin.

72. Sergio and I were invited to El Encuentro con Rubén Darío, a gathering of poets and literary scholars hosted by Casa de las Américas. Sergio returned to Mexico when it ended. I stayed on for two more weeks, taking the Cubans up on their offer to take us across the island to see the changes that were in process.

Mexico City—3/13/68

Dearest Susan:

The repression here is devastating. They are trying to destroy me. I am absolutely broke and working like hell, getting very little mail (including many checks for articles that I do to keep alive) and sometimes it depresses me. Also, the Mexican Olympics, which are milking us dry (car tax, house tax, water bill, etc. all doubled without warning last month). The repression is meant to discourage, but in the long run one is only committed more.

I am translating the complete work of Otto René Castillo, a marvelous Guatemalan poet who would have been 31 this year. He was exiled at 17, studied in Germany, was involved in the Communist underground his whole adult life. Finally returned to Guatemala early last year and joined the FAR in the mountains. He and a woman comrade, after 15 days of eating only roots, were caught in an ambush in March. After they were tortured for four days, they were burned alive. This March 19*th* marks the first anniversary of that death, one of so many. For me, he is the best guerilla poet to have come out of the Latin American scene. I enclose some translations with this letter. Maybe you can use them there.

Nineteen sixty-eight unfolded in a direction I couldn't have anticipated in March. In July, student protests exploded when the police killed a young student during a march in solidarity with the Cuban Revolution. Throughout the world, young people were taking to the streets, and in Mexico it was no different—except that the Summer Olympics, to be held in October, made the government frantic to clean things up before the expected crowds were due to arrive. *El Corno Emplumado* took a strong stand in defense of what rapidly became a movement, and I got involved in other ways, as well—translating flyers and passing them out on city buses, hiding and feeding those fleeing the repression, engaging in ideological discussions with some of the leaders. When the athletes arrived, I even tried to sneak into the Olympic Village, hoping to convince some of them not to participate as a way of showing their solidarity with us. Vain hope.

In September, the government invaded and occupied the vast campus of the National Autonomous University. *Autonomous* wasn't an idle term. Since the 1918 University Reform Movement in Córdoba, Argentina, Latin American universities enjoyed a tradition of autonomy; they were places people could take refuge, expecting to be protected by the law. But, as we know, the law invariably bends to protect the powerful.

The Mexican student movement had spread throughout the country's major cities. Everywhere, people were protesting. And it was no longer only students. Unions and farmworkers had joined the demonstrations, demanding better working conditions, higher salaries, attention to their many issues. By early October, the government feared for the enormous investment it had made in new sports installations and luxury hotels; many prospective visitors to the games were canceling, fearful of the violence.

On the second of that month, a peaceful demonstration at a place called Plaza of the Three Cultures was suddenly attacked by air and ground forces. The name refers to the fact that a central plaza is built over the site of an Aztec ruin, there is a colonial church, and it is surrounded on all sides by a modern high-rise housing complex. Rumor had it that as many as a thousand had been killed. Blood soaked the paving stones and ran down the steps leading to the buildings into which frightened demonstrators had fled, trying to escape the bullets. The following morning, long lines of people could be seen leaving the area, many carrying what they could. It looked like a scene from the aftermath of World War II.

Our movement was dead. The Olympics went on as planned. For me, personally, the massacre at Tlatelolco[73] taught me my first serious lesson about what a government will do to its own people when its power is threatened.

Meanwhile in New York, Susan continued to spread the word about what she had seen in Cuba and involve herself in the struggles consuming the nation: the war in Vietnam, increased police harassment of the Black Panthers and other Left political organizations, and the beginnings of women coming into their strength and agency. Her economic situation was as dire as ours, the need she felt to contribute to progressive change as intense. But Susan was burdened by an isolation we didn't suffer. In Mexico and throughout Latin America in general, diverse groups of disenfranchised people were combining their energies. In the United States, Communists, socialists, labor union members, students, women, hippies, and an incipient gay movement still tended to operate separately. This would continue well into the following decade. An outrider commitment was necessary to continuing to struggle.

In 1969, I was attacked in my home by two men, who stole my passport at gunpoint, eventually forcing me into hiding and making us feel we had to send our children to Cuba for their safety and my mobility. I finally managed to leave Mexico and join my children on the island, where we would live for the next eleven years.

Cuba also figured prominently in Susan's life. René Vallejo had established an epistolary relationship with her and was

73. The official name of the plaza.

concerned about the health problems she was having and her inability to get the medical attention she needed. He invited her to come to the island for several months, where she would have access to free medical treatment. Susan and Vallejo continued to correspond, and he wanted her to return to Cuba the following year. Thirty years later, his daughter contacted Susan and told her that, at the time of her father's death, she'd found a half-finished letter to her in his typewriter.

On May 17, 1974, Susan wrote:

> New York is strange and tense and quiet. Without direction. But I know it is just a pause, a break, as if events are moving so fast really people can't keep track of them. And then because of the alienation of the country, of the people, for numbers of reasons, the diversity and multiplicity of the country, and no one strong central issue, IDENTITY becomes for most people the strong central issue. Or, in some of the so-called leftist groups, a strangling of identity, a real confusion between assertion of self and the concept of individualism. People are strangled in their own consciousness. A confused way to put it, but it takes a PERSON to fight, and that's the real problem here—something I think the women's movement saw but parts of it went off in the wrong direction. A starting place, an important place, but only finally in relation to other things. A good starting place, a good building place but a bad ending place.
>
> Please write and keep in touch. Your letters mean a great, great deal to me. And I think our magazine could be something of very great importance here. As any piece of something real is, especially in the vacuum that exists now.
>
> What can I say, Margaret? This letter is only a faint shadow, sounds silly really, but you know what the words are between

the lines. The doubt that is part of it. The love that is behind it. A lot of years.

Love, Susan.

The magazine Susan referred to was one we hoped to produce together. *El Corno* had been threatened by the repression that followed in the wake of the 1968 student movement. It had been able to sustain itself for a few more issues, mostly due to support it received from writers and artists all over, who held benefit readings, art sales, and other events that kept us going into the following year. When I left Mexico, it died. The magazine Susan and I dreamed of collaborating on was doomed before it began by the perennial problem of money. In the 1980s, she would launch a second series of *IKON,* this time as a feminist journal that featured women's work but was inclusive enough to publish that of the occasional man when appropriate.[74]

We continued to correspond with each other and our letters, when censorship and the deficiencies of several postal systems allowed, were bridges of sustaining friendship and real information.

Havana, September 13, 1971
"Year of Productivity"

Dearest Susan:

This has been a tremendous year here. For me, for us. So much discovery, past the things that are easy to talk about. Also, a sense of re-belonging to the States, a new understanding of what's happening there. This has mostly happened through the largely different people we've become in our two years here. Not to deny everything that went before. But I'm getting very abstract now. I'll try to be more specific. I feel

74. For example, *IKON*'s second series issue 5/6, "Art Against Apartheid."

much more whole. The revolution has explained a lot that used to be questions. It's not like "finding the answers." It's just that now, rather than questions they are statements. I have a whole new feeling about work. And about people.

This new way of relating to people includes, in the first place, the children. They are four extraordinary, curious, independent, happy beings. Gregory is in sixth grade at a swimming beca,[75] and also working with Cuba's only astronomer at the Astronomical Institute (she is 32, was a door-to-door salesperson before the revolution). Sarah is brilliant, funny, very much off on her own, attends another beca, Seguidores del Che, but may transfer to Gregory's swimming school as well. Ximena just had a major operation on her ear. They grafted a new eardrum from her own tissue. She was in the hospital for a month, showed a strength and resourcefulness I never imagined she had, and is home now, completely healed. But she won't go back to school for a couple more weeks. Little Ana isn't so little anymore. She's two and a half, funny, very talkative, one of the happiest toddlers I've seen: a real product of a Cuban círculo.[76] Robert is working hard at Radio Havana. He's also opened up in many ways. We've been through some struggles in terms of male chauvinism, and he's changing in that regard. He's also less dogmatic, easier with people and with himself. I've been sick on and off—an infection in the remaining kidney—but feel better now and am working hard myself.[77]

---

75. A school where the students live during the week, coming home on weekends.

76. Day-care center for children of working mothers.

77. While I was underground in Mexico, I was quite ill but couldn't seek medical attention. When I got to Cuba, I was able to see a doctor and it was determined that my left kidney had failed. It was removed and my health improved dramatically.

There's a sense of maturing in the revolution, a settling in, and much more depth of understanding on the part of more people. After that very hard year (with the failure of the 10-million-ton sugarcane harvest), we begin to see our hands and minds actually making change. But it's not just production alone. It's the connection between consciousness and physical work. And criticism that means something. A consciousness of the role Cuba is playing, not just within the country but also on the world scene.

I think you could tell me a lot about the Gay Liberation movement there, and I wish you would. There's so much confusion here. And so much lying about Cuba, even by people we once saw as comrades. I'd really be grateful for your thoughts, observations, feelings. It's clear to me that while the gay movement in the States is authentic and necessary, it's not by its nature revolutionary, by which I mean anti-imperialist, and also very susceptible to infiltration. Of course this could also be said of the women's movement, but it pretty much seems to have defined itself now. Gay people in Cuba have been hurt tremendously by the accusations made by gays in the US.

I wish I could send you some poems, something of myself. But I haven't written many, hardly any as a matter of fact, in the past year. I wrote one out of rage when they murdered George Jackson and our brothers and sisters were being assassinated on the streets of Bolivia at the same time. I have been writing a lot, just not poems, mainly in a huge journal, thousands of pages long now. And I'm working on the English translation of my book on Cuban women which is about 500 pages—such good stuff there.[78]

All my love, Margaret.

---

78. Shortly after my arrival in Cuba, I began the fieldwork for a book of oral history with Cuban women. It was published there in Spanish as *La*

Havana, July 10th, 1974

"Year of the XV Anniversary"

Dearest Susan:

How is our magazine going? I'll be going to Vietnam in September (spending a few days in Paris on the way). Needless to say, this is a privilege and I've been studying a lot, trying to prepare as well as I can.[79]

Susan, be well. Don't let yourself get depressed. Keep working.

Much love, Margaret.

Paris, 9.2.74

Dearest Susan:

I send you strength and love from this distant city, where I'm walking, looking, listening, and learning a lot. The contradictions so much more hidden than in our poor raped nations. At one and the same time marveled and angered by the pillaged wonders at the Louvre. I continue my journey in about a week. Thinking of you a lot and hoping everything is going well there. I'll be in touch, as much as possible along the way.

All my love, sister, and strength, Margaret.

---

mujer cubana ahora (Havana: Editorial de Ciencias Sociales, 1972) and in English in Canada two years later (Toronto: The Women's Press, 1974). Subsequently, it also came out in editions in Venezuela, the Dominican Republic, and the Netherlands.

79. After my book *Cuban Women Now* appeared, I received an invitation from the North Vietnamese Women's Union to visit their country in the fall of 1974. I spent several months there, traveling from Hanoi in the north all the way down Highway 1 to Friendship Bridge, which divided the North from the South, and crossing over into the liberated zone of Quang Tri. This trip, just months before the Vietcong defeated the U.S. invaders, was a life-changing experience and resulted in my writing a small book based on interviews with Vietnamese women, *Spirit of the People: Vietnamese Women Two Years from the Geneva Accords* (Vancouver: New Star Books, 1975), and *El espíritu de un pueblo* (Mexico City: Siglo XXI, 1975).

Paris—October 5th, 1974

Dear Susan:

Left Vietnam behind, and after more than 30 hours of planes, airports, etc. am back in this "city of lights." The real light is in the DRV. I'm still in a pretty heavy state of culture shock but thinking of you and of our magazine. Hope all is going well. Soon I'll be sending you poems and things from this beautiful experience.

Love, Margaret.

Spending that time in Vietnam was a turning point in my life. I had to fight my way through inevitable guilt as someone from the United States, the country waging a brutal war on that of my hosts. The Vietnamese I met were unfailingly gracious and generous; they constantly told me what it meant to them that I had defied the wrath of my government by visiting. The magazine Susan and I had planned on doing together after *El Corno*'s demise never happened; we were unable to raise the money. But we continued to collaborate on her *IKON.* I never did write a poem about Vietnam that satisfied me. It was as if the experience was just too profound and complex for me to put into words.

During those years of important changes—problems of self-realization as well as those having to do with the broader political panorama—Susan and I were able to talk to each other about things I wasn't able to verbalize with many other people. The connection we'd made in Mexico and our experience of Cuba provided a bedrock of understanding. Sometimes we didn't even need words, but the words in the letters we exchanged always felt like solace to me. On June 24, 1974, Susan wrote:

> How much I wished when I read the letter you wrote that I could have then, at that moment, been able to say how much I understand—on another level, of course, in another place,

another time—what you are facing and how much I wish I could help, if only as a friend. How much I would like to be able to talk to you about these kinds of things, that I too have been having troubles with, from both ends—the sense of isolation, broken by only a few people who really understand. This last two years has been a difficult time for me—a real identity crisis in a way—and the inability on my part to be able to write through it, to express the confusion, because always before I was SURE in one way or another of many things. I am still sure of them, but they seem distant, and much more difficult in action than in words. And the words finally don't mean as much to me except as they express that action, with all its doubts and struggles. And now with the book out[80] finally it's as if a part of my life has really closed, the late 60s as well and the early. And now I must face and write about here, now, what all that means. I see much hope too through the book, already many wonderful reactions, and so that RESPONSIBILITY to work, to write, and not to compromise as you put it so well. Although now, as I grow older, that seems harder. Just from habit really.

My main project now is to work on the book Creativity & Change, which probably won't be the final title. The first essay?—prose?—will be the one in the book, the second a remarkable experience I had with time many years ago. Something I can write about now that it's a little more distant, that I hope will get me back to the habit of being able to express—one which I have lost in that deeper sense, or better said misplaced.

---

80. *With Anger/With Love: Selections, Poems and Prose 1963–1972* (Amherst, Massachusetts: Mulch Press, 1974). The book went into a second printing and sold close to four thousand copies, extremely unusual for a poetry collection then and even now.

It keeps the words from being too smooth, too fluent, for me, I think. It keeps things closer to the truth.

I'm glad of the poem "Reminiscences." It will also be in an anthology that the University of Massachusetts is printing on the Women's Festival last March. It remains one of my favorites, and I'm sure one of my best, certainly one which conveys the hope, the enthusiasm, I felt through that talk. A poem I go back to and read that gives me strength now and makes me remember when it's easy to forget.

Please keep writing. It is awful knowing it will be a full month before you receive this letter. But I will continue writing, continue to be in touch.

My love, as always, Susan.

And then, on December 30 of that year:

I have been through a very hard time but have gained, I think, from it. A new strength and certainly a new and renewed sense of the very beautiful support I have gotten. And it's really helping me to grow. The financial situation here is impossible to describe. I was laid off from my typesetting job with all the other employees, and now we will have to retain a lawyer to fight for our rights to unemployment insurance because they offered to rehire us but without paid lunch time, sick leave, no phone calls or talking to other employees, no raises in the foreseeable future, strict hours, will be fired if fifteen minutes late four times, no medical insurance unless we pay for it, etc. etc.

With my work, the new book, things are going very well.[81] It has been received in a very beautiful way. I have begun to write again, which was a little like learning to talk again. There is so

81. *With Anger/With Love.*

much I want to say, to express, that only the impatience, the too much need, stands in my way.

MORNING POEM

There's always plenty of time
until it runs out on us
But you can't rush things either
They grow at their own speed
reaching for a point of contact
of their own

I am plagued with impatience
inertia
          the two extremes
the edges of everything
Those two things also
being one

Some people build homes   houses
of themselves   I think of Jung
his circular walls
                    years of
thought enclosing his body
Trapped in his own ideas

Others travel the streets
planting themselves in their
sidewalks
          Their bodies a motion
more like a dance

And some try both worlds
multiple existences
                    are makers of life

Patience is part of it   but more
To have a vision   To make it
real

        Can you see what I'm saying
How time itself is our enemy
our friend   How we trap ourselves
in vision
                But how it also opens
                                        out
can lead us forward
How we lose things only to find
them again
                Only to find ourselves
different   at the same place

Listen   this morning the world closes
and opens at my fingertips   The sun
is bright   draws me to it
But I sit in a room cluttered with
memories books old pieces of furniture
old pieces of myself

I am inside
                        and outside
of it all
I reach out
with what is behind me
I live my death
                        am captured
in my life

SPRING SONG

Let's put it another way
The street breaks with ice
It is cold tonight   quiet
This first day of spring

Burdened with clothes
I would shed them   My coat
long blue wraps me into
                    myself
Holds me together

How much we are lied to
Lie to ourselves
How much we hide How many things
are hidden
        in these layers
of cotton wool rayon
skin

I am startled by differences
a lack of correspondence
As I was before by what
                    binds us
But things change
Ten years   twenty   thirty
Some drop away   others grow
stronger
        Faces change
& names
I change   remain
What makes us unique

This first day of spring
alone I wrote
            this poem
patched a coat of words
stitched a song
Tried to find out what is beneath it
what it means
At the end of it
            finally
what I would want
to say

This woman tried to grasp life
balance her days
            the worlds
that sprang from her hands
broke from her lips

She was burdened as we all are
by ends and beginnings
But she never turned away

March 28, 1975

Dearest Margaret,

I got embroiled here in a real political fight in the women's movement. I don't know if you read anything about Jane Alpert turning herself in.[82] Anyway, Flo Kennedy, Ti-Grace Atkinson,

82. Jane Alpert was a political activist who took part in a series of bombings in opposition to the war in Vietnam and authored the letters released to the press to explain those actions. Because she was being sought by the police, she went underground for four and a half years. In November 1974, she turned herself in, was sentenced, and served time in prison. She turned against the Left, blaming her crimes on having been influenced by a male

some other friends, and I got together and I wrote a statement, a collaboration of ideas of the four of us, strongly attacking Jane and the movement that supports her. I used a line of yours in the statement; I'm sure you'll recognize it. The upshot was that it caused a minor explosion in the women's movement and Gloria Steinem and Robin Morgan, basically Robin, circulated a petition against us which was signed by 83 women prominent in the movement and also very unfortunately by many women I considered friends. The petition itself was virulent, accusing us of advocating censorship and all kinds of nonsense. A lot of pressure and lies were circulated. It has been very difficult. I have thought of you often, Margaret, during this time particularly. How simple these things are, finally. How hard it is to make some people understand. How much I would have loved to talk to you, just heard your strong voice.

It is so hard to speak, not knowing how many people, which ones, will read this letter. As it will of course be read. The papers here finally admit what we all know—how mail is opened, phones tapped, jobs lost and more. At the same time, many grand juries across the country are trying to make people speak, setting group against group. This is why we felt the statement on Jane was so important. To define the enemy. To say some of us aren't sisters. That this is deadly real. To break through, somehow. Our society in every way is reinforcing these weaknesses—almost in the air we breathe here. Some supposedly "progressive" people are so blocked into their own tight little worlds. A time, I think, for real sorting out.

With love, as always, Susan.

---

comrade, made derogatory statements about prisoners killed during the Attica uprising, and it was rumored (although never proved, and she denied it) that she had given sensitive information to the FBI.

For a while, Susan was what we call today "canceled" in some feminist circles because of this controversy.

Havana—April 26th, 1975

"Year of the First Congress"

Dearest Susan:

I read your letter to the movement, the one about Jane Alpert, and was happy to get it. If anything, I felt it wasn't strong enough. It's so important that this be said, made clear. Several years ago here, I was talking with Julie Nichamin and we were looking at Robin Morgan's book Sisterhood Is Powerful. I remember Julie looking at that title and muttering almost under her breath: "Yeah, sisterhood is powerful all right; it kills!"

On my trip to Vietnam, I had an experience that underscores this whole issue, which is a political question and vital for us. I will share it with you but please don't share it at this point with anyone else. I was traveling with another US American woman, Arlene Eisen Bergman and we had many differences. She was married for several years to a man named Lincoln Bergman who was then working at Radio Havana. Radio Havana gave airtime in English to the Vietnamese, and Lincoln often worked on those programs. In Hanoi, some women from the leadership of the North Vietnamese Women's Union asked us about our husbands and children, a common question there. One of them asked Arlene: "What does your husband do?" Arlene, rather than say that they were separated, spat out: "He's living as a bigamist in Cuba."

To understand the impact this had, you must know what bigamy means to the Vietnamese. It is something that has weighed on women there for generations and the Union is doing a lot of grassroots work, with men especially, to try to eradicate it. I thought it outrageous that Arlene would present Lincoln in

> that way to the women there. Later, when we were alone, I told her so. In fact, she and Lincoln had been separated for several years by then. She raged at me: "How can you feel so much for Lincoln? You should be feeling for me, for my hurt!" This was only one of many run-ins she and I had on that trip, and they remain unresolved even now. I don't want this story spread because basically she and I are on the same side. She has done so much good work for Vietnam and for the antiimperialist movement in general. I share it with you as an example of what I'm sure you've faced many times: the idea that women are somehow better, that men are the enemy.
>
> Love, Margaret.

On October 23, 1981, Susan wrote about an event that—although I didn't know it then—would have a major impact on my life. Kathy Boudin was a member of the Weather Underground. She and several others took part in a political robbery that went bad. They were arrested and given long prison sentences. In the late 1980s, I was teaching at Trinity College in Hartford, Connecticut, just a few hours' drive from where Kathy was being held at the Bedford Hills Correctional Facility. My friend Ruth Hubbard visited her there occasionally and thought Kathy and I would have a lot to talk about. She took me to the prison, and that began another important friendship that would last all Kathy's remaining years behind bars, through the surprising moment of her release, and until her death, in 2022. Kathy was another outrider: brilliant, a profound thinker, compassionate, and someone who contributed to society even in the most difficult circumstances. Here is a fragment of Susan's letter from 1981:

> A whole explosion in the news the last three days over the arrest of Kathy Boudin who was picked up with two other

> Weatherpeople when they tried to rob a Brinks truck. The police and FBI are having a field day, tying everything together, saying Assata Shakur was involved. Breaking into apartments. Trying to stop The Freedom of Information Act, which is currently up before Congress. I just hope this isn't the excuse for a witch hunt on the left, which is what they're really pushing for.

In another part of this letter, she spoke of painful tensions around the power of art for social change:

> There is so much prejudice in the movement in general, left and feminist, against art and poetry in particular—no idea of the power of poetry, even though at rallies and benefits it is freely used. A bad tension in the women's movement still left over from the seventies against the left in general, even though there are wonderful new things happening. Difficult but possible. And the real friendships, the real understanding that finally doesn't need to be spelled out, a lifeline really.

In an undated letter that I deduce was written sometime in 1982, Susan mentioned an incident with Susan Sontag that took place during her second trip to Cuba. I think I had written to Susan about disagreements I had with Sontag's book *On Photography.* She responded:

> When you mentioned Susan Sontag, it brought up memories I really haven't thought about for a while, and the fact that I never really told you much about that second trip to Cuba. I'll never forget flying over that green, green island—one forgets what green is here in New York—and the plane landing and Vallejo standing there waiting for me at the door. I couldn't really believe it. You know, all the letters he wrote me were stolen from my file cabinet in the late 60s. What a terrible loss. But then, they can't steal memories.

Anyway, to the best of my recollection, as they say here, when I got to the Havana Libre Vallejo checked me in and then I spent a month at the National Hospital, and when I got out, I received a phone call from Ms. Sontag. Oh, she was here in Havana and didn't know a soul and had heard about me, and did I know this one and would I introduce her to that one and would I come over to the National Hotel where she was staying for a drink. Sweet, nice, friendly, ingratiating etc. So, I went over and met her, and we drew up a list of people—Miguel Barnet and Pablo Armando Fernández and others—and I called and arranged the appointments. And of course, I never heard from her again. And she almost pretended, once I had done these things for her, that she didn't even know me. From then on, in my mind, she was a first-class opportunist, and I suspect now that I was right. First of all, I don't think she's all that intelligent. I think she knows how to parrot the male establishment very well, so clever would be more the word. I think her book on photography is awful, but it's one of a series of books like that.

Susan and I continued to correspond throughout my years in Cuba. At the end of 1980, I moved on to Nicaragua, then in the throes of the first years of the Sandinista revolution.

Managua, Nicaragua—January 15th, 1983

Dearest Susan:

This a.m. around five we all emerged from ten days of having worked night and day with the foreign journalists here for the Non-Aligned summit. Many of us were taken from our usual jobs to help out. We even lent our own cars to the effort. And it meant working all day, all night, with a bare hour or two of sleep out of each 24. I am exhausted, have no voice, and only today to catch up on sleep and a lot of other things before I return to work tomorrow. Ana is coming home from New York tomorrow. I hope she at least called you. Ximena is picking coffee in the war-torn zone of Jinotega (in the north).

All my love, Margaret.

On May 21, 1983, Susan wrote:

Dearest Margaret:

So many things to say, it's hard to know where to begin. Two days ago, your letter and in the same mail one from Rosario Murillo and Leonor Huper with the invitation to attend the meeting in Nicaragua July 12*th*—and of course I'll be there.[83] I would like to stay an extra week or so but this is such important news for me. Second, about your tour here in the fall. I would love to organize a reading for you and Gioconda through *IKON*.[84]

I suppose someone has sent you the horrible review written by Richard Elman for *The American Book Review*. If not, let me know and I will send it. I am composing an answer today to send to the paper; I can't imagine how they ever printed it. He picks out you and Gioconda for attack along with his indescribable attack on Nicaragua. I must say even for Richard this is a new low. I'll never forget my first and next to last meeting with him—I've only seen him twice—when he laid into me for no reason at all except that's generally how he deals with women.

Love, Susan.

---

83. Rosario Murillo headed the Sandinista Cultural Workers Association, and I worked on and off with her there. This was many years before she and her husband, Daniel Ortega, took over the country and became de facto dictators. To show off the Sandinista revolution's accomplishments, the Association hosted a gathering of intellectuals in July of 1983. This was the meeting to which Susan is referring.

84. Gioconda Belli, one of Nicaragua's best-known writers. This tour didn't materialize.

Susan was ever alert to what topics would be important in the United States. Upon her return from Nicaragua, she wrote:

October 27, 1983

Dearest Margaret:

About the next issue of *IKON*, I would love to have something from you on liberation theology, some rewriting or even part of your new book perhaps,[85] although an article based on the information and directed at a US audience would be better. There is little known about it here and I feel it is an exceptionally important phenomenon for many reasons: for what it means to the Latin American struggle, particularly in terms of the Church's influence in the region, its traditional position in keeping down struggle, and because of its possible effects on Marxism in general. The questions of course that are immediately raised for women are in terms of the Church's patriarchal oppression, its position on questions like marriage, sexuality, abortion, birth control, etc. And is this just putting in power a more benign but still oppressive authority as far as women are concerned?

I am still trying to digest the trip—the contradictions between "here" and "there." I hope you realize just how important your presence there is for the people here who visit, Margaret. I've heard it over and over since I've been back and even before I left. It serves as a kind of contact, a base, a point of understanding in an experience that might otherwise be overshot—that's just the right word—it's hard for Americans to understand simple things—how complex and profound they

85. *Christians in the Nicaraguan Revolution* (Vancouver: New Star Books, 1983). It also came out in Spanish the same year from Editorial Nueva Nicaragua in Managua and Poseidon Editores in Caracas.

are—our experience here is so unnecessarily and premeditatively complicated—things aren't respected unless they are very complex—very specialized—very technical and very intellectual in the bad sense of the word. So it's easy in an experience like Nicaragua to get lost, unless there's a point of contact.

A whole lot of love, Susan.

FROM NICARAGUA, A GIFT

for Margaret Randall

If you were to ask me
to name a color for that land
I would say it was green
But the color you sent was yellow
A plane descending into green
The sun rising golden beyond its wings

Many things are made of gold
A voice sometimes is known as golden
A wedding ring
Even silence
(when chosen)

But "to be silenced"
That's a different matter
That's to choke on one's own words
erupt in violence
an act of war

Margaret today in your letter
folded in a press release
COVERT ACTIONS AGAINST NICARAGUA
CHALLENGED BY INTERNATIONAL LAW

a small shard of foil falls out
slips to the floor
                    I can't make it out
It puzzles me
What is it? What does it say?
A rectangular shape in the center
a golden face
circled by yellow edged by red
—a cigar band—
                    a cigar band?
Sol Habana
The Havana Sun

Margaret in the midst of war
both yours & ours
How my country is trying to silence yours
How the silences here are many
& growing
          & the violence
not limited by nationality borders names

How people are more and more refusing
to be silenced
                    in both our lands
Margaret in the midst of war
from your letters of anger
                              & triumph
death struggle hope
you have sent me/shared with me
perhaps even as an afterthought
who knows?
          (& I will treasure it always)
a gift of light

Susan was always very generous with my children when any of them went to New York.

November 25, 1984

Dearest Margaret:

We see Ana now and then.[86] She stopped by last weekend for a short visit. She looked fine but was very upset by what she thought was the imminent invasion of Nicaragua. My real fear is that the US is playing a war of cruel and horrible nerves while using the Contras to inflict real economic and human damage, and taking the edge off criticism here by looking like it will invade and then not invading, pretending to back down so as to induce relief. Like threatening death and then making you feel lucky because you're only being starved and tortured. It's an atrocity and it looks like a lot of people are being taken in by it. At the same time, they are playing up Soviet "intervention" and militarism to break people's sympathy with the Sandinistas.

I don't know how I can feel simultaneously that I am working way too much and way too little. It's like being in a state of fatigue and guilt all at once.

Love, as ever, Susan.

As the years unfolded, many of the social experiments that had given Susan and me and those like us such hope were defeated. The United States, through its covert and overt actions, inflicted the fatal blows, but corrupt leaders of the revolutions themselves also sometimes aided the destabilization. Meanwhile, our personal and writing lives continued.

86. My youngest daughter, who was living in New York at that time.

Albuquerque
June 13th, 1985

Dearest Susan:

Since this book is for you, I thought I should at least send you a copy in manuscript.[87] I'm not sure about the title. I certainly don't expect you to sit right down and go through it but want you to have it for whenever. I'm sorry I embarrassed you on the phone yesterday when I mentioned that the book is dedicated to you. For me it's important because it acknowledges a friendship with one of the people in the world I most treasure.

Love, Margaret.

p.s. I sent a copy to Michael Ratner just in case he thinks it should be read by someone in the office looking for things I've included that could hurt the case.[88]

9.15.86

Dearest Margaret:

Finally, a chance to write at least the beginning of the long letter that I want so much to send. I have been thinking of you often these last few days—really these last weeks. I had a wonderful day with Sarah.[89] I took her to the Cloisters restaurant for tea and then to Washington Square Park. She was fascinated by the teenage dope peddlers plying their trade around the fountain. At a certain point when the crowd thinned out, I felt it was time to leave and could hardly tear her away. And

---

87. *Albuquerque: Coming Home to the USA* (Vancouver: New Star Books, 1986). This book is based on a selection of my journal entries written during the first year after I came home. I also included some of my photographs.

88. Michael Ratner (1943–2016) was one of my lawyers.

89. My eldest daughter.

> then we met Colleen[90] and all went to see "Aliens" which Colleen spent mostly with her eyes closed—I liked it more than she did—and Sarah really enjoyed. She really got into it. We were trying to find something that was fun and that she wouldn't have to know too much English to understand. Although I must say her English is pretty good, certainly better than my Spanish.
>
> Thinking about it, it seems to me that you have been bound up in, responsible really, for many of the most important experiences I have had. Cuba, Nicaragua, *El Corno, IKON*. It's something I don't forget, Margaret. It's funny how isolated one can feel in a city as big and full as New York. I love you a lot. Please take care. Susan.

After twenty-three years in Latin America, my reentry into the United States was exciting and also fraught. One thing I had to do was figure out how to earn a living. I discovered I could teach, but that had its own problems. In December of 1984, I wrote to Susan:

> By now you know that I finally did get the course, although there was criticism of my syllabus on the basis of minority ghettoizing (I'm revising it this week). Tomorrow I should finally know if I will be teaching the American Studies course as well. All for 1/3 of what a regular professor gets for the same amount of work.[91]

---

90. Photographer Colleen McKay and Susan were partners for more than a decade.

91. I started out with adjunct courses at the University of New Mexico in Albuquerque before being hired to more lucrative and satisfying positions at several other universities. From 1986 to 1994, I had a visiting professorship at Trinity College in Hartford, Connecticut.

I returned to the United States to live in 1984 but had to wage a five-year battle to regain my citizenship. Susan and I saw each other more frequently after that. I traveled to New York and other cities to read poetry and lecture, and she sometimes visited me in Albuquerque. Over the next decade, I taught at half a dozen U.S. universities. In 1989, I had a Distinguished Visiting Professorship at Macalester College, in St. Paul, Minnesota. On April 12 of that year, I wrote to Susan from that northern city:

> Let me tell you how extraordinary your book is.[92] I felt compelled to call you between planes, to tell you that, and I feel compelled to repeat it now after a careful reading of the whole and a rereading of certain parts. It is a major book, your major statement to date. It must be done perfectly. I very much hope that Curbstone will do it justice (both in production and marketing) and will try to exert whatever influence I may have as a board member to see that that happens. They are good people, both of them, and she is very smart. They often end up making very fine books. Sometimes their sheer overload and lack of expertise in certain areas causes them to slip up. You need to be careful and vigilant. Fortunately, they both welcome a close relationship with the author. They actually need the help, often ask people who drop in on them to fold, collate, and so forth. Love, Margaret.

On July 8, 1988, I wrote:

> Dearest Susan:
>
> Two issues run through our conversations like a continuous leitmotif. We often talk about extreme compartmentalization, how people today tend to isolate themselves as

92. *The Color of the Heart: Writing from Struggle & Change 1959–1990* (Willimantic, Connecticut: Curbstone Press, 1990).

revolutionaries or feminists but rarely both (or, even more narrowly, as a revolutionary member of a pro-Albanian pre-party organization or a disabled Black lesbian or a feminist interested only in women's spirituality, etc.). The renaissance personality seems to have gone out of style with the covered wagon. This tendency to limit one's identity—and consequently one's interests—means that a literary magazine like IKON, which is politically progressive as well as feminist, retains a terribly small readership. People on the left may find it "too feminist"; feminists (who seem more and more to be interested only in the less "threatening" areas such as women's spirituality) find it too left. Inevitably, when this tendency toward extreme compartmentalization comes up, we bemoan the shallow (or nonexistent) sense of history most people have. And this brings me to the other issue, the ways in which monopoly capitalism—using education, mass media, and even religion—erases or distorts history right before our eyes, so that it is a "natural" thing these days for people to believe that their best interests are served by visualizing only the world most immediate to their current experience.

In dozens of ways every day we see history broken apart, reshaped, leveled to a kind of bland mush concocted to make us feel "patriotic" or proud or hopeful. Up until a couple of years ago at least some of us basically caught on to the misrepresentation of great dramatic events: the McCarthy era, the execution of the Rosenbergs, the US dropping the first atomic bombs on Hiroshima and Nagasaki, the Korean and Vietnam wars, World War II, the history of Chinese/US relations, Cuba/US relations, Soviet/US relations. A presidency. Human rights abuses in Central America. The story about each of these events would change, almost imperceptibly, as time went on. More recently, we can watch the network news for two or three nights in a row and from day to day observe the ways in which we are told first one thing and then something completely different, with no explanation given that in any way accounts for the contradictions.

Something happens, like the shooting down of Iranian commercial airliner #655 by a US warship in the Persian Gulf. First, we are told the airbus was flying outside the commercial flight path. Then we are told it wasn't really outside the path. Dan Rather or Peter Jennings tells us the plane emitted a commercial signal and then that it gave off a military signal as well. A commentator tells us the commander of the US warship couldn't find the flight listed in his commercial log. That same commentator then says that it took him exactly thirty seconds to find the listing. While President Reagan declares the incident closed, our irresponsible news sources suggest that the Iranians ("everyone knows revolutionaries value martyrs!") emitted the military signal as a kind of hari-kari to provoke the attack. i.e., the Iranians shot down their own commercial plane. Now, those responsible for 290 civilian deaths are them, not us. Comparisons with the Korean commercial airliner shot down by the Soviets several years back are rejected with a tone of authority that silences further reference to that other accident upon which newscasters capitalized to such an extent. Soon the Iranian airline "incident" will be forgotten, displaced on the news by other more captivating stories such as a small boy living in a germ-free bubble or the rescue of a baby who fell into a well. The individual is always more important, in our society, than a nation or a group of millions, especially if those millions aren't white and don't speak English.

As teachers, you and I have often exchanged stories about the almost total lack of historical perspective our college-age students seem to have. It's not difficult to understand how and why young people have such a poor historical sense. History that would effectively give them an idea of where they've come from and where they may hope to go is purposefully erased so that young people today are much more aware of more immediate fabricated need: what to eat (so they can keep the food and fitness industries going), what to wear (so the fashion industry may flourish), what to buy (so the range of gadgets, with all their built-in obsolescence, will continue to make millions for their manufacturers). Your wonderful poem "Facts" speaks of all this much better than I can here. You really zero in on the tragedy of kids being told how things happen (i.e., a finger pulled a trigger, and a bullet was fired from a gun) but never why (whose finger, whose gun, in whom the bullet landed, whose interests are served).

I'm often shocked when a student of mine doesn't know who the Rosenbergs were, or Che Guevara, or what really happened in Vietnam. Several years ago, an intelligent, community-active young woman in a class of mine admitted she had never heard of Gandhi until she saw the movie. Then I remind myself what that student studied, how she was taught, what appears in the papers or on TV, and how many people even read beyond the comics or sports page or listen to more than the soaps. I am angry when people who do read, who consider themselves responsible and even conscious, political, literary, say they are "not interested in feminism" or "don't want to talk about politics" or "that's too left for me." Then I try to remember how much scientific calculation and money goes into the system's ongoing efforts to keep us memoryless and ignorant of our own histories, separate from one another.

Current language usage reflects and encourages this "here and now" atmosphere. Illegal Contra criminals are "freedom fighters." The shooting down of the Iranian passenger plane is an "incident," something that just happened. A woman "was raped"; rarely are we told by whom. Passive tense, the co-optation of words (such as "revolutionary" to describe a new deodorant or "magic" to describe a painkiller) are important in shifting responsibility, giving people the sense that we have no control over our world. We must eat until we burst and exercise until we disappear. We will go on destroying earth, air, water. We will wage the ultimate war. Change is not in our hands.

You and I have always felt empowered by the possibility of change: creativity and change—that's been the central theme of IKON. In many ways it's been the theme of both our lives. And in looking at how we change and create, at how we are products of a changing world and committed to creating a better one, we have wanted to build or be bridges from one to the other.

My whole life has been bridge-like. Early on, when I had my first child in the way in which I chose to do that, I was bridging need with act and totally defying social convention. In Mexico I edited a bilingual literary magazine that bridged much more than Spanish and English; it brought poets and artists of different cultures, ages, writing styles, and political visions together in a shared space. When I lived in Cuba and in Nicaragua, I was interested in understanding how revolutionary socialism affects people's lives, how it changes what it means to be a child, a woman, a worker. And I wrote about those things and explained them to people who traveled from one culture to another. The bridge role. It's something that *IKON* has been interested in as well, and powerfully. You've told me how the magazine fails to engage many feminists because it focuses on issues such as self-determination in Central America or apartheid in South Africa. How it has been ignored by many on the left because it is a magazine of women's voices, women's ideas. A sad commentary on the feminist movement and on the left.

All this has nudged our memories, made us want to remember who we have been and how we have lived, the great events of our lifetimes already distorted—if not omitted—from our contemporary history. You're 49 and I'm only a couple of years older (51), yet we've already spoken of how those couple of years sometimes make a difference when looking at certain issues. I hope we can begin to write to one another about the times we have lived and what we think they mean.

This letter is an invitation. Let's go back to the events of our childhood, yours in Los Angeles, mine in New York City and its suburbs, the similarities and differences in the families from which we came, class and cultural considerations, relationship to people and places, the things that influenced us in important ways. What Berkeley and the San Francisco renaissance meant to you. What the Beat scene, the Black Mountain poets, and Abstract Expressionist artists meant to me. What it was like to have been women in such male-dominated milieus. What doing our respective magazines said about our lives and meant in them. What going to Cuba when we did meant to each of us. And whatever else that comes up.

I'm more interested in the public history than the private details, but we'll need to touch on the private in order to locate our particular views of the public. I remember the first time in my life I was aware of the real possibility of imminent doom was at the time of the Suez Canal crisis. I can conjure a vivid image of sitting around a kitchen table with friends; it was here in

Albuquerque and of course it was 1956 or '57 (it will be easy enough to reference the date, harder to recall exactly what information we were getting and how real or distorted it was). How often since then has official reportage given us a crisis situation? How often did we find out, months or years later, that the news was contrived even as it was being given? And how has that history been altered even more as it faded into the oblivion of the past? I don't want the things we've lived to disappear into a story that serves them. There is so much that we can retrieve and look at in these letters. I look forward to doing that with you.

Love, Margaret.[93]

This is Susan's poem to which I refer in my letter:

FACTS

1

South Africa September, 1984
A story in the *New York Times*
South Africa
40 miles south of Johannesburg
28 dead 600 detained
Picked up at the funerals of their loved ones
and their friends

The photo shows death
rebellion
Black people moved again
as they were before

93. Susan told me that my letter was an initiative for her writing her memoir, *America's Child: A Woman's Journey through the Radical Sixties*.

and continue to be
(except in our press)
                    to action
resisting
the lie

Underneath the photo   a caption
No explanation A statement of fact
A lie of omission
"Police Quell a Riot"
as if implying they were doing
a commendable act

So many injured So many killed
& how many times in our papers
do they tell us

"Why?"

2

In my class I ask
"What is a fact?"
A student answers
"What you hear on the 5 o'clock news:"

I laugh but it isn't funny
& I am the only one
who gets the joke

3

"Why!" is not "How!"
is not a recital of physical causes
physical effects
              It is meaning

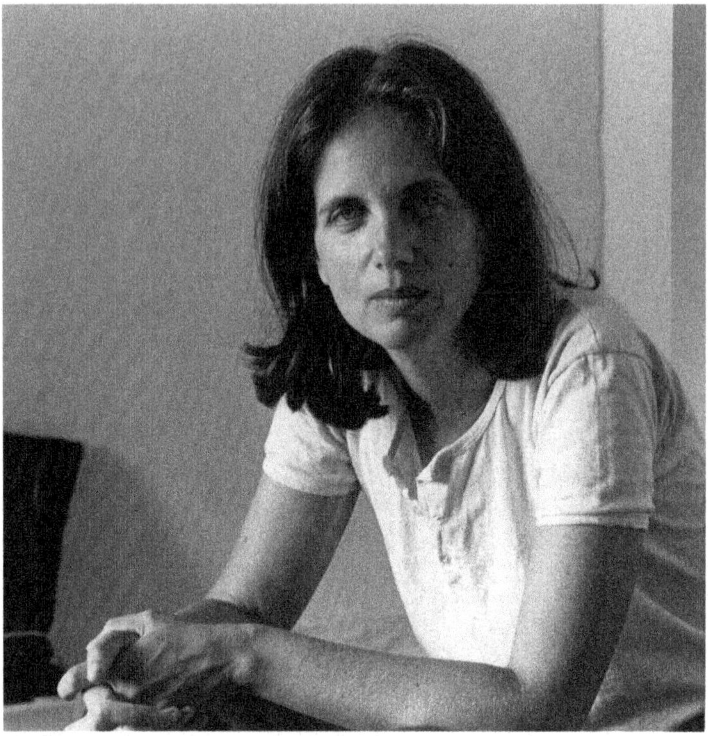

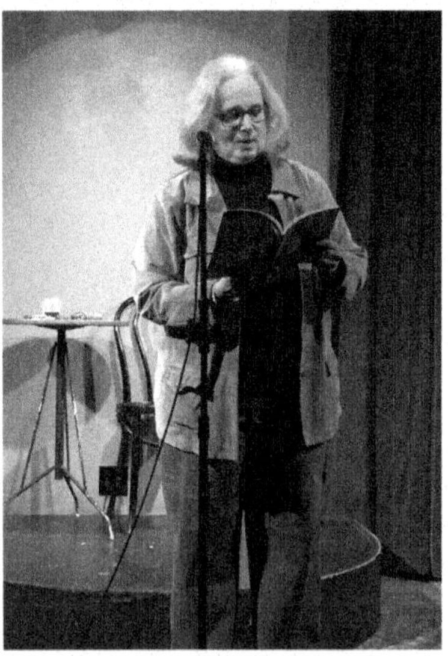

Above and right: Susan Sherman in 1980s, photos Colleen McKay. Left: Susan reading in Albuquerque 2015, photo Margaret Randall.

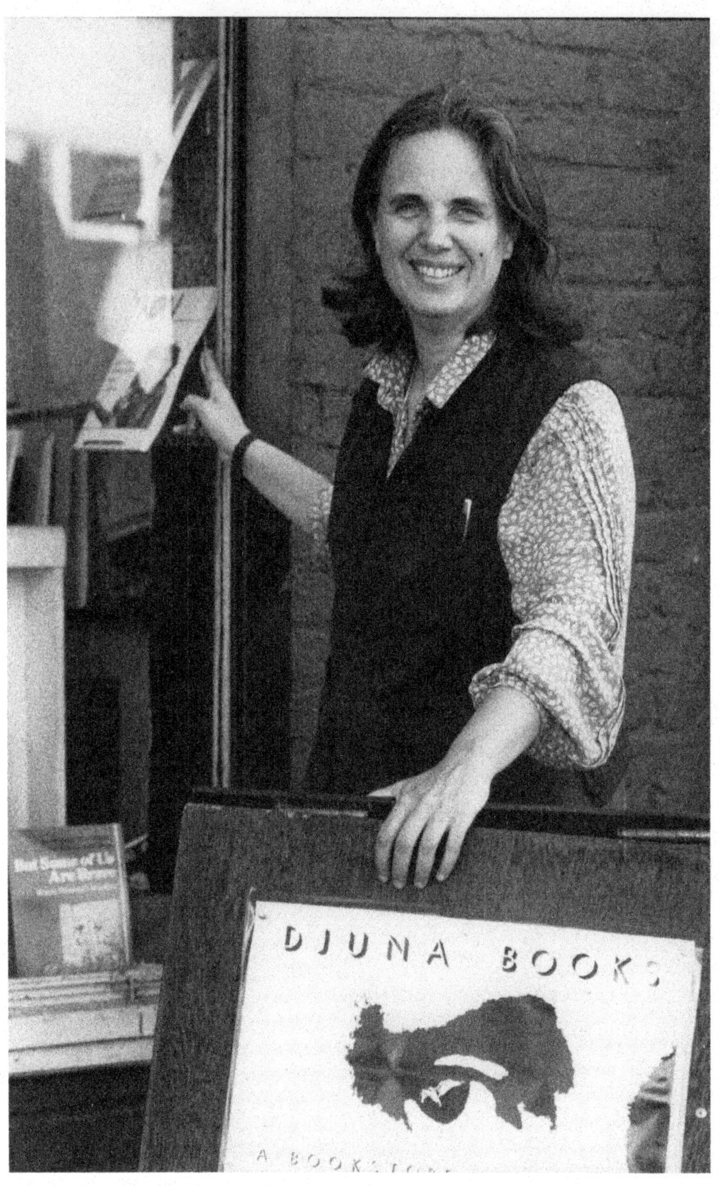
DJUNA BOOKS

The bullet pierced her flesh
because a finger pressed a trigger
& she was in the way
is "how"

Why that gun was there at all
why she was in front of it
why that policeman's finger pressed the trigger

not muscles but years are behind the answer
not reflexes
            people

4

October 6—
"Pretoria Will Use Army to End Riots"
"Military called in to support the police"
80 now are dead

October 23—
2 o'clock in the morning
7,000 South African soldiers
(along with police) surround a town
Standing 20 feet apart guns in hands

Two more townships follow
over 150,000 are interrogated
Their hands are stamped
Their thumbs dipped in orange ink

A general strike is called succeeds
Now whites also are detained

In Soweto The people continue to rebel
In Soweto The people continue to fight back

In Manhattan
My student looks at the 5 o'clock news
His head is filled with facts
He knows nothing He learns nothing

He doesn't even know "*Why?*"

When I wrote that long letter to Susan in July 1988, I was asking for a conversation that had already begun long before and would continue for as long as we both live. I just didn't realize at the time that it existed in the hundreds of letters we've exchanged over the years.

IV

GREG SMITH: A PAINTER WHO LISTENS TO SILENCE

Art is never an entertainment or pastime for boredom.
It redeems us by existing solely beyond the banal.
We see art. We cannot say it.

—Greg Smith

WHEN I RETURNED FROM Latin America at the beginning of 1984, my parents gave me a piece of land next to theirs in the foothills of the Sandia Mountains. They also lent me the money to build a house, a profound act of faith, since the U.S. government was trying to deport me at the time.[94] Eventually, I won my immigration case, regained my citizenship, built the house, and began the relationship with Barbara that has sustained me now for almost four decades.

---

94. In Mexico, when I was married to Sergio Mondragón, I took out Mexican citizenship. In the process, I inadvertently lost my U.S. citizenship. So, when I decided to come home, I had to do so on a tourist visa and apply for a change in status. The government decided that the content of several of my books was subversive and ordered me deported. The Center for Constitutional Rights took my case, and after initial defeats, we won in 1989.

Barbara and I lived in that house for nineteen years, until my parents had to move to an assisted living facility, and we lost them as neighbors, the subdivision's wealthy Republican vibe made staying in the area uncomfortable, and we, too, moved into the city. While we lived in that foothill community, though, we developed the Sunday-morning habit of breakfasting at a bagel bakery and then dropping in at a nearby bookstore, Page One, where we perused the shelves for new releases and spent far too much money on books.

At Page One, a friendly young man often engaged us in conversation. We quickly discovered that he wasn't the usual salesperson, primarily interested in getting us to buy. He was deeply knowledgeable about books and much else. He would approach us with his shaved head, always dressed in Levi's and a dark blue or brown shirt and with friendly eyes and a broad smile that invited conversation. He was an extraordinary listener as well as immensely cultured. We found we agreed about politics, art, literature, and the dangers we face as creative people.

This was our introduction to Greg Smith.

For several years, it was just those Sunday-morning encounters. But we frequented Page One as much for the pleasure of them as we did to seek out books. I later learned that the store manager reprimanded Greg for "talking too much to the customers," but he wisely ignored her complaints. Eventually, we met outside Greg's place of work. Our relationship was deepening. It was still a few years, though, before we met Greg's partner, Rich Gabriel, an artist like him. And longer still before the four us began to regularly share evenings of food and conversation.

Rich is from a New Mexican family in the state's northern town of Questa, which was hardly more than a village when he was growing up. His parents owned the only restaurant, and he learned to cook there at an early age. Today, among many other talents, he is a gourmet chef. He is a big man, quiet but with a compelling presence. It took a while for him to fully engage in our conversations, but when he did say something, it was always right on the mark. As we got to know him better, his brilliance emerged. Like Greg, Rich recognized his gay identity when he was young, and resisted letting others decide who he was. He also knew early on that he was an artist; he paints and excels in the Spanish colonial genre of tin punch work.

Greg and Rich are one of those couples who, as soon as you've been in their presence a short while, you know belong together. Not only because they complement each other so effortlessly and seem so completely at ease with each other but also because they retain their individuality while doing so. And it's not simply that each of them supports and encourages the other's full self. Who they are together constitutes a world in and of itself, one that is made richer by their connection and radiates a magnetic charisma.

Over the past several years, the four of us have become inseparable, sharing meals, followed by several hours of passionate conversation a couple of times a month. We've also traveled together to see art exhibitions in Santa Fe; on an overnight to Roswell, New Mexico, to visit Herb Goldman's *Henge*[95]; and to Marfa, Texas, the unique arts community made famous by Donald Judd,[96] who purchased a decommissioned army base and

95. Herb Goldman (1922–2012) was a sculptor who began training at the age of twelve as apprentice-assistant to Samuel A. Cashwan. During his career, he created over one hundred commissioned works of art. He taught at the University of New Mexico, where, as a very young woman, I modeled for his sculpture classes.

96. Donald Judd (1928–1994) was a U.S. artist associated with Minimalism. In 1973, he began purchasing properties in Marfa, Texas, where he

turned into a permanent home for art installations by him and artists whose work he loved. Greg and Rich have been to Marfa a couple dozen times and were the best-possible guides to its riches we could have had.

After years in which everything Greg and Rich earned went into paying off their land, making their home livable, and building studios, Rich's tin art has come into its own. He sells out each year at Santa Fe's Spanish Market, teaches classes that are always filled with grateful students, has pieces in major museum collections, and is able to support the artist lifestyle he and Greg have chosen. They even have enough money to travel, and frequently fly across the country to see an art exhibition by someone whose work they admire.

Conversation with Greg and Rich has become a necessity in these times of increased violence, commodification, capitalist assault, and the extreme polarization that makes it so difficult for people to talk to one another. We don't have many friends in Albuquerque who share our ideas, fear, and rage at the increasing assaults on our freedoms, and we treasure our time together. We are often forced to say good night before fully exploring an issue, and Greg and I—the most verbal of the four—have taken to writing to each other as a way of going deeper into our thoughts and feelings. In this age of instant digital communication, writing letters the old-fashioned way, sealing them in envelopes, affixing a stamp, and sending them through the U.S. postal system has proved to be a slowed-down practice that nurtures thoughtful expression.

The first letter I wrote to Greg was in October 2008, after Barbara and I visited his and Rich's home in the Manzanita

---

would permanently install his work and that of others until his death. The Chinati Foundation there preserves his legacy and perpetuates his ideas.

Mountains southeast of Albuquerque. I'd known of their decision to live simply so that they would be able to prioritize their artistic practices. Having met Greg when he was working two jobs—the one at the bookstore and the other at night in hotel hospitality—had given me a sense of the sacrifices he and Rich had made over many years in order to be able to acquire the land, purchase, gut, and renovate an old single-wide trailer, and build two small studios where they could make their art.

On that October day we visited, Greg was hosting a studio show of his work. Seeing their dream realized with such grace was a revelation to Barbara and me. It deepened an already important relationship.

The bulk of the letters from which I have transcribed relevant portions are from 2020 and 2023. The first letters aren't in order; the excerpts respond more to theme than they do to dates. Gradually, though, I began following a chronology because I wanted to try to re-create something of the ongoing conversation they represent. We write about what concerns us in these dangerous times: art, encroaching fascism, the isolation caused by capitalism, human relationships, place, landscape, light, age, legacy. We are relaxed in knowing we are not writing for publication and thus are willing to risk expressing tentative ideas, try them out on each other. I hope the reader will keep this decision to publish a part of our correspondence in mind when reading these letters. These aren't always finished thoughts, but an open-ended discussion between friends.

October 20, 2008

Dear Greg:

It was wonderful to finally be able to visit that cherished space where you and Rich make your home—literally make it, with hearts and hands. One can feel the love and sense of purpose, the creative use of space, and wide-ranging future possibilities. The site itself is lovely, and what you are doing with it inspiring. Barbara and I felt your hospitality from the moment we stepped out of the car.

We liked all the art we saw. Barbara was particularly grateful for Rich's generosity in talking about his tin work. And that shrine he made for you just off the path leading up the hill to your studio is fabulous. But we were both powerfully struck by your paintings, Greg. They are spectacular. Entering the small triangular space of your studio, at first seeing what appeared to be empty pieces of clear acrylic hanging on the walls, then turning and allowing the light to draw our eyes to the minimalist strokes of your masterful brush, was an experience in and of itself. The paintings make one want to stand there in silence, for hours, slowly absorbing the clear on clear. I was interested also in the dialogue between the pieces themselves and the slight imperfections visible behind them on the walls; although Barbara later wondered what those paintings might look like hung slightly out from a black wall, and the idea also struck me as interesting.

I couldn't help but think of Ad Reinhardt's work. I'm sure you must be familiar with his later minimalist black-on-black canvases. Except you have gone way beyond what he did to create a much lighter, luminous, experience. Where one can lose oneself in a Reinhardt work, one can find oneself in your subtle patterns. I remember Lucy Lippard once quoting Reinhardt to the effect that he felt his paintings were "the last," that after him no one would be able to paint. I never believed that even then, but in that context your paintings would be like a rebirth, making everything once again possible. I was also somewhat reminded of Sol Lewitt's work. I don't mean to imply that your work emerges from theirs or is limited by those visions. You have your own unique voice. Just that within the continuum of art history, I sense a moving thread.

It was so clear to me, when I gazed at that grouping of panels, that the act of painting, skilled and purposeful as it is, is but the final moment of a lifetime of experience, belief, worldview, and conscious and unconscious systemization. Not at all in the sense that they represent a final effort—I'm sure that you have many more creative years ahead—but in the sense that they hold so much: kind of like a compendium of years of thought and meditation.

Love, Margaret.

November 16, 2021

Dear Margaret—

Aside from the fact that my paintings cannot be photographed (this is not a hyperbolic metaphor—it is true). Cameras do not click because they are unable to locate an image before them, and artificial light in front of them reflects only a flash of light—behind them, makes them entirely disappear. Sometimes a reflective image from an angle to the side of them captures a likeness—but never the real thing, a photograph is always a reproduction. It is not the real thing.

Photography is essentially intrusive—or better put, a distraction from actual existent experience. A photograph of New York City is not New York City. It can provide us an image—perhaps beautiful—of the City, but it is not the City itself. A photograph cannot replace reality.

Photographs can be useful documentations—even likenesses that acknowledge a certain reality—or promote the possibility in our minds of a reality. My paintings resist all these.

My paintings are only what they are in actual reality. They appear and disappear in one's presence before them only. They are completely present wherever they are.

Photographs are incapable of replacing the actuality and totality of presence.

Love, Greg

2 May 2022

Dear Margaret—

Just after I was born in Pueblo, my father was transferred by Mountain Bell to Springfield—a small town on the high plains of southeastern Colorado. There was nothing but horizon, sky and the perfect straight lines of gridded farm roads. I was pre-lingual and, thus, unable to remember the actuality of his favorite story of me in that place. As he told it, one day I was in the garage amongst a red riding tractor and sedan, both with pedals, that my grandparents just purchased for me. I was uninterested in driving them, but promptly picked up a paintbrush resting in a can of clear cleaning solution. It was translucent, still retaining some of the white paint he used to paint the garage the weekend before (serendipitously looking similar to the raw form of clear acrylic I paint with now). I simply painted the brand-new tractor and car with this solution. My mother watched, but said I was so elated in my painting she could not bring herself to stop me. When my father returned from his work of stringing phone lines along the seemingly infinite rural roads of that particular part of the world that evening, he said I was so happy to show him the work I had done he could do nothing but be happy with me. Apparently, I was covered from head to toe in this paint and didn't care. I do remember both these vehicles still retaining this transparent paint through several generations of Smith children who, unlike me, wanted to use them for their actual purpose. But I was never interested in use—or lots of things—or perhaps better put—the use of things. I prefer useless things of beauty. And, fortunately for me, my parents knew this and let me be. This story came softly back to me after our lovely evening last Friday, when you said: "art is who you are, not what you do." Margaret, it was one of those moments when I felt the line of my life is true and ever present.

And mirroring your lovely note of the next day, I feel such gratitude for the long line of your and Barbara's presence in both Rich's and my life. This only really happens with other artists. I didn't fully realize what Agnes[97] meant when she constantly said it is "important for artists to be with our own kind." We felt the truth of this with you and Barbara on Friday. I also recall one of the happy entries in "The Warhol Diaries" when he described an evening he spent with just artists. "There is nothing else like it," he wrote. Reading your own letter about Warhol, I am amazed at how in sync we are and appreciate your insight into how his work was also a form of political resistance, at the very least resistance to living a life of banality.

Love, Greg.

7 May 2022

Dear Greg:

Your letter of May 2*nd* arrived today, one week after you mailed it. Perhaps the slowness with which our letters move says

97. Agnes Martin (1912–2004), Canadian-born U.S. abstract painter who lived for much of her life in Taos, New Mexico, and was an important mentor to Greg.

something about this sort of correspondence, written on paper, placed in envelopes, and sent through an antiquated system that nevertheless served us for many years: a time when thoughtfulness fit in the medium that carried it. I read your letter out loud to Barbara. I had to stop after the first paragraph in which you so beautifully describe that scene in your childhood garage and how you preferred even then to paint rather than to do what children were expected to do with toys. I'm sure that having the parents you had, people who knew and cared enough to let you be and celebrate your desire, must have something important to do with who you are today.

This is a poem I finished recently that I hope speaks to some of what we are losing in this speeded up world of ours:

IN REMEMBRANCE

Make it small. Invisible. Store it in a tiny device
where a thousand books reside
and one click of the cursor greets you
with full-color cover, variable type size,
background either black on white,
white on black, or a calming
shade of gray.

Make the word itself brief as you can,
a single exclamatory example
like *cool* is all you need in response
to any situation. Even *huh* can stand
as a question now, or *hmm* make do,
no actual thought required
for meaning's sake.

Make it quick. No need to waste time
or tell the story from start to finish,

retrieve memory from its hiding place,
coax it to dance in your jaded eyes
or swim to the far shore of an ocean
of mimicry, only to emerge brushing sand
from your naked body.

Be modern, keep up with your children
who know nothing else,
have never seen a book
but in a museum, never held
its precious weight in hand
or smelled the endurance of ink
across its pages.

Make it efficient, practical. No need
for leather bindings,
scent of centuries, titles embossed in gold,
tissue-thin end papers and nameplates
no one cares about today.
And when there are no more books
who will need bookstores?

No one will have time to browse through
their stacks so libraries too
will be delights of the past, everything
can be done from home,
that is if you have a home
and don't dream of taking refuge
in places where wonder lives.

Greg often surprises me with his insightful looks at the lives of artists who interest us both. In a subsequent letter, and stemming from a conversation begun on a previous evening the four of us spent together, he relayed some of his thoughts about the U.S. artist Andy Warhol[98]:

20 April 2022

Dear Margaret:

Warhol's gift was that he took every day mass-produced products and popular images and put a little glitter on them, made us look at them as beautiful. Even in his electric chairs and car crashes he made us see our own propensity for being too at ease with violence—how media and mass images anesthetize us to its reality—making it seem all too normal.

Warhol's sensibility was unequivocally gay—even as he did not openly embrace this in himself. He used the gay urban subculture of the time and turned it into art. His Catholicism was a gift and a curse. It gave him an early sense of beauty in icons and the particular beauty of repetition. His portraits are retablo-esque. It also held him back, as all religions do, from being fully in his physical life. One might argue, as many do of religion in general, that it gave him solace in the world. I say religion always devolves into an abject denial, if not disdain, for the beautiful world we inhabit. It promoted an addiction to photos rather than a trust in his pure sight. His films let him adore the young men he loved but stopped him from actually embracing them. Rather than solace, his Catholicism led him further into the darkness of depression.

And depressed he was. In his monotone and his demeanor. But I don't think the advancement of his depression was due so much to the Christian violence toward gays as it was to his

98. Andy Warhol (1928–1987) was a leader in the Pop Art movement, a painter and filmmaker, known as much for his self-representation as he was for his work. He turned his New York studio into a space he called the Factory, where a coterie of like-minded artists worked and played.

detachment from actually making his art. After his initial soup can splash, he turned his attention to the celebrity it gave him. He became the acceptable gay artist at establishment parties, partly because he never threatened to say he was gay. And this became his brand. He became a business.

Andy wanted money. He became a commercial success. He was honest about this. Many artists claim these don't matter. But all artists want our work to be seen. The difference is the business swallowed his art. And he knew it. He knew the difference between fine art and commercial art. He chose the latter. And the critics knew it.

Many say Andy was prescient in his foretelling how media would overtake our sense of reality. He certainly advanced the fraudulent conflation of art as entertainment. Oddly, his actual paintings feel more real than a mere prediction, party, or movie. They possess an innocence. Others say his greatest work of art was himself. But we are not works of art. What artists actually make are. And what we make is how we are judged. It's that simple.

Love, Greg

26 April 2022

Dearest Greg:

What a joy this morning to receive your text about Warhol. Your observations about religion are absolutely in tune with my own. But reading and rereading what you wrote, what strikes me most deeply is what you say about artists not being works of art, despite the fact that our mainstream audience often pursues the romanticized notion that we are.

Barbara and I also watched the limited Netflix series, "The Warhol Diaries." I found it interesting that Andy dictated his entries for those diaries to one of his many assistants, a woman named Pat Hackett. Beginning shortly after he was shot by Valerie Solanas[99] in 1968, upon waking Warhol often picked up the telephone and called Hackett, who typed up his ramblings for posterity. I always think that when artists depend on someone else to print their work, transcribe their words, or in some other way engage in the real work of "making," a distance emerges that dilutes the work.

I should say something about Solanas. She was a mentally ill radical feminist separatist whose "Scum Manifesto" of the year before advocated for a world without men or monetary exchange, thereby equating half humanity with a bartering tool. She served three years in prison and a psychiatric hospital for seriously wounding Warhol, and after her reclusion she remained a heroine to a certain fringe anti-male following.

Warhol himself came from a rather drab childhood in Pittsburgh and was mercilessly taunted as a child. His was an immigrant family and he was queer in a world that couldn't accept anything but the most traditional social, sexual, and religious identities. At a young age, he moved to New York City and never looked back. But his origins pursued him.

As the Sixties ended, Abstract Expressionism was losing its allure. Social and cultural contradictions generated a new aesthetic and Pop art was coming into its own. Warhol's early contributions to that movement are legendary: the Campbell Soup cans, the repeated images of Marilyn Monroe, and his portraits in general. His Mao Tse Tung. A lone electric chair, small but menacing on a murky ground. Images that showcase figures and objects representative of the times and repurpose them for

99. Valerie Solanas (1936–1988) was a U.S. feminist separatist known for the *SCUM Manifesto,* which she self-published in 1967, and for her attempt to murder Andy Warhol in 1968.

viewers in ways that provoke and challenge. Although not really accepted into the consecrated art world, he quickly began to make money and surround himself with a group of other outsider artists, among them Jean-Michel Basquiat and Keith Haring.

Almost all the men were gay, but Warhol's sexuality—like other aspects of his identity—was always a bit different. He often said he was asexual, that he would prefer to be a machine, and was severely hypochondriac. He also frequently proclaimed that his main interest was making money, and his flamboyant life-style suggested an obsessive identification with the rich and famous. Shame loomed large in his life. The religious iconry—rather flat but colorful images of saints like those in the church he attended as a child—would influence his work to the end.

Many people feel that Warhol's most complete work of art was himself. He developed a look and style of dress designed to mask his professed shyness and what he considered his ugly looks: weak body, bulbous nose, craggy skin, sallow complexion. From his earliest days in New York, he always wore an unruly wig, a disheveled shock of white hair that stuck out in all directions. He once elaborately made himself up as a woman, took photographs in that disguise, and made a self-portrait in drag. An extremely humiliating moment was when a young woman at a book signing reached across the table and grabbed his wig. In his diary he spoke about the incident as if it were a major catastrophe.

Did he have values? Yes, although not always the ones we hope those we admire possess. The ways in which his values emerge in his art are still being studied and discussed. His work belied his professed interest only in money and fame. Throughout his career he showed the US American consumer society in all its seductive madness. One of the Last Supper panels depicts the familiar scene overlaid with military camouflage. What better imagery linking religion and war! So much of what he produced was in the context of his frequent comment that he wished he was a machine and in the raucous frivolity of his lifestyle. Yet there was also real pathos. A series of love affairs with beautiful young men ended badly, leaving him alone with his celebrity friends. Photos of those boys and men are often lovely and very sad.

The six episodes of this series are often very drawn out and move too slowly, but just as the viewer is about to give up, they reveal some tragic friendship, event, or element of the artist's personality that kept me watching. Warhol simultaneously comes off as childlike, miserable about aging, self-centered to an extreme, in love with celebrity, racist, new-age, irreverent, banal, brilliant, and extraordinarily incisive. In terms of the art itself, there is no taking away from the genius of his early work or the perfect symbiosis of his later collaborations with Basquiat.

As the episodes progress, HIV/AIDS comes onto the scene, bringing tragedy into gay male communities. Tens of thousands were dying, often without feeling they could even pronounce their killer's name. The AIDS epidemic of the 1980s crossed class and racial lines although, as medication was developed, the richer and whiter you were the more access you had to it and the more likely you were to survive.

Rethinking that time now, in the light of the current Covid pandemic, inevitably leads to some observations and comparisons. All in all, "The Warhol Diaries" gave me a lot to think about in terms of the way artists are or believe we must be, difference and representation, the role the market plays in creating and supporting artistic icons, and how hard a time talent and discipline often have in helping us gain a creative edge.

As an artist myself, I inevitably thought of my own journey. From around the same early age, I knew I wanted to be a poet. I too came from a provincial childhood—although my homelife was richer—and I traveled to New York which I saw as the place to be an artist, know other artists, expand my cultural horizons. I also rebelled against many of the strictures of society, in my case first as a woman in the stifling 1950s, and much later as a queer person in a heteronormative world.

I have been fortunate to have been able to draw on a self-confidence Warhol seemed to lack. Progressive politics and a yearning for justice took me in a very different direction from his self-centered celebrity-seeking hunger. Living in Mexico, Cuba, and Nicaragua gave me life experiences that helped me overcome US America's sense of exceptionalism and superiority. Becoming a mother gave me the priceless gift of plurality. My atheism and distaste for religion in general allowed me to avoid the trap of religious lies and guilt-tripping. Childhood sexual abuse played its part in shaping the woman I would become, but I was clearly able to deal with it more productively than Warhol was able to deal with having been ostracized and bullied as a child. Thinking about someone such as Warhol, it's tempting to forefront his difference. Watching this series, I found myself relating to him as an artist. Despite the dissimilarities of our backgrounds, beliefs, values, longings, temperaments, and fears, I felt the connections all creative beings share.

Those who admire Andy Warhol try to put him in their column, so to speak. Social activists want to believe he was one of them and find signs of that in his work. Those engaged in art for art's sake claim him for their own. Those who want to shock the world into awareness see him as a model. Despite his insistence that he was asexual, the queer community looks to him as a pioneering figure. Long after his death, the arguments continue to rage. There is evidence enough to support or defy them all.

As you can see, I needed four times as many words to express half of what you managed to express much better.

Still, an interesting conversation.

Love, Margaret.

22 February 2022

Dear Margaret—

I completed #81—a painting I began just before my father's passing in early autumn of 2021. I immediately felt it as a homage to him, but there was something in the composition that clearly delineated a before and after. Certainly, this is due to the last of my parent's dying and a definite sense of the life before this and now, the life after. But it is also connected to some deeper transition, not yet fully realized. Most of this concerns the continuing conundrum of my paintings in the world, but some of it is directly related to the pandemic. That event, or more specifically the cloistered quarantine associated with it, prompted an already deepening silence in me and my work. As we are aware, as soon as we are enveloped by it, silence is completely sufficient unto itself. I found—and still do—reading and writing not quite adequate during this time as our collective reality is still too strong, too present, too physically enveloping to remove ourselves long enough to articulate this reality in language.

Covid-19 was the first event in my life that is common to all humanity. It affected the entire world. We all stopped. And this stopping provided a universal platform for individual stillness. Unable to distract ourselves from the constant entertainments we consume, we saw them for the distractions they are. Unable to run to the jobs we thought we needed to purchase those distractions, we experienced how little we need to survive. Of course, those of us who are serious artists have always known this. It was interesting to observe what we know surprisingly embraced by the mainstream. And even more surprising that many didn't miss what they thought constituted their "real lives." This, I feel, is the real reason many people have not returned to the "work force." The "rat race" was revealed as an exactly appropriate name. Stopping allows clear sight. And our collective stopping temporarily saved us—albeit barely—from fascism in America. Without the pandemic we would have continued to be palliated and Trump's march to victory assured. The question now is: will our clear-eyed stillness turn into another short-sighted distraction? Will the after be the same as before?

Although this was diminishing, largely through my painting process before the pandemic, I personally have no more fancy for magical thinking. I am happily empirical. One of the results of this is a sober sight about the very real difference between civility and religious barbarism. I have no tolerance for the latter.

In America, perhaps, the pandemic allowed the myth of capitalistic benevolence to be exposed for the fraud it has always been. Most of us were helped in some way by the federal government. Without it, total societal collapse seemed inevitable. The huge gap between the financially secure and insecure has been made visible. On our road alone, those with high paying "professional" jobs didn't lose a thing. In fact, their lives got better. They were allowed to work from home, didn't have to commute and be further exposed to the virus. Those who are hourly front-line workers, however, had to go to their jobs—in some cases holding more than one—and were placed in more harm of contracting the virus. Rich and I deliberately moved to the mountains to devote our time to our art. We paid off our land and trailer and built small studios to do this. A friend once told me, "If you have shelter, you can always find a way to eat." And we did. We received small government loans and some friends helped as Rich's business is largely determined by tourism. And tourism stopped. But our real lives did not stop. We continued our studio rituals even though, in Rich's case, it wasn't paying. My studio work does not pay, so nothing changed for me. I did learn, though, that I adore a blank calendar and in the absence of any other obligations painting's primacy in my life was reaffirmed as the true sustenance it is.

My love to you and Barbara.

Love, Greg.

10 June 1922

Dearest Greg and Rich:

We've been talking a lot about censorship and self-censorship. The brilliant Nicaraguan novelist Sergio Ramírez,[100] forced into exile by his country's dictatorship and currently living in Spain, recently made a prescient comment referencing the history of free expression: "Carthage's tyrant Hanon ordered citizens' tongues to be cut out to prevent them from conversing among themselves. Citizens then found ways of getting around the prohibition by making gestures with their heads or hands, raising their eyebrows, and expressing their feelings with their eyes, all to taunt or defy the law. So, the ruler issued another decree, prohibiting gestures. People then gathered one morning in the public square and with a single voice

100. Sergio Ramírez (1942) is a Nicaraguan intellectual and writer who played a key role in the 1979 revolution. He served in the government's Junta of National Reconstruction and was vice president of the country from 1985 to 1990.

broke into a great and bitter cry. This is how words, gestures, and even the natural freedom of eyes to spill tears were rendered illegal."

Ramírez goes on to say this story came to mind when the despots who currently rule Nicaragua illegalized all manner of civic organizations including the Academy of the Language. He pointed out that the consequence of prohibiting words is silence. And he quoted the director of Spain's Academy of the Language, Santiago Muñoz Machado: "Cutting out people's tongues is one further step in their oppression." In Nicaragua, language has been forced underground.

If or when the current system of deception cracks and shatters here, will this become our future in the United States?

Love, Margaret

10 June 2022

Dear Margaret -

I was inspired by your piece on the Colorado Plateau—how the reality of rocks outlives the systems of time. I loved your inclusion of the fact that Icelandic has no word for "please." Donald Judd has an extensive library in Marfa. He was an avid reader of the world's philosophies and myths. He observed that of all the world's myths, the only ones without a deity were Icelandic. Is this related to their not having a word for "please?" If there is no power above us, do we need to falsely pay homage by saying "please" for what is already ours?

Again, Agnes Martin: "The most troublesome anti-freedom concept is our belief in a transcendent supreme authority. But when we see that all the authority there is, is within ourselves, then we are free."

Love, Greg

22 June 2022

Dear Greg:

I love this culture of letter-writing we have developed to exchange ideas, continue the conversation.

I hope I didn't spend too much time last night ranting. This week's congressional hearing struck me as yet another exercise in futility, and totally predictable from the beginning. Many of the women and men who traveled to Washington to testify had lost family members, including young children, in the recent mass shootings. Buffalo. Uvalde. And the tired parents of Sandy Hook who, ten years after their tragedy, continue to plead for sanity. I listened to a few of them on the New York Times live feed. And I forced myself to listen, as well, to those who defend the status quo. I knew the hopes of those urging change would be defeated. I can only imagine they knew it too, although desperation tends to birth hope. I tried to imagine what those who have suffered such irreparable loss must have felt as they struggled through the session. After the agreed-upon time for witnesses ended, the House of Representatives began discussing suggested measures, all woefully small and inadequate. As predicted, they voted in a watered-down bill which will now go to the Senate where it is sure to be thrown out. And that will be that. Another in a long line of promises doomed before they materialize.

What gripped me—what still has me in its grip—is the utter deception of the entire "democratic" process. We are witnessing a carefully contrived drama in which we can pretend we live in a country in which open discussion and diversity of opinion are respected. It's become a game, refined by the most vicious and retrograde minds. Indeed, it has become a dogma, one by which we increasingly and blindly operate. We have the elections, the committees, the models meant to convince us that we can choose; while we have become non-persons to a power that plays us as if we were figures in a video game. The form continues to be important to some image of "freedom" while the outcome is predetermined. And this is true in all areas of life: civil and gender rights, abortion, the implacable threat of climate change and global warming, the economy, education, health care (including management of an ongoing pandemic), and on down the line. We are treated to expensive shows that try to make us believe we have a say, when the status quo, which only benefits those who get richer and more powerful at our expense, results in things staying the same or getting worse.

Then last night the long-awaited hearings on the January 6th, 2020, coup attempt finally began. Trump has been subpoenaed to testify. Two years' worth of investigative findings will be on display. Millions have been spent on getting to this point. And the outcome will be exactly what it is in all the other cases: absolutely nothing. Some believe that putting the details of the coup on display will demonstrate Trump's criminality and influence voters, including Republicans, to turn against him. I am sure this will not happen. A few followers may be indicted but the real leader will remain untouchable. Trump loyalists will become more entrenched, while Democrats and others who see him for what he is will continue to founder and engage in diluted and ineffectual actions destined to fail.

This farce extends beyond our borders. It is the very recipe by which we interact with other nations. How US interests abroad are framed and discussed. The information we are allowed or prevented from having. One example: On May 20th, a draft bill called the Puerto Rico Status Act was announced. This is a forced "compromise" between the statehooders and the supporters of HR 2070, the Puerto Rico Self-Determination Act written by Alexandria Ocasio Cortez and others. Majority Whip

Steny Hoyer pushed for this "compromise" which eliminates HR 2070's plan for an extended deliberative process of an elected constituent assembly in Puerto Rico itself to consider that country's future. The new proposed legislation pays lip service to the "education" of the Puerto Rican people but is basically just a plan for another plebiscite. This plebiscite is currently scheduled for November 5th, 2023, and would list three choices: statehood, independence, and "free association" (like Palau). The "compromise" was designed to kill HR 2070 and take self-determination off the table. If this bill goes forward and results in a binding plebiscite in 17 months, it is clear the votes will replicate past ones, with a substantial vote for statehood, which will never happen. In other words, once again no change. Money and play-acting invested in a process the outcome of which is assured. Of course, most US citizens don't care or even think about Puerto Rico . . . or Ukraine or the Middle East or Cuba or Latin America or any of the other places in the world where our tax dollars support and defend situations that oppress human beings, do damage to the earth, and increase the profits of our wealthiest. The amount of money spent on this farce, and the length to which our lawmakers go to make sure the process appears democratic, would go a long way toward solving real problems. But that is not the goal.

Thus, we are witnessing a progression toward fascism dressed in today's emperor's new clothes, which are nothing more or less than a giant deception. I don't know enough about the history to understand if this is how fascism came to power in 1930s Germany. I know the changes were as incremental as they were implacable. Language plays an important part in this. Words describe acts once deemed unacceptable or hide those acts altogether. Concepts that twenty or thirty years earlier would have been socially unthinkable become more acceptable.

Perhaps even glorious or patriotic, at the very least put forth as "necessary evils." Most people are only concerned about their own economic survival: the price of necessities, a roof over their heads, minimal wellbeing."

Love, Margaret

29 June 2022

Dear Greg:

These letters we have been exchanging have provided a beautiful space for open-ended expression. And not even necessarily polished expression. One of the things I value so much in our conversations and in this written exchange is that we trust one another to try out ideas and opinions. You have been, and continue to be, a brilliant sounding board for me. You always make me think.

Love, Margaret

23 July 2022

Dear Margaret -

The first show I had out of my studio was in the early 2000s. An old friend of mine from my Taos days surprised me and came with her parents and her husband who is Hopi. He walked around my studio and said: "Did you know your studio is surrounded by metates?" I was pleasantly surprised, thinking the smooth concave grey stones were from water that old maps indicate once flowed on our land. I have often looked at these stones—feeling their solid presence—and wondered about the people and their hands slowly making something smooth out of the rough. I have also wondered what it might have been like to be here and to be so connected to this exact place—and the mystery of the extra luminous stars we have at night (we can still see the milky way above us) and to trust their being here as being the world. I know I am projecting my own sensibility onto a people I know nothing about. I also know I feel my own being as enough and connected to all this is working in my studio each day. This is not a romantic intention. It is often what I feel.

I am not suggesting we abandon the world. We are in it and a part of it. As an artist especially, one must come to the exact truth of what this essential responsibility is. The world always asks us to betray this by being "useful." I wrote in my small journal yesterday: "A painting's solitary uselessness is an unintended resistance to the tyranny of usefulness anywhere."

Love, Greg

25 July 2022

Dear Greg:

The story you tell about the metates around your studio is very moving. How powerful that you and Rich are living and working on land that was inhabited by people who came before you/us, people who still have things to tell us if we can learn to listen.

Love, Margaret

16 August 2022

Dear Margaret:

Tao Luther was an antiquarian book collector. I knew him when I was a bookseller at the Taos Book Shop. He had what I believe was then the largest collection of first edition books by DH Lawrence—most of them signed—and was also a Lawrence scholar. Lawrence's main theme is that love does not work. This is not a cynicism I share and, thus, I have never been drawn to his work. I feel his negation of love is most probably because he never embraced the real possibility of gay love within himself. This is also reflected in his hyper-sexualized heterosexual paintings that were banned in good ole Britain and bought by Saki Karavitz, the former owner of the La Fonda Hotel on the Taos Plaza. Saki displayed them in a room off the hotel lobby. When I saw them, I couldn't blame the Island for rejecting them as paintings. They are simply bad. Of course, I blame them for banning them based on their sexual content. At any rate, the owner of the Taos Book Shop bought the collection of Lawrence first editions and housed them in a room of their own, adobe dust regularly settling on the shelves. I recall going in there, pulling the chain of the single bulb light to clean the shelves, opening a few books, looking at Lawrence's beautiful signature. But mostly I remember Mr. Luther telling me how Lawrence had what he described as a remarkable ability to size up a new place immediately and then describe it. This is true of his writings on place, particularly on Taos. I do not feel, though, that this ability, except for his acumen in the written word, is singular. I feel we all have this ability if we allow ourselves to become mind-free when first physically present in a new place—or one where we have been absent for a long time. This is how I try to travel.

Love, Greg

23 August 2022

Dear Greg:

What you had to say about D. H. Lawrence is fascinating. I'm ashamed to say that my own ignorance prevented me from understanding that he may have been repressing a homosexual nature. Without your discernment, however, I too have long been troubled by his reputation as an author who writes compellingly about love. I agree that his writing about place is very fine. But love, no. Yet so many heterosexual women swoon over his books. The following is a poem that appears in the recent collection that Barbara and I did, Stormclouds Like Unkept Promises:

WAITING OUR TURN

Lawrence, he of Lady Chatterley,
said the way to eat a fig
was open it until it becomes
a glittering, rosy, moist, honied,
four-petalled flower,

then after raping the blossom
hold it in your mouth
lick the crack
and devour the flesh
in a single bite.

Every fruit has its secret
said the poet women loved,
then turned us into luscious fruits
to be peeled by hungry lips
and spit out.

Neruda, he of communist
solidarity, wrote
of women's bodies as white hills
and white thighs, promised
to forge us as weapons—

arrow to bow, stone in its sling—
so he could outlive himself.
This poem is my reply.
Neither seductive fruit
to be savored and discarded

nor white in a world of brown
and never ever weaponized,
we sharpen our tongues,
imagine our revenge
and wait our turn.

I would love to see the show you talk about titled "Doubles." I remember a piece I have always loved called "Untitled (Perfect Lovers)" by Félix González Torres.[101] I saw it years ago at the Wadsworth Atheneum in Hartford and wrote a poem about it too. Félix's lover died of AIDS (as he would later, as well) and the piece consists of two very simple kitchen clocks next to one another on a wall. One has stopped and the other is still keeping time. It was the artist's way of expressing his loss and the fact that his clock would also wind down and stop soon. I have never forgotten the impact that piece had on me.

Love, Margaret

27 August 2022

Dear Margaret—

Not chance, but choice. We make decisions and they do determine much of our lives. And isn't this, at base, what Roe is all about. I am not suggesting that we control life, nor that there aren't things that are entirely out of our control. We do, though, respond to life in our decisions. I am thinking of the Greek Stoic philosopher Epictetus—"It is our conviction which compels us; that is, choice compels choice."

Love, Greg

---

101. Félix González-Torres (1957–1996) was a Cuban-born U.S. visual artist. He lived and worked in New York City between 1979 and 1995.

27 September 2022

Dear Greg:

There is so much that I want to share about my time in Mexico. It was life-changing for me in many ways, not least of which was discovering that at almost 86 I was still able to make such a trip on my own and successfully navigate 12 public events in as many days, all different and all in Spanish. Of course I had a lot of help. The time with family was also important.

Rafael [Mondragón][102] had organized the launch of my memoir in its Spanish edition (Nunca me fui de casa), so that three young women who had read and absorbed the book sat with me at a table in front. Each made a short presentation and then asked questions, which I answered. They were Ave Barrera, Nayalí García Sánchez, and Alejandra Retana Betancourt. Nayalí initiated the conversation and one of the things that stays with me was her description of Mexico as a narco-state. News of the power of the cartels reaches beyond the country's borders, of course, but truly understanding that people there live with what that means in their everyday lives is tremendous. There are so many countries in the world right now where the terror of extreme violence is part of life's fabric. Alejandra went next, and finally Ave who belongs to the Nahua tribe of Milpa Alta, also known as Momoscas, the only indigenous people with a cohesive community in the capital city. Each emphasized different aspects of my memoir that they found relevant to their lives. There was time for a few questions from the audi-

102. Rafael Mondragón is a professor at the National Autonomous University of Mexico, a writer, translator, editor, and member of Heredad, a publishing collective in Mexico City that produces titles in various genre and distributes them in innovative ways designed to further popular education.

ence as well, and a woman in the back raised her hand to say that she was our neighbor 60 years ago when we lived in Mexico! She is Fabiola Escárzaga, the daughter of a woman who lived at the end or our street. Today Fabiola is a leading authority on the Latin American guerrilla movements of the 1970s and '80s!

An extraordinary performance at the MUAC, the art museum on the UNAM campus, was organized by Julio García Murillo. I read poetry and three young women performance artists joined me in a large theater-in-the-round space surrounded by a robust audience. Two of the women did corporal movement while the third sketched and painted on two different mural-like surfaces. They interpreted my words through their own creative media and, although I couldn't see what they were doing because they were behind me or off to the side much of the time, Ximena tells me it was brilliantly effective. This whole performance was quite extraordinary. During a brief Q&A afterwards, one young woman posed a question I've never before gotten at one of my events. She asked: "Have you ever been afraid of the power of your own words?" I knew she was telling me that she was sometimes afraid of the power of her words. I had to think quickly and hard to be able to give her a response she might find useful.

Another event was a public conversation with Gabriela Silva about my photography. It was held at a wonderful feminist bookstore in Coyocán. It didn't take long for the store's small meeting room to fill, and by the time we started every seat was taken and there were folks standing four-deep outside. Gabi spoke about how she conceived the program and then projected a selection of my photographs—most from the memoir but some from my web site—and asked me questions about each. This event drew a varied and interesting audience. Rafael's whole family was there, and Sarah, Sebastián, Richi and Sofia as well. Tatiana Coll, the niece of Laurette Séjourné's assistant in the 1960s and someone I saw almost every day back then, surprised me. She had seen an interview with me in the paper that included an announcement of this evening and said she wouldn't have missed it. She told me that the first photograph of her daughter, at nine months of age, was taken by me in Havana. Roberto Citlali Rodríguez, formerly of Tucson and now living in Teotihuacán, showed up; I had no idea he had relocated to Mexico. A middle-aged woman introduced herself as a niece of Teresa Proenza, someone I knew years ago at Cuba's embassy in Mexico City. Sergio and Marina came, and many others with whom I've had connections—casual or deep—over the years. I am always amazed by the vast web of relationships that weave in and out of one's life, reappearing when least expected.

Love, Margaret

30 October 2022

Dear Greg:

Lately I've been obsessed with a question about human development, and almost every conversation I have, book or article I read, even what I choose to cook for dinner or how the weather announces itself when I part the blinds each morning, tickles this question in some way. My question, simply put, is: Why and how did the earliest humans stray from the necessary self-involvement required to protect themselves against danger—bitter cold, extreme heat, hunger, pain, the threat of wild animals—and begin to factor into their natures a concern for others, what we define as generosity of spirit, kindness, or love? In other words, when and how did humans become human?

It's clear that caring qualities vary from person to person, ranging all the way from those who seem to have been born without compassion and thus possess none of them to the most altruistic among us. In general, though, as Anne Frank is quoted as having said in her darkest days, "I still believe most people are good at heart." In every culture, independent of the formalistic attributes they may project, a majority will share what they have if presented with someone in need. Someone who is hungry, cold, ill. If not personally taking the needy individual into their homes, they will at least try to get help from an agency established for the purpose. The most dramatic situations often result in the most extraordinary gestures, for example during World War II when so many non-Jews risked their lives hiding Jews, or much more recently when the small town of Paradise, California, was destroyed by fire in 2018, and people in nearby communities took those who lost everything into their homes, often for months. Or in the context of Russia's invasion of Ukraine, in which families throughout Europe have welcomed Ukrainian refugees into already crowded apartments and houses. Way back in the shadows of history, where did this practice of lending a helping hand come from? What motivated it? How did it develop? Perhaps loneliness played a role; unless we help others, we have no friends. When we wonder, we wander. This is where I wander today.

My obsession with when and how our earliest ancestors first began thinking of their contemporaries as well as themselves leads to further questions. For example, when did we begin to think in abstractions rather than only in terms of the practical? The answers to all these questions seem to be hiding just out of sight. As if I might turn a corner and find them waiting in unexplored memory.

Love, Margaret

November 4, 2022

Dear Margaret—

I genuinely like people. I feel most people are essentially good. This makes our current times challenging. It is not in my disposition to easily dismiss people even when I am dismissed. This does not mean I suffer overt cruelty nor that I am not able to remove myself from those who consciously mean harm. These times, however, have unfortunately exposed what many people truly believe and the harm they are willing to vote for and be part of. As gay people we are innately aware of the reality of hate. Many of us have learned to survive and even thrive amidst it. I have to remind myself that we are our own best example right now.

I cannot love fascists, though. These times have made me very clear that I cannot change them or forgive their willful delusion. These times have also taught me that once fascism's darkness is released, it cannot be put back in a bottle.

The midterm elections have shown, again, that there is an awareness in our country about the current precariousness we are in. It confirms a certain goodness and that this good is the majority. But we are naïve to rest easy as the Republican religious desire to take over the country remains firmly in place.

Love, Greg

2 December 2022

Dear Margaret:

These low-light late autumn days leave me struggling with patience. I realize how my own patience over the years has acted as a panacea for outrage—in more benign ways as a practical way of getting by. I also see how "patience" is a Catholic religious vestige of my childhood—how it colludes to keep me complicit when I need not be. I have always thought of anger as our bodies' very practical way of letting us know what we should not be involved with. I don't always trust it immediately, though. There is both common sense and suppression in this. These days Adrienne Rich's beautiful line "a wild patience has taken me this far" has been humming within me. When I looked the line up, "Integrity," the poem that bears this as its first line appeared. And I thought of you, Margaret—your deep integrity—how you continue doing your work of making history less false—and how you do it with such kindness. May we continue to strive for integrity—"the quality of being complete: unbroken condition, entirety."

Love, Greg

5 December 2022

Dearest Greg:

I love those lines by Adrienne Rich.[103] A beautiful birthday gift. Thank you. Adrienne's poetry has been vital to my wellbeing, as she herself—her friendship and support—was vital to me when she lived. I will never forget how she traveled to El Paso for my immigration trial, and how active she was there that whole week on my behalf, taking on tasks when I had to be in two or more places at once. Her poetic voice accompanied me on my return to the US in a way no other did. I felt that a couple of the long poems at the end of *The Fact of a Doorframe* were about me or that she was speaking directly to me in them. Of course they weren't. Perhaps many others feel the same way. I remember reading one of those poems out

103. Adrienne Rich (1929–2012) was a U.S. poet, essayist, and feminist. She is credited with having brought the oppression of women and lesbians to the forefront of poetic discourse.

loud to anyone who would listen; it was my "coming out poem" in very tangible ways.

Love, Margaret

9 February 2023

Dear Margaret—

Rich and I are so touched and honored to have your new book, Luck, dedicated to us. Appropriate since we are all lucky to have one another. We discussed what luck is on our way up the mountain from our last dinner. Rich said he feels you and he have experienced luck because each of you has been willing to see the doors open before you and walk through them. Luck, it seems to me, is always optimistic. Not the fake positivity of prosperity, platitudes, and preaching, but the real fearlessness in doing what one truly wants. I do know that fear and its attendant delusions block open doors. I recently heard a linguist say that in most languages the word for fear and religion is the same. Luck is grounded in reality. You and Barbara are largely living the life you want, and Rich and I are too.

I recall walking through our trees on a warm autumn day in 2021, having just completed stacking our wood for winter and gathering kindling that had naturally fallen from our pine and oak branches. A wave of quiet gratitude filled me as I saw that we have done and are doing our work. This is not a wish but a reality. We moved here to devote most of our time to making our art, and we've been doing it for over 22 years. I know that just because one is responsible to one's own life does not guarantee luck or success. It is random and does not always follow what we have done or not done. I wonder, though, if the possibility of greater luck is associated with our ability to let go—to not linger in—that which has failed us? I wonder, too, if luck is physically tied to a specific place where there is a greater chance for our own possibility to take root?

I felt such synchronicity with you when you asked me near the elevator if I ever ask dreams to answer questions or solve problems. I do not do it very often, but I will share with you two of the most lucid dreams I have had. In 2004, just before Agnes [Martin's] passing and in the year that I began my clear paintings, I dreamt I was looking for some validation of my art. I was looking for Agnes in Taos. I found her house and was welcomed in. She was on her death bed and looked at me with one clear blue eye in the center of her forehead and said, "take my brush."

In May of 2014 I was earnestly looking for ways my paintings could enter the wider world. At the end of the month, I received a rejection letter from the Roswell Artist in Residence Program. Just before bed that evening I asked Agnes for advice and had what is the most clearly lucid dream I've ever had.

Agnes, my mom, Rich, and I are in Agnes's studio which is located in the Taos Moccasins building in between where I lived in Taos and Agnes's studio. Rich, who is Agnes's studio assistant, is painting Japanese calligraphy onto one of Agnes's band paintings. I would paint over the calligraphy as I dislike language in art. Rich continues painting and my mom takes Agnes and me to lunch. We arrive at a restaurant that is in the location of the present Michael's Kitchen, a Taos landmark. We go to the back of the restaurant to a single table next to the swinging kitchen door. The tabletop is pale yellow and there is a skylight directly above us. It is the most illuminated part of the restaurant. After Agnes and I sit, my mom immediately retreats to the kitchen, leaving Agnes and me alone to talk. Agnes tells me I must take my paintings to New York City. When I ask why, she says, "you want to be in the mix." I continue to question her, asking if other places might do. She is insistent on New York City and tells me a story about how she and her partner (she is very open about being a lesbian in the dream) were once in Houston and that did nothing for her paintings; she had to be in New York. We rise from the table, and I say I'd like to show her my paintings. She says she'd like to see about four (I can confidently make four or five a year). We begin to exit. There are two glass doors we can go through. Each has an enclosed glass entry. The one to the south has a toilet in it (privacy) and the one to the north is open. These two ways out are side by side. Outside in the parking lot the sun is shining. I look at Agnes and am amazed at how youthful she looks—I think she will live forever. I tell my mom and Agnes I need to buy a new pair of shoes at a store next to the restaurant, called Mor. An uncle who is deceased works there. We get into a red car. My mom drove us to the restaurant, but now I am driving. There is fresh wet snow on the road—it feels like a New Mexico spring storm. I turn south and then decide to turn east. Every time I ask Agnes for advice about my paintings she tells me the same thing.

Love, Greg

15 February 2023

Dear Greg:

I share Rich's conviction that we have experienced luck because we have been willing to see the doors open before us and walk through them. At the same time, luck to me, is a very complex quantity. In our cultures, luck clearly flows more readily toward those who are white, male, able-bodied, cis, healthy, educated, not destitute, and free enough to know there is more out there than what society tells us should be our destiny. But I also think that often being part of a discriminated group may bring us luck in that it forces us to struggle with adversity, something that can produce a fierce edge of will. We are immensely lucky when, like the four of us, we recognize that we are artists and understand that it's not just okay but imperative that we find a way to build our lives around that expressive need. We are lucky to live in a country that hasn't experienced war on home ground for hundreds of years. We are lucky to live in a landscape that speaks to us. We are lucky to have been able to find and nurture friendships that matter. I feel immensely lucky to have four amazing children who in turn have produced grandchildren and great-grandchildren—to see my lineage extending itself across distant lands, making and doing and giving back to society. I feel lucky to have survived the revolutionary struggles with which I have been involved when so many of my comrades didn't. Last week, when the Nicaraguan political prisoners were released, and I saw photos of them—emaciated and haggard—having escaped the jaws of the Ortega/Murillo dictatorship, I saw their release as good luck. And I also felt, intimately, our luck that the international campaign we kept going for more than two years and against complicated odds finally seemed to have paid off.

And yes, I absolutely agree with you when you link optimism with luck. But luck, as I see it, is also random and too often ignored. I hate it when someone is diagnosed with a serious, even terminal, illness and friends and family tend to blame them for it. "Well, he smoked like a chimney; what did he expect?" Or: "You know she was obese." The truth is, it was bad luck. I am even more outraged when extremely religious folks ascribe everything that happens to "God's will," implying that some fictitious supreme being was responsible for the torture and deaths of millions in every one of our Holocausts, or even the lesser ills that batter people every day. I was astonished when I read your line about having heard a linguist say that in most languages the word for fear and religion is the same. Makes perfect sense to me.

Thank you for sharing your two dreams about Agnes. What beautiful intimate gifts! Each, in its own way, is a map to be endlessly explored. I feel so grateful that you had/have Agnes in your life. I think she did for you what Elaine [de Kooning] did for me: provide us with the knowledge that we can and must nurture our creative selves. Enabled us to believe in ourselves and our work. I also think that you were born with that proclivity, as I was. In some important ways, perhaps, your meeting Agnes and my meeting Elaine were like the "chicken and the egg" conundrum. It's hard to know if we sought out these important mentors because we were determined to find the influences we needed or if meeting them was simply luck. By which, once again, I simply want to enumerate some of the many ways in which I feel that luck is complicated. It happens, and we also make it.

Love, Margaret

24 February 2023

Dearest Margaret—

Thank you for your elucidation that luck is just luck—that it is not conditioned on anything we do or don't do. Luck cannot be planned or controlled. We can only know it once it has occurred. You showed me how easy it is to fall into the "prosperity speak" so prevalent now—a biblically-based language that falsely asserts we are responsible for everything that happens to us—that we are "blessed" if we "prosper"—all a disguise to maintain the present power structure.

Love, Greg

4 March 2023

Dearest Margaret:

The "Dearest" chapter in Vertigo of Risk was stark and moving. I recognized some of the names from years of conversations with you and can't imagine what it must feel like to have lost so many of your friends. I liked the somewhat dreamlike quality of the poems. Each was a beautiful combination of the total person—no denials—and ultimate love. In "Dearest Mark" I was moved by the first lines of the last stanza—"You showed me love of oneself leaves space / for the presence of friends if they can listen / to their own truth." As I do with most books of poetry, I first randomly opened to any page. The first poem I opened to was "Your Love of Here"—a lovely tribute to Sabra and Roger—and a deep listening to their connection to their home in Abiquiu. I thought of my dad who was equally connected to his home—it was enough for him to be there and tend to his trees and roses. My sisters always said he would not live long if he left. Although it was physically necessary for him and my stepmom to leave, he never fully felt at home in their new house. Your poem beautifully illustrates our connection to place, and that without that connection we would perish. It also speaks to our need, even amidst real concerns, to let people live their own lives without our interference—bad or good.

I was struck by the two poems about your parents—each starkly different but full of love. I felt a palpable compassion for your mom—and your adult understanding of her plight as a woman in her time—even in our time. You do not judge her—as is the tenor of all the poems in the book. You seem to be at a very peaceful level of acceptance. "Just People"echoes this. Our parents do not leave us. Yet another physical connection to our being here. "Every Morning" and "Twilight" speak to your continued spirit of living each day fully awake—a spirit you share with all of us lucky to be around you. The Dine weaving metaphor in "Life is a Two-Way Street" marries form and content wonderfully—the inner and outer are the same and equally important. "When I Die" is beautiful—along with "The Business of Dying"—each a strong statement amidst a stream throughout the entire book—on mortality. "Still, you may be surprised / to know my certainty / also possesses its quota / of magic, / landscape of wonder / in cosmic energy" does not surprise me. I have always seen you as clear-eyed and encouraging the possibility of each of us in this world. Of course, your time in Latin America must have seeped the notion of magic and reality as continually moving and interchangeable deep in the bones of your psyche. It is amazing that you write with such ease and grace about aging and death. I had to pinch myself occasionally reading these poems since I don't see you as old. You are the very same as when we first met over twenty years ago.

Love, Greg

9 March 2023

Dearest Greg:

I got your recent letter yesterday, opened the envelope and began to read. Before I knew it, my breath was coming in short bursts, and I was tearing up. It's rare that I receive such detailed feedback on my poems. Your response makes me feel deeply heard. Thank you.

Much of your commentary has to do with what you call a lack of judgment or attempt to understand as well as love the people in my life. This is interesting to me, because I absolutely hate the dictum from the recovery movements of the 1980s that posited judgment as something negative. I believe I am extremely judgmental and am proud and determined to be so. I have very strong feelings about what I consider right and wrong, especially politically but also in terms of ordinary human interaction. But I also try to see people in their historic context, to understand the destructive and self-destructive tendencies all of us fight against. I try to give people the benefit of the doubt and am even beginning to learn to do that with myself.

The "dearest" poems are special to me, and you get that in a way that both excites and humbles me. As we age, death comes closer. It's kind of you to say that you see me the same as when we first met at Page One so many years ago. In many ways, I get that, because I feel that you and Rich are "my age" in that strange way that years have of disappearing when there is a profound identification between people. You are the ages of my children, yet I feel us as equals. At the same time, age is real because it embodies history and experience. I feel what my age represents. And a sense of being closer to death is naturally a part of that.

Your description of writing a poem for Agnes, giving it to her, and having her read it in your presence, almost made me hold my breath. It was as if I could feel your anticipation about what she would say. I'm sure you needed time to absorb her response and be able to refer to the incident as simply your story that didn't match the reality for her. As we know, there are many realities. Although Agnes didn't recognize what you wrote as reflecting hers, it did reflect yours. I am always nervous when I write about others and know they will read what I have written. Being in their presence as they read can be terrifying.

Personally, I have never experienced the dilemma Martin expresses. I have always seen politics as important in that it affects our lives. I do believe art is art, to quote Ad Reinhardt. The two can and must coexist. If artists don't speak about social conditions in their art, it's fine with me. I look at the art. If it moves me, I'm grateful. But in art or outside it, if people aren't concerned with the conditions and decisions that affect their lives, I feel they do so at their peril. We all want to live in a sane world, where difference is respected, and freedom valued.

Love, Margaret

8 April 2023

Dearest Margaret—

The clear water washing gently over the perfect diamond grid of whites, grays and blacks set the tone for one of the most beautiful films we have seen in a long time. Thank you, amidst our talk about Mexico in particular, for suggesting "Roma" to us. We watched it the evening after our last dinner with you and Barbara and were entranced. We couldn't believe we missed it the year it came out, but realized it was because of the title. We thought it referred to Rome instead of a neighborhood in Mexico City. Cleo has stayed with us—her serenity, her inner strength, her complete presence, her innocence that does not betray her innate intelligence and her kindness amidst her awareness of the shock of patriarchy's classism. I was struck by the buddhas in the home of the family she served—and of Fermin's obsession with some form of Tai Chi—and how each of these religious pronouncements betrayed her in their fundamental hypocrisy. And yet, she was the only person in the film who was truly buddha-like without practicing any religion. The scene where she is waiting for Fermin to finish his rather military-esque training in Tai Chi—where the leader demonstrated the focus required for standing still with one foot on the knee of the opposite leg while holding one's hands above one's head—was beautiful. She was the only one, without any particular interest or training, who could maintain this posture. Her nature was simple focus, while all the men who were trying to focus could not. The tragedy of Fermin's cruelty to her was hard to bear—as was the hypocrisy of the doctor she worked for. His pretending to care when she was in labor by saying he could not accompany her to the delivery room, when her female doctor said he could, said it all. The men abandoned her, while the women and children in his house came to embrace her on relatively equal grounds. But only after they themselves were betrayed by the doctor, son, husband, and father. The ocean washing them all clean—and perhaps renewing them—ended the film where it began. What is it about black and white film that captures light more truly than color? I recall seeing a black and white film on the Cuban revolution that made me feel I was actually in the Caribbean. You would know the technical reason for this more than me.

And I am thinking deeply about all the women in our country this weekend. The deafening clamor of fascism marches on in the Amarillo judge's singlehanded attempt to impose Christian white authoritarianism onto all the women of America. And what enrages me the most, Margaret, is that Merrick Garland could have stopped this. I do not know the exact protocol, but legal scholars say he could have immediately stopped the possibility of this happening by upholding the right of the FDA to control all drug regulations—thus stopping the red states from shoving Jesus down our throats on Easter weekend. The Washington state judge's counter ruling assures that this case will go almost immediately to the Supreme Court. One former Democratic judge, now at Harvard Law School, had the audacity to say she thought the Supreme Court would overrule the Texas judge! When is the Democratic party going to start to defend the women of this country? When are they going to see this as the war it is? The problem since bubba Bill Clinton's tenure is that Democrats are afraid of Republicans, but Republicans are certainly unafraid of Democrats because they know they won't fight. We need two things from Joe Biden right now.

Number one—he needs to summon Merrick Garland for a private dinner at the White House and inform him that if action within the week is not taken on Trump and the Republican insurrectionists, he will replace him with someone who will act. Number two—he needs to immediately begin the process of expanding the number of justices on the Supreme Court while the Democrats control the Senate. While I am very supportive of our own Democratic governor, the national party needs to realize it cannot expect those of us who constantly vote for it to continue if it cannot fight for us.

I was very intrigued by our conversation about language last dinner. Barbara's recalling reading something and thinking it said one thing, but when she read it again, it said something completely different. I am beginning to experience how unreliable memory is—and our explanations about those memories. This in no way undermines our need to talk—nor the absolute necessity of stating facts. But the incessant barrage of "information" makes all information seem the same. It makes language itself banal. Perhaps this all began with the printing of the Bible. But the current proliferation of information seems to drown us into forgetting facts. This is a profound dilemma in our time. We are descending quickly into a corporate theocracy where the consumption of beliefs supersedes reality. Perhaps this is just the human dilemma of being enticed by superstition. This always makes our eyes cloudy instead of clear.

Love, Greg

13 April 2023

Dearest Greg:

I'm glad you saw "Roma." I think it's one of the best films of recent times. But not everyone who saw it agreed with that assessment. One of the requirements of public art, such as film, is that it work for a public that might not have any knowledge of Mexico City in the period covered. But then of course there are other levels of interpretation. If you know Mexico City, and in particular the neighborhood called Roma, you have an advantage. If you are familiar with the political and cultural period portrayed, you have another. And if you lived in that city for eight years as I did and had maids working in your home, your understanding is even deeper.

The Roma neighborhood is a very particular one. When someone says Roma, people know what they are talking about. It is upper-class, with beautiful old houses, many of them built in the early years of the twentieth century. This is old money. Conservative money. There are neighborhoods in that city that are more appealing to me, such as Coyocán or San Angel, where many artists and writers live. The houses in those are also colonial in style but with big interior courtyards, lots of tile work, etc. Lomas de Chapultepec, once on the outskirts of the city, is for those with new money: ornate, flamboyant, and ugly. In the center of the city, narrow streets are lined with houses that are centuries old; the paving stones in that area are among the oldest on the Continent. So, when inhabitants of Mexico City talk about Roma, they immediately know they are talking about grand homes on quiet streets: old money, old values.

One thing I know from my intimate relationship to the history of the period is that the rather militaristic Tai Chi that Fermin was involved with was actually a cover for creating a paramilitary group able to attack the political protestors of the era. This comes out in some of the Spanish-language reviews that were published in Mexico, but in none of the English-language reviews that appeared here. The leader of the group is based on a notorious figure who was known at the time to be involved in paramilitary repression. I remember hearing about him back then. And so, the film evokes the connection between political repression, ordinary everyday classism, racism, and sexism, and the individual characteristics of those who are being portrayed.

The whole time I lived in Mexico and took full advantage of having poor women working in my home, I struggled with this. I talk about it some in my memoir, but there is so much more to say. The women who worked for me ate at my table, shared my clothes, we traveled to get to know their families, and I helped them realize their every ambition even when it meant losing them as workers. But it was never possible to erase those insidious lines between exploiter and exploited, rich and poor.

I know what you mean about black and white films conveying light in a way few in color can. I think this is also true of still photography. Which is why once the world switched from film to digital processing, I soon lost interest in photography as an art form that thrilled me.

Memory is such a complex thing. I must find and read Donald Judd's essay. When he points out that the discussion of science is scientific while the discussion of art is superstitious, he creates a brilliant and very useful way of thinking about the issues.

Love, Margaret

17 May 2023

Dearest Margaret:

There is a mostly quiet on and off rain on the mountain today—an appropriate weather for my still slow reentry into the rest of the world from Marfa. Part of the slowness this time is the fact that we were able to be with you and Barbara for a beautiful block of time and we cherish that.

As we discussed briefly on the phone yesterday, we always experience a sadness at leaving Marfa and a consequent period of adjustment when we return home. This, I suppose, is always true when one is on a trip to a place one loves. It is always true for us with Marfa. Driving back through the endless cumulus clouds and the clarity of the row upon row of bare mountains all the way to Albuquerque reminds me again of how much I deeply love the landscape of the northern Chihuahuan desert. The light is always "New Mexican" in Marfa, but this time we noticed what is distinctive from Marfa to El Paso. There is a soft, barely discernible haze that makes the light bounce differently. It is not as harsh and is almost otherworldly.

We never feel like watching TV in Marfa, so turning it on at home has been a real shock. I always see the cruelty of the banal clearly after returning. This time, we can hardly bring ourselves to watch the news. Is all of America nothing more than a marketing machine where entertainment is conflated now with everything we behold and do? Marfa's isolation and the singular clarity of Judd's (and a few others') physical work reinforces the fact that doing our own work and living our lives in that simple act is sufficient. The critic Robert Hughes, while admiring Judd's art, said Marfa felt utopian to him. I disagree. Marfa is always most real to me. It states over and over that if one makes the creation of one's art primary, one is able to live as one wants. This is all that's necessary. One may be isolated from the incessant "entertainments" of the world, but one is making what is real. Marfa makes the speedy barrage of illusions apparent.

I shall never forget the look on your face when you entered the first shed of Judd's milled aluminum boxes. It was a wide-open gaze into infinity. And you're saying that nothing I could have said could have prepared you for what the boxes do is the most perfect lingual response. Later in the evening you made another beautiful response by saying how you wished at one point amidst the boxes that you were not a writer. The silence of those physical responses is all that can be said.

I am grateful—and the world is lucky—that you were born a writer, though. Your devotion is a continued inspiration—as was so exemplified in Tim Johnson's physical embrace of you. We look forward to the Agave Festival next June when Marfa will celebrate your real contributions to all of us.

Love, Greg

1 June 2023

Dearest Margaret—

During our trip to Colorado this past weekend I felt this flow while passing through my hometown of Pueblo. It now, literally, feels like a place I pass through. It is no longer a place where I have a home in my parents' homes. Strangely, this did not provoke a sadness, but a reality. The reality that life moves on. Unexpectedly, a profound sense of gratitude for the strength and kindness of the people I come from lingers in me. Visiting with family and friends, seeing the beauty of Denver and the bones of the Front Range of the Rocky Mountains magnifies what is in my own bones for life. I have noticed since the deaths of both my parents I see my own individual life more clearly. I feel a freedom that isn't obligated to any narrative of the past. My parents, unlike many, did not impose a heavy narrative on us. And I was not of the disposition to accept others' definitions of me. But none of us can deny the places that shape us—particularly when young. I feel the working-class union sensibility in my own work habits. I feel the discipline of swim team training. And for all its evils, I feel the influence of the Catholic Church's veneration of art and ritual. I don't feel any of these is determinative, but they remain in the landscape of my childhood.

I was also reminded of how slow progress is—how it ebbs and flows. We stayed in Trinidad the last few days and walked its red brick streets—could be any city in the northeast of our country. One historical marker spoke of how Mother Jones visited Trinidad in solidarity with the coal miners' efforts to form a union. Some of those miners are distant relatives. She was involved in the rally at Ludlow which some mark as the beginning of worker's rights in America. It was, of course, not without tremendous bloodshed. This was in the early 1900s. Workers did not have the right to form unions until 1935. And today unions are virtually gone.

It was hard to reconcile that Lauren Boebert is the congressperson for this district now. And yet Jared Polis, our nation's first openly gay governor, was reelected overwhelmingly in this district. I did feel a great pride at looking at the shining pure gold dome of the Colorado State Capitol from the top of the Denver Art Museum, knowing that a gay man is leading my home state. I could not have imagined this as a child. And he has passed some substantial gun legislation in a state that loves firearms.

It reminds me, too, that progressivism has always been alive in America. I am once again proud of Alexandria Ocasio Cortez and Bernie Sanders for voting against the debt ceiling bill because it hurts the poor and they don't feel Democrats should negotiate with fascists. I was also heartened this week by a statement by Maryland's new governor, Wes Moore. He said the state of Maryland will not engage in any policy that seeks to force people to justify their humanity. I understand he is passing progressive legislation. I recall working the phones with a gay activist to help elect Federico Peña mayor of Denver in the mid 80s. He was the first public official to address the gay community in Colorado. And today a gay man holds the highest office in the state. During Barbara's and my childhoods, Colorado was ruby red. It is now rock-solid blue.

Once again, I am grateful that my childhood made me see the tyranny of punching a perpetual time clock. It also made me know I had to find meaningful work within myself—the only way here out of the isolation of capitalism.

Love, Greg

Los Angeles
10 May 2024

Dearest Margaret -

"First thought, best thought." Allen Ginsberg's entreaty is most often true. But what does that have to do with Ed Ruscha? Rich and I saw both Ruscha retrospectives—at MOMA in New York City in December and at LACMA in Los Angeles in May. I did not like the show at MOMA. I liked it less at LACMA. I read a favorable review by a critic I respect that said, basically, the show at LACMA was better because it was in Los Angeles—the place Ruscha depicts and draws inspiration from. I, too, love Los Angeles and thought seeing it here amidst its singular light, low apartment buildings and iconic palms would make Ruscha's work somehow more relevant—more present—better than my first impressions. Perhaps I was wrong in Manhattan. But being in the locus of his work did not help it. It made it more banal—far, in fact, from the actual beauty of Los Angeles. Some would argue that is Ruscha's gift—presenting us with the sloganeering mundanity of celebrity obsessed America. I feel this vacuousness is already all too present and we need not be reminded of it in art. This was Warhol's singular gift—and Lichtenstein's perhaps. Except they were the first and last of the

Pop artists. And they did it better. Took it as far as it could go. And they did it with a beautiful hand—the mark, outdated as it may seem amidst the fast traffic of current technology, of any true art. The only revelation in the LACMA show was that Ruscha is really a photographer. Which is not really art.

In my experience, photographs always make what they represent seem far away - unreal. A few brief recent examples from our trip: we were amazed by Lake Tahoe, in part, because all the photos we saw of it completely betrayed its reality; the same was true of the intimacy of the Cochella Valley near Palm Springs - and the Frey House itself; and the show about gay/lesbian visibility/invisibility, while great in concept, was largely made up of photographs which I have forgotten- the concept remains, but not the work itself. I acknowledge the creative "eye" of many photographers - their perspectives - I see it as largely a technical skill, not an art.

Ruscha's documentary catalogs of Los Angeles parking lots and apartment buildings are his best work. Los Angeles is a beautiful city. I wanted to give him another chance to celebrate that fact in painting. I do not expect depictions of sunsets—which Ruscha does averagely—or palm trees, which he did well once as black and white drawings, but only in a small book. The beauty of Los Angeles is in its singular physical phenomenology. It is its abstract artists, with no intent at intent, who have rendered this feel more realistically. The first and best of these is John McLaughlin. Then Benjamin, Feitelson, and Hammersley (Langsner's four Abstract Classists). And, of course, there's Ahn, Bell, Corse, Irwin, Lundeberg, McCracken, Pashgian, Pelton, Valentine and last but certainly not least, Norman Zammitt. There's even Hockney with his swimming pools and grand "Mullholand Drive." Outside his iconic gas stations—regional art at its finest—Ruscha fails. My first thought in New

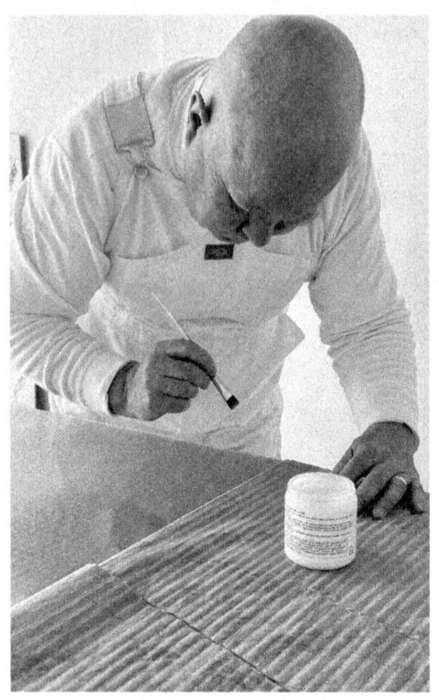

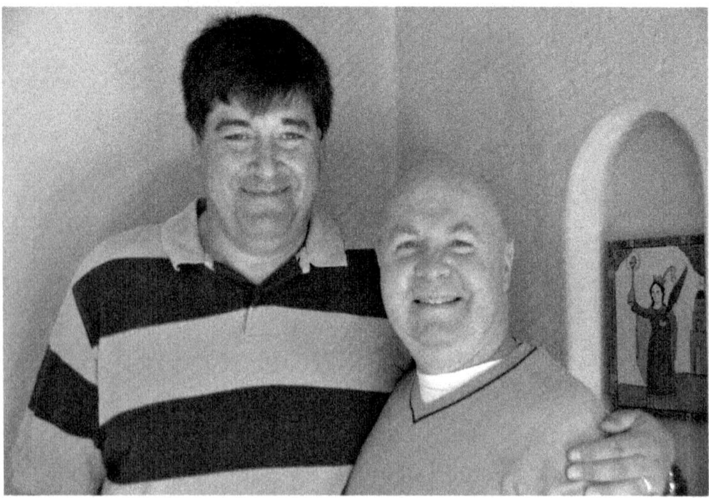

Left: Greg Smith in his studio, photo Rich Gabriel. Below: Rich and Greg, photo Margaret Randall. Right: Greg in his studio, photo Margaret Randall.

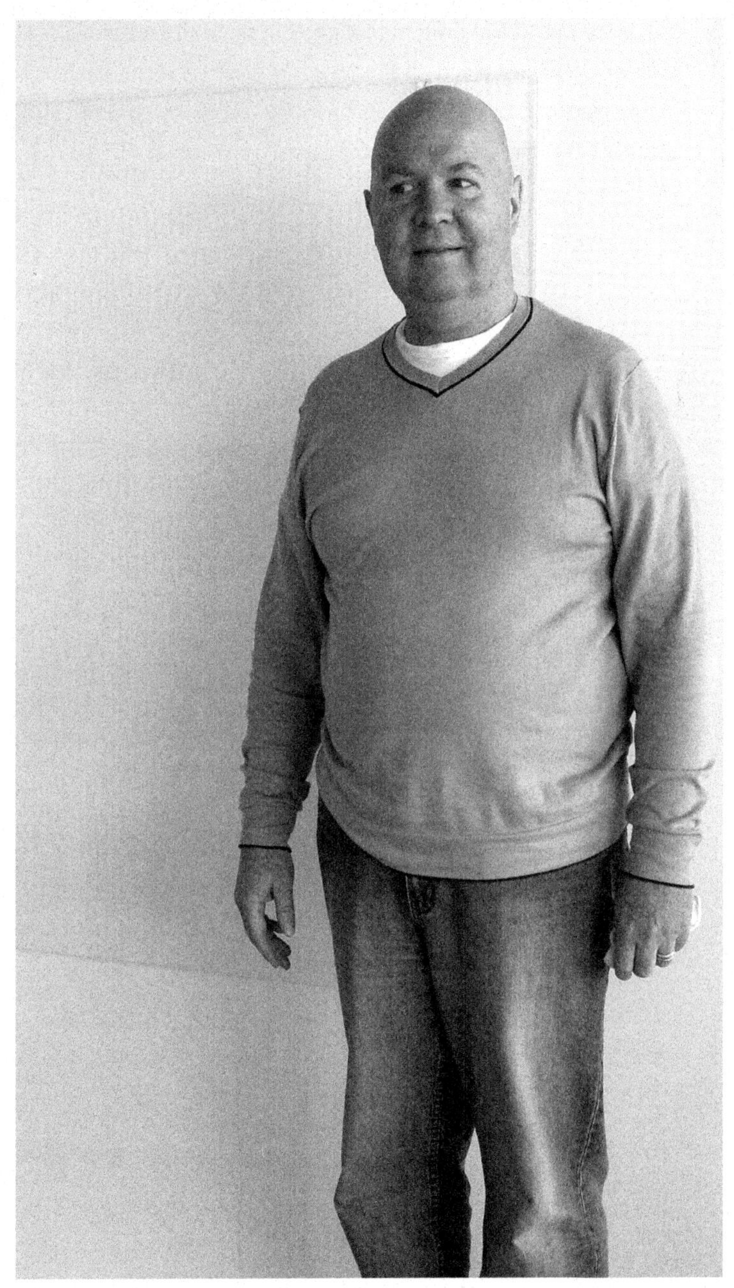

York City was in fact my best thought. But then, all great art—even if it depicts a place—is placeless. Or great art is the same in any place we see it. And that is why we search across continents to behold it. To see something so real it transcends the utility of us.

Love, Greg

Palm Springs

May 17, 2024

Dearest Margaret -

One has to look closely to glimpse Frey House II on the bare mountain just above the Palm Springs Art Museum. It is invisible and so small as to be simply a one room hermit's hut.

Seeing it—barely—from the bustling shopping intersection of Tahquitz Canyon Way and Palm Canyon Drive, a sublime and complete emptiness rose within me—I did not want to buy anything—I need nothing.

The next day I read that a writer who visited Frey in 1995 observed that the house remained exactly the same for over 34 years—Frey had not bought one thing to change it. He quietly responded—I like it the way it is.

Upon entering the house Rich and I immediately felt we didn't want to leave—

It and we were sufficient unto ourselves—

Love, Greg

FINAL THOUGHTS

IT'S BEEN A REVELATION to reread these letters, in three cases decades after exchanging them. In the fourth, our correspondence is much more recent, but revisiting some of the ideas expressed has been equally interesting. I hope these conversations will provide windows into past eras as well as issues with continued relevance today. And I hope they stimulate in readers their own thoughts about some of the events and ideas discussed.

Locating the letters, thinking about the relationships they describe, selecting fragments to reproduce, and in some cases translating convoluted passages entailed veritable detective work in some instances. In others—those involving people who are still alive—I was able to construct the chapter with their valuable help. They aided me in gathering the material, responded to questions about interpreting certain episodes, and read the final conversation. I am immensely grateful that they allowed me to use our correspondence and for their confidence in my ability to portray them authentically. I'm also grateful to the many people who aided me in obtaining the materials I needed to reconstruct the chapters on the three outriders who are no longer alive. Some of this help resulted in new friendships generating their own epistolary richness.

I want to return to what I mean by the word *outrider.* Every generation has its quota of brilliant, innovative, and creative people in a variety of fields. Those conditions alone aren't enough for outrider status. Those in the category must also have suffered discrimination of one kind or another and have resisted its damaging isolation, continued to grow, and left their mark, fueled by an inner conviction and sharpened by the obstacles they've been forced to overcome. Discrimination itself, when it doesn't destroy, can play a part in strengthening resolve. This combination of talent, strength, resistance, and rebel spirit places such people ahead of their time, in a place that can be extraordinarily lonely but is often visionary.

Those I call outriders aren't outlaws; they aren't defined by crossing legal lines or engaging in unlawful acts. Neither are they flamboyant or attention-getters. But they are unusual. They generally don't pay attention to society's prescription for success. Defying pressures to conform, they allow their passion for what they do to lead them to unexplored territory. Their iconoclasm has helped them prioritize a discipline in what they make and do. Their devotion to a practice engenders rich exploration and their persistence helps imbue that practice with originality and power.

The epistolary genre is unique. It is immediate and not overly polished, reflecting the place, time, and history propelling each letter writer. Letters aren't written for publication, but carry a spontaneity and authenticity not often found in the more formal literary genres. They are by their nature a dialogue, depending on both correspondents to push it forward. They are generally not produced for posterity but may turn out to be a more interesting mirror because of this. Most of the letters in this book were written long before digital communication. They traveled long distances, sometimes by unsophisticated means, and carried with them a desire to sit down with the other for a face-to-face conversation. Nostalgia and desire live between the lines. The thoughtfulness generated by slow travel imbues them with a quality that is often missing today.

We are in an age in which the transmission of history has become more and more distorted. All sorts of spurious interests are involved, among them fundamentalist religious and right-wing political influences. In several southern U.S. states, school texts have rewritten the country's shameful era of slavery, outrageously claiming that kidnapped Africans lived happily in their bondage because they felt safe and protected. Our First Peoples are still often portrayed as savages. Periods of successful people's struggles—such as the civil rights movement, the protest movement against the war in Vietnam, and the rebel sixties—are routinely lied about and misrepresented.

The truth behind such important events as the United States dropping nuclear bombs on the Japanese cities of Hiroshima and Nagasaki has never been fully explored in our history books. Motivations for such monumental events as our Civil War and World War II are told in a biased fashion. Crimes such as the murders of John F. and Robert Kennedy have been buried in official rhetoric meant to protect the guilty. Zionism has succeeded in rewriting the story of Israel and Palestine, resulting in Israel's genocide against Palestine, which is polarizing the world right now. Gay and transgender people, too, often aren't mentioned at all. Many of the egregious acts perpetrated by a succession of U.S. administrations are covered up by a more flattering view of governmental policy. Even such a flagrant crime as the January 6, 2021, attack on the United States Capitol is ignored by many who continue to support its perpetration.

And it's not only textbooks and media coverage that are affected. Literature is also routinely targeted. Censorship periodically raises its ugly head in our society, and—following the fascist trend of the Trump administration—has only gotten worse. The books that have most often been banned across the country are *Adventures of Huckleberry Finn,* by Mark Twain; George Orwell's *1984; To Kill a Mockingbird,* by Harper Lee; and *The Catcher in the Rye,* by J. D. Salinger.

Between 2022 and 2023 alone, school boards in Florida banned three hundred titles. Many were about LGBTQ+ life, but others dealt with such themes as explaining sex to teenagers, speaking openly about death, or showcasing any nonwhite hero. On the list were such classics as *Anne Frank's Diary: The Graphic Adaptation,* adapted by Ari Folman; Toni Morrison's *The Bluest Eye* and *Beloved; The Fire Next Time,* by James Baldwin; Bernard Malamud's *The Fixer; The Handmaid's Tale,* by Margaret Atwood; *The House of Spirits,* by Isabel Allende; *The Absolutely True Diary of a Part-Time Indian,* by Sherman Alexie; *The Color Purple,* by Alice Walker; *Push,* by Sapphire; and Judy Blume's *Forever. . . .*

When we lose the connection to our history or refuse to face it honestly, we forfeit our identity and are easily coerced into acting against our own best interests. When young people don't see themselves represented in what they read and are forbidden to read great literature—or any literature—it stifles ideas and discourages critical thinking. As this distortion of who we have been and are becomes more entrenched, the voices of those who were there are needed to tell it like it was. We need to hear what it felt like at the time. This is the additional value of letters such as these.

Memory, both collective and individual, is the most obvious victim of this cultural coercion. When our relationship to our past is severed or distorted, we flounder in a morass of guesswork and uninformed supposition. We may be easy prey to conspiracy theories. Constructing each of the chapters in this book reconnected me with my memories of people and places and of the events in which we took part. Certain letters enabled me to relive moments I'd forgotten and surprised me with their references to incidents and feelings long lost in a shadowy past. In some cases, they triggered memories of painful struggles; in others, they awed me by their power and conviction, reenergized me to reclaim a pride of accomplishment, or simply allowed me to revel in the warmth of long-ago relationships.

In most cases, letters don't pretend to be great literature or historical texts. They reflect the experiences and viewpoints of those writing, who don't believe they are writing for posterity. If they did think they were writing for future readers, they might display a self-consciousness that would belie the honesty of their casual truth. The way they transmit what was happening at a particular time and place may offer a different take on an era or its events.

We need to be reminded that there was a time when a political witch hunt ruined many lives in our country and that there were individuals such as Walter Lowenfels who refused to give names or allow the attack to defeat him. That as recently as the mid-twentieth century, to be a brilliant innovative woman like Laurette Séjourné was an impediment to be overcome, and that even a man of the dimension of Arnaldo Orfila may suffer censorship if he publishes books offensive to the powers that be. That even more recently, the male-dominated literary establishment accepted only those women who conformed to an image of womanhood it could tolerate and the Left had no interest in or understanding of gay identity, making life difficult for a marvelous poet like Susan Sherman, who embodied both conditions. And that even today the art world can be as exclusive and competitive as the worlds of politics and commerce, leaving a deeply thoughtful painter such as Greg Smith in relative isolation with his nonconformist art. And this is not simply history but also sadly relevant today. Following a period of relative freedom, fascism looms large on our current horizon.

Each of the people in this book is an example of the ongoing struggle against such silencing and death. The political scene, nationally as well as internationally, has only gotten worse since the correspondence that makes up this book. The creativity, ingenuity, courage, and tenacity displayed in these letters exemplify the qualities we need in order to confront the ongoing crises. There really is no substitute for the outrider presence among us. As Margaret Mead famously said, "Never doubt that a small group of thoughtful, committed citizens can change the world. Indeed, it is the only thing that ever has."

INDEX

ACKNOWLEDGMENTS

I HAVE MADE EVERY effort to give credit to those who helped me locate these letters and to others who have been willing to share their own memories, enabling me to shed additional light on the times and their protagonists.

I am immensely grateful to Mai Jacobs, who inspired this book by sharing my correspondence with her grandparents Walter and Lillian Lowenfels. She also provided copies of family photographs. Susan Sherman and Greg Smith, the two correspondents who are still alive, consented to my using our letters and helped me obtain copies; I am grateful for their confidence that I would represent them authentically. Rich Gabriel provided just the photographs I wanted to illustrate the chapter on Greg.

Several years ago, my son-in-law Javier Pérez Siller, a historian who studies the French migrations to Mexico, came across some of my letters to Laurette Séjourné when he was doing research for a book of his own. When I embarked on this project, I asked if he could find and copy more of our correspondence. He went to great effort to do so and sent me several hundred pages of letters to Laurette and Arnaldo from me and other family members.

I want to thank Adrienne Leigh Sharpe-Weseman at the Yale Collection of American Literature, Beinecke Rare Book & Manuscript Library, for making available copies of letters from the Walter Lowenfels Papers; Belem Fernández and Itzel Cabello Garduño of the Instituto de Investigaciones Estéticas at the National Autonomous University of Mexico for facilitating copies of my letters to Laurette Séjourné and Arnaldo Orfila Reynal; the Special Collections at Princeton University, in particular Charles Doran and Emma Paradies, for copies of letters from Laurette and Arnaldo to me; Shannon O'Neill, curator for the Tamiment-Wagner Collections at New York University Special Collections, for a portion of my correspondence with Susan Sherman; and the Center for Southwest Research at the University of New Mexico—at the latter, in particular Dr. Margie Montañez, curator of Latin American Collections, and graduate student Daniela Geovanna Galvis Garzón—for their attention and help in facilitating copies of additional letters between Susan and myself. Greg Smith had copies of our correspondence and kindly copied them for me.

Lynne Elizabeth, my perceptive editor at New Village Press, committed to this book before it existed as such. Her suggestions made it better in every way. More important, her faith in me as a writer whose ideas may be interesting to a general readership and her support for this project have been invaluable. Sofia Marie Matson read an advanced draft and made valuable suggestions. I am grateful to the numerous friends and family members with whom I've discussed ideas along the way and to some who have connected me with people who could help in one way or another. Among these, I especially want to mention my daughter Ana Cohen Bickford, Tatiana Coll, V. B. Price, and

Rafael Mondragón. My son, Gregory Randall, often reads my manuscripts; his critique and suggestions always make for better books. And I can never give enough thanks to my wife, Barbara, whose insightful conversation helped me define the book's major theme and whose ongoing input helped me shape it. My heartfelt gratitude to you all.

ABOUT MARGARET RANDALL

MARGARET RANDALL (New York, 1936) is a poet, essayist, oral historian, translator, photographer, and social activist. She lived in Latin America for twenty-three years (in Mexico, Cuba, and Nicaragua). From 1962 to 1969, she and Mexican poet Sergio Mondragón coedited *El Corno Emplumado/The Plumed Horn,* a bilingual literary quarterly that published more than seven hundred writers and visual artists from thirty-five countries—some of the best new work of the sixties. When she came home in 1984, the government ordered her deported because it found some of her writing to be "against the good order and happiness of the United States." With the support of many writers and others, she won her case, and her citizenship was restored in 1989.

Randall's most recent poetry books include *Against Atrocity, Out of Violence into Poetry* (both from Wings Press), *Stormclouds Like Unkept Promises, Vertigo of Risk,* and *Home* (from Casa Urraca Press) and *This Honest Land* (Wings Press). *Che on My Mind* (a feminist poet's reminiscence of Che Guevara, published by Duke University Press), *Thinking about Thinking* (essays, from Casa Urraca), *Artists in My Life* and *Luck* (New Village Press), and *Last Words* (Casa Urraca) are other recent titles. In 2020, Duke published her memoir, *I Never Left Home: Poet, Feminist, Revolutionary.* A second volume of selected poems, *Time's Language II: Poems 2019–2023* (Wings Press) follows *Time's Language Poems 1959–2018* as compendiums of her best poems. Many of these titles have appeared in Spanish translation from Siglo XXI, Alforja, Ediciones de Medianoche, and Heredad in Mexico; Casa de las Américas, Ediciones Matanzas, and Vigía in Cuba; Abisinia and Tinta Limón in Argentina; Rumbo in Uruguay; and small independent publishers in Cuba, Nicaragua, Brazil, Ecuador, Peru, Colombia, Venezuela, Spain, Holland, Japan, Turkey, and India.

Margaret also translates from the Spanish. She has translated poetry collections by Roberto Fernández Retamar, Roque Dalton, Otto René Castillo, Carlos María Gutiérrez, Daisy Zamora, Kelly Martínez, Israel Domínguez, Alfredo Zaldívar, Laura Ruíz, Chely Lima, Rita Valdivia, Reynaldo García Blanco, Yanira Marimón, and Gaudencio Rodríguez Santana, among others; novels by Freddy Prestol Castillo, Juan Antonio Hernández, and Tomás Modesto Galán; memoirs by Gregory Randall, Lurgio Gavilán Sánchez, and Stefano Varese; and anthologies of Cuban poetry and short stories, Ecuadorean poetry, U.S. poets for Mexico, and Beat poets in Spanish. She has read her own work and delivered keynote addresses in hundreds of venues throughout the United States, Latin America, and occasionally in other countries.

Two of Randall's photographs are in the Capitol Art Collection in Santa Fe. In 1960, Randall was a recipient of a Carnegie Fund for Authors aid grant, and in the same year a grant from the American Academy of Arts and Letters revolving fund for writers in need. In 1989, she was a cowinner of the

Mencken Award, and in 1990 she received a Lillian Hellman and Dashiell Hammett grant for writers victimized by political repression. The Barbara Deming Money for Women Award was given to her in 1997, and in 2004 she received the PEN New Mexico Dorothy Doyle Lifetime Achievement Award for Writing and Human Rights Activism. Randall received the 2017 Medalla al Mérito Literario from *Literatura en el Bravo,* Ciudad Juárez, Mexico. In 2018, she was awarded the Poet of Two Hemispheres prize by Poesía en Paralelo Cero in Quito, Ecuador. In 2019, she won an honorary doctorate of letters from the University of New Mexico. In 2020, she received the George Garrett Award from the Association of Writers & Writing Programs (AWP) and the Paulo Freire Award from Chapman University. In 2022, she received the city of Albuquerque's Creative Bravo Award. Randall lives in Albuquerque with her partner (now wife) of more than thirty-eight years, the painter Barbara Byers, and travels extensively to read, lecture, and teach.